JEAN ANDERSON'S GREEN THUMB PRESERVING GUIDE

BOOKS BY JEAN ANDERSON:

The Art of American Indian Cooking
    (with Yeffe Kimball)

Food Is More Than Cooking

Henry the Navigator, Prince of Portugal

The Haunting of America

The Family Circle Cookbook
    (with the Food Editors of *Family Circle*)

*The Doubleday Cookbook (with Elaine Hanna)

Recipes from America's Restored Villages

The Green Thumb Preserving Guide (1976)

The Grass Roots Cookbook

Jean Anderson's Processor Cooking (1979)

**Half a Can of Tomato Paste & Other Culinary Dilemmas
    (with Ruth Buchan)

Unforbidden Sweets

Jean Anderson Cooks

Jean Anderson's *New* Processor Cooking

Jean Anderson's Green Thumb Preserving Guide

*Winner of the R. T. French Tastemaker Award,
Best Cookbook of the Year (1975)*

**Winner of the R. T. French Tastemaker Award,
Best Specialty Cookbook of the Year (1980)*

JEAN ANDERSON'S GREEN THUMB

PRESERVING GUIDE

How to Can and Freeze, Dry and Store,
Pickle, Preserve and Relish
Home-grown Vegetables and Fruits

Quill · New York

Library of Congress Cataloging in Publication Data

Anderson, Jean, 1929–
  Jean Anderson's Green thumb preserving guide.

  Rev. ed. of: The green thumb preserving guide.
1976.
  Includes index.
  1. Canning and preserving. 2. Fruit—Preservation.
3. Vegetables—Preservation. I. Anderson, Jean,
1929–   . Green thumb preserving guide. II. Title.
TX601.A49 1985   641.4   84-15883
ISBN 0-688-04190-6

Printed in the United States of America

First Quill Edition

1 2 3 4 5 6 7 8 9 10

For Aunt Florence,
whose thumb is green and pantry full

Acknowledgments

I would like to thank the following individuals, institutions and corporations without whose valuable assistance this book could not have been written: Kate Alfriend, U.S. Department of Agriculture, Office of Communication, Washington, D.C.; Dr. Donald B. Anderson, Professor Emeritus, Plant Physiology, University of North Carolina, Chapel Hill, N.C.; Ray Davis, Marketing Manager, Anchor Hocking Corporation, Lancaster, Ohio (for supplying preserving jars for recipe testing); Mrs. Peter Dohanos, East Hampton, N.Y.; Mrs. Harry Flegel, Le Roy, Ill. (for sharing old family and farm recipes); Cooperative Extension Service, New York State College of Human Ecology at Cornell University, Ithaca, N.Y.; The North Carolina Agricultural Extension Service, North Carolina State University, Raleigh, N.C.; John W. Snyder, CBS-TV, New York, N.Y. (for sharing old Nebraska farm recipes); Mrs. Gratz Spencer, Swan Quarter, N.C.; Elaine Stahl, Upper Saddle River, N.J.; and Mrs. Mary Lou Williamson, Director Consumer Service, Ball Corporation, Muncie, Ind. (for providing information as well as preserving jars for recipe testing). And a very special thanks to Claire Del Medico for typing the manuscript.

CONTENTS

Part TWO   DOING

Introduction

Not since the "victory gardens" of World War II have so many Americans begun to grow their own vegetables and fruits, not just in suburbia but also in city centers where neighborhood corps are jointly farming vacant lots, where windowboxes and rooftop planters, once greened with geraniums, now yield mini harvests of tomatoes, salad greens and herbs. Today's return to the soil, like that of the 40s, is a war effort, only today's battle is against the high cost of eating and the suspected perils of commercial processing.

What many greenhorn gardeners are discovering, to their surprise and delight, is not only the superiority of home-grown produce, but also what green thumbs they have. That there really are carrots down there in the ground waiting to be pulled. That those green marbles on the vine are developing, day by day, into tomatoes. That overnight, almost, there is a new batch of beans to pick. Or limas. Or peas.

They are learning, as you have perhaps already learned, how bountiful a postage-stamp plot can be. That it often produces more than you—or your neighbors—can eat during the growing season.

Which brings us to the point of this book. What should you do about the surplus? (Indeed, what about that other "surplus" that you *don't* grow yourself, the beautiful produce that still does flood into local roadside markets at low, low prices during peak harvest seasons? It's no economy to buy it by the bushel unless you know what to do with it.) Can it? Freeze it? Hold it in cold storage? Not every method of conserving food works equally well for every fruit and vegetable.

Because most new hands at gardening are also new hands at canning or freezing, pickling or preserving, I discuss in detail in the pages that follow only the surest and most suitable methods of conserving those fruits and vegetables most easily grown in home gardens. I do not cover meats, poultry or seafood (this is, after all, a "green thumb" preserving guide). Nor do I include exotic vegetables and fruits that must be tracked down in specialty produce shops.

This guide, unlike others, does not attempt to describe every possible method of conserving every fruit and vegetable. Rather, it is selective (opinionated, if you will) because it recommends only what I consider to be the very best ways of conserving each. I am quick to say which fruits and vegetables can well and which ones do not. Which ones freeze well and which don't. Which can be held in cold storage. Or which can simply be left in the field all winter long.

I also suggest how to cope with the unexpected. What, for example, can you do with those end-of-the-season green tomatoes that never will ripen properly? (Make them into pickles or piccalilli.) And what about that prize zucchini? The one measuring twenty-two inches? Can it ever be anything more than a conversation piece? (It can, if you cook it, purée it and freeze it, then use the purée for making soups or soufflés.)

Summing up, this is your guide to conserving what you have grown, to saving money—and, to eating better, perhaps, than you are accustomed to eating. THE GREEN THUMB PRESERVING GUIDE is not concerned with conserving food on a massive or marathon scale. It is geared to small gardens, small kitchens and limited pantry space. My purpose, simply, is to prove that there is nothing very mysterious or complicated about putting food by. That it does not require cupboards full of special equipment, or particular skills, or any more time than *you* choose to give it.

JEAN ANDERSON

New York, New York

part
ONE

LEARNING

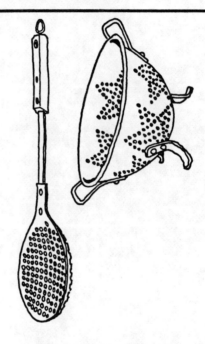

Food Conservation: What's it all about?

It's about saving money . . . knowing (indeed *controlling*) exactly what goes into the foods we eat . . . and about sharing with family and friends not only the work of gardening, canning and freezing, but also the fun and fruits of our labors.

Our grandmothers were old hands at canning, pickling and preserving. But our own skills lie more with the can opener. (Americans, it's estimated, open about 26 *billion* cans and jars each year.) Most of us haven't the foggiest notion what home canning is all about. And most of us are terrified to try it. Freezing food doesn't intimidate us, although how often do we do more than toss a couple of steaks or chops in the freezer? As for drying food . . . well, does anyone really bother? And root cellars? Do they *work?*

Indeed they do, as do Grandmother's other "old-fashioned" methods of putting food by. Even freezing, generally considered to be a World War II innovation, is an ancient way of preserving food. Eskimos have been freezing food for centuries (it was from them that Clarence Birdseye, "the father of the modern frozen food industry," learned the secrets of quick-freezing).

Which method, then, is preferable? That depends upon the particular foods you have and plan to conserve. In the chapters that follow, I will discuss the various vegetables and fruits, alphabetically, one by one, recommending the best ways of conserving each. Asparagus, for example, cans poorly and I say so straight out. Why waste time, not to mention perfectly good asparagus, in canning when frozen asparagus spears are the next best thing to fresh? Tomatoes, on the other hand, are terrible frozen because they disintegrate into tasteless mush. It's far better to can them—whole, as juice, pasta, catsup, chili sauce or Bloody Mary mix. Sweet corn dries beautifully and so do apples (you will find here not only directions for drying each, but also recipes that show how to use them once dried .

But before we proceed with specific fruits and vegetables, let's examine the different methods of conserving food and prove, hopefully, that there is nothing very mysterious or complicated about any of them).

CANNING, PICKLING AND PRESERVING

It's been said that if Napoleon could have kept secret the process of canning food safely, he might have ruled the world. Napoleon is, in a way, responsible for the discovery of canning although his motives, to be sure, were less for the advancement of mankind than for the advancement of his own armies. With as many of his troops dying unheroically of starvation as heroically in battle, he determined to find a way of keeping them well-fed and strong. So in the early 19th century, Napoleon offered a prize of 12,000 francs about $250,000 at the present rate of exchange) to the man who could devise a way of preserving food safely. The man who did was a French confectioner named Appert. His breakthrough discovery, as guarded a secret in Napoleon's day as the A-bomb during World War II, was simply to seal food airtight inside bottles and boil it. Appert had no inkling why the process worked. That remained for Pasteur to explain some years later—that microorganisms spoiled food and that they could be destroyed by heat (sterilization). Appert's method is what we know today as "the boiling water bath," and among man's earlier historic discoveries, it ranks right up there with fire and the wheel because it meant that man was no longer dependent upon fresh food. Harvest surpluses could be safely preserved for future use.

Why Food Spoils and How to Prevent It

Thanks to Pasteur (and too many others to name), we now know that the microorganisms that spoil food fall into three categories: *yeasts, molds* and *bacteria.* We also now know that *enzymes,* organic substances existing naturally in foods, must be dealt with, too. Call them ripening agents, if you like, for they accelerate color, texture and flavor changes in foods as they mature. Enzymes must be considered in canning because unless their action is checked, ripening continues within the preserving jar. And it continues to the point of decomposition.

Heat has the power to destroy yeasts, molds, bacteria and enzymes, which is why canning remains one of the safest and most effective means of conserving food. Enzymes are destroyed at a comparatively low temperature. That of a hot or simmering water bath (185° to 190° F.) will render them inactive and it will also kill the actively growing cells of bacteria, yeasts and molds. It will not, however, kill their spores (dormant, heat-resistant germ cells or "seeds"). A *boiling water bath* (212° F.) will kill the spores of molds, yeasts and *most* bacteria. *Most* must be stressed because a temperature of 212° F. will not faze the spores of such dangerous thermophilic (heat-loving) bacteria as *Clostridium botulinum,* the culprit in the often fatal form of food poisoning known as botulism. They are killed at a temperature of 240° F., well above the boiling point of water and attainable only in a steam pressure canner.

The various microorganisms of spoilage do not grow equally well in all kinds of foods. The dangerous *botulinum,* for example, thrives in low-acid foods (vegetables, meats, fish and poultry), but it is not a problem in high-acid foods (pickles, relishes, fruits, jams, preserves and jellies) because acid inhibits its growth. Yeasts and molds, on the other hand, *do* grow well in the presence of acid, but they are both less dangerous and more easily killed.

The acidity of a food (whether that acid is natural, as in apples, grapes and other fruits, or added, as in pickles and relishes), thus determines which microorganisms may be troublesome in canning and that information, in turn, determines how—and how long—a specific food must be processed.

Two Important Rules of Thumb:

1. *Process All Low-Acid Foods in a Steam Pressure Canner* (10 pounds pressure, the equivalent of 240° F., is the pressure most often recommended).

2. *Process all high-acid foods in a water bath* (with the exception of jellies which need no processing after they have been boiled down to the proper consistency). Pickles and relishes require a boiling water bath (212° F.), as do tomatoes and other canned fruits. Such sugar-rich mixtures as jams, preserves and marmalades may be safely processed in a hot or simmering water bath (185° F.) because high concentrations of sugar help prevent spoilage.

NOTE: As for processing times, they vary from food to food. Specific times and temperatures are given in the vegetable-by-vegetable and fruit-by-fruit canning instructions that appear later on (see index for page numbers).

A List of High-Acid Foods and Low-Acid Foods

So that you can see at a glance which foods belong in which category—high-acid or low—here's a handy list (it is arranged alphabetically, *not* according to acid content).

HIGH-ACID FOODS	LOW-ACID FOODS
(Process in a water bath)	*(Process in a steam pressure canner)*
Apples (also apple juice and applesauce)	Asparagus
Apricots	Beans (all varieties)
Berries (all varieties)	Beets
Catsup	Broccoli
Cherries (both sour and sweet)	Brussels sprouts
Chili sauce	Cabbage
Chutney	Carrots
Citrus fruits (all varieties)	Cauliflower
Conserves	Celery
Currants	Corn
Fruit butters	Eggplant
Fruit cocktail	Greens (all varieties)
Fruit juices	Hominy
Grapes	Meats (all varieties)
Jams	Mixed vegetables
Jellies *(do not process jars after they are filled and sealed)*	Mushrooms
Marmalades	Okra
Melons (cantaloupe, Crenshaw, honeydew, Persian, watermelon)	Onions
	Parsnips
Nectarines	Peas (all varieties)
Peaches	Peppers (all varieties)
Pears	Pimientos
Persimmons	Potatoes (all varieties)
Pickles	Poultry (all varieties)
Pineapple	Pumpkin
Plums	Rutabaga
Preserves	Salsify (oyster plant)
Quinces	Seafood (all varieties)
Relishes	Soups (all varieties)
Rhubarb	Spinach
Sauerkraut	Squash (all varieties of summer and winter squash)
Tomatoes (also tomato juice, sauce and paste, but *not* stewed tomatoes)	Stewed Tomatoes
	Stews (all varieties)
	Turnips
	Yams and sweet potatoes

NOTE: Certain modern varieties of tomatoes are lower in acid than tomatoes of years past. It is advisable, therefore, to can with particular care, and to add ½ teaspoon of citric acid to each 1 quart of canned tomatoes or tomato juice to compensate for any lack of natural acid. For specific information about the acidity of tomatoes grown in your area, contact your local home economics extension agent (obtainable through the county government offices).

THE *HOW* OF HASSLE-FREE CANNING, PICKLING AND PRESERVING

Get Set:

Assemble all canning equipment and check to make sure each piece is in perfect working order (pay particular attention to the pressure gauge of your pressure canner; have it checked by the manufacturer's representative or, if there is none in your area, by your local home economics extension agent). See, too, that your candy thermometer is accurate (you'll need it for making jams and jellies).

Lay in a good supply of preserving jars (or if reusing old jars, make sure they are not cracked or chipped). Check the closures, too. You can reuse the porcelain-lined, zinc screw tops and you can also reuse the screw bands that accompany dome lids. *But you should never reuse either the rubber jar rings or dome lids.* Order a brand new supply. If you wait until the middle of the canning season to buy jars and closures, you may discover that they have already been snapped up and that you will have to wait for a reorder.

Stock your cupboard with whatever vinegars, salts, herbs and spices you will need in the course of canning, pickling, preserving, jam and jelly-making. As with preserving jars, if you wait until mid-season, you may find that those mustard seeds and cinnamon sticks you so desperately need are sold out.

Refamiliarize yourself with the use of your steam pressure canner. Reread the instruction book carefully, then keep it out where you can refer to it. Also make certain that you know how the different types of preserving jars and closures work (again, reread the manufacturer's directions).

Set aside one canning day—or perhaps two days—each week to conserve your garden surplus. And try to keep those days free so that you can devote yourself to the project. Can only one type of food each day and never more than two or three canner loads of that. Otherwise, you may wind up with more food than you can put into jars, you will hopelessly clutter the kitchen, and you may confuse the recipes or directions for preserving one type of food with those of another. NOTE: Never try to make jam or jelly on a humid or rainy day. They are apt not to jell because they will absorb moisture from the air.

Gather whatever fruits and vegetables you intend to can just before you are ready to begin. Once picked, they shrivel, soften, lose color, flavor and vitamin content. If for some reason the canning must be put off, store the fruits or vegetables in a cool, well-ventilated spot—*do not wash them first.* Be very choosy as you pick, selecting only those vegetables or fruits that are ripe and firm, free of blemishe and insect damage.

Wash and, if necessary, sterilize enough preserving jars and closures to see you through the day's session. Directions for washing and sterilizing are included in The Kitchen Conservatory; see index for page numbers).

Go!

Read carefully whatever recipe you intend to use and review the canning procedure so that you know the sequence "cold" and won't have to stop at some critical point to refresh your memory. Canning, pickling and preserving should move like clockwork—and will, once you get the hang of them.

Sort the food you intend to can according to size. It will not only be prettier in the jar but it will also process more evenly.

Wash the food well in cool water—whether or not it is to be peeled. It's easiest to do small batches at a time, sloshing up and down in a sink or dishpan full of cool water. Lift out and drain so that all grit and sediment remain behind in the sink or pan. Repeat several times. Never allow vegetables or fruits to soak any length of time in the wash water; they will lose color, flavor and nutritive value.

Peel, core and cut the fruits and/or vegetables as individual recipes direct. TIP: Tomatoes, peaches, apricots, nectarines, plums and onions will all peel zip-quick if first blanched 30 seconds in boiling water, then plunged immediately in ice water.

Pack the jars by whichever method the particular recipe or directions recommend. And lift each jar from the simmering water (used to preheat the jars) as you are ready to fill it—don't lift them all out at once.

The Two Methods of Packing Jars:

1. *Cold (or Raw) Pack:* Fill hot jars as quickly as possible with raw food leaving the recommended amount of head space. (This method is preferred for canning fruits because they will retain more of their natural color, flavor and texture than they would if heated or partially cooked before being packed.) Pears, peaches, and other large fruit halves are more beautiful if arranged hollows down and slightly overlapping. They should be as snugly packed as possible (although not to the point of mutilation) and so should all other foods *except* green peas, lima beans and whole-kernel corn, all of which will expand in the jar during processing. Berries, in particular, should be firmly packed and the best way to do so without crushing them is to fill the jar in stages, shaking the berries down as you go. Once a jar is filled, pour in enough boiling syrup, juice or pickling liquid to cover the food, at the same time leaving the required head space.

2. *Hot Pack:* Pack hot jars loosely with hot or cooked foods (vegetables, pickles, and relishes) or simply pour in boiling hot preserves, jams, chutneys, catsups or jellies. Fill one jar at a time, leaving the recommended head space, and do so as fast as possible.

Two Tips:

1. Use a wide-mouth canning funnel (obtainable at any hardware store) when packing small or cut-up foods because it enables you to fill a jar fast without spilling or splattering the rim.

2. If you should find that you have insufficient liquid to cover food in a jar, as sometimes happens with the very last jar, simply add enough boiling vinegar (for pickles and relishes), boiling water (for vegetables) or boiling syrup (for fruits), leaving the required head space. On an average, you will need from ¾ to 1½ cups liquid to cover the food in a 1-quart jar. The reason foods must be covered with liquid is that if they are not, they will discolor and/or shrivel.

Seal the jars. And seal *each* jar as soon as it is filled. But first, run a table knife or small, thin-blade spatula around the inside edge of the jar to remove any air bubbles (any air trapped inside a jar is apt to darken or discolor food). *How do you seal a jar?* That depends upon whether you are using dome lids and screw bands or the more old-fashioned screw tops and rubber jar rings. Or, as in the case of jelly, melted paraffin. Here, then, are the three techniques:

1. *To seal a jar with dome lids and screw bands:* Wipe both the jar rim and the threaded neck with a clean cloth or piece of paper toweling moistened in hot water, removing any spills or fragments of food that might prevent the jar from sealing vacuum-tight. Place the dome lid on top of the jar, flat against the rim. Screw the screw band on *tight,* making sure that it goes on straight, not askew.

2. *To seal a jar with screw tops and rubber jar rings:* Fit a hot rubber jar ring (these should be kept immersed in hot water and fished out one at a time as needed) on the ledge of the jar just below the rim and press flat. If a ring bulges or buckles, reject it and try another. In order for the jar to seal vacuum-tight, the rubber ring must lie flat. Wipe the jar rim and rubber ring with a hot, moist cloth, screw the top down tight, then unscrew (turn counterclockwise) ¼". After the jar has been processed, you will "adjust the cap," or "complete the seal," which means in plain language, "screw the lid down tight."

3.   *To seal jelly glasses with melted paraffin:* Because paraffin is flammable, it should be handled with utmost care. Never melt it over direct heat, but in the top of a double boiler. Or, if you prefer, buy an inexpensive little coffee pot in which to melt the paraffin and use it expressly for this purpose (the spout makes pouring the hot paraffin easy). Set the coffee pot in a pan of boiling water to melt the paraffin. Melt paraffin *slowly* and never heat it to the point of smoking because noxious fumes are given off. Too-hot paraffin will also become brittle as it cools and is far more apt to crack, chip or shrink from the edges of the jelly glass than paraffin heated just to the point of melting.

When sealing jelly glasses with paraffin, it's far better to use a thin layer (⅛" is the recommended thickness) than a thick one. If too thick, the paraffin will not adhere to the jelly or to the glass as it hardens. Thus, the seal won't be airtight. If there are any air bubbles in the surface of the paraffin, prick with a sterilized needle. NOTE: You can pack jelly in half-pint can-or-freeze jars, if you like, and seal them with dome lids and screw bands. Simply pour the boiling hot jelly into the *sterilized* jars to within ⅛" of the tops, wipe the jar rims with a hot, damp cloth, fit the dome lids in place and screw the screw bands on tight.

Jelly is not processed after it is packed into jars (processing would break down the jell), so to kill any microorganisms that might exist in the ⅛" of head space at the top of jars fitted with dome lids and screw bands, turn each jar upside down as soon as it is sealed and let stand 10 to 15 seconds. Then turn right side up and cool.

4.   *About those old-fashioned bailed or "lightning" jars:* As we have stressed elsewhere (The Different Kinds of Preserving Jars and Closures; see index for page numbers), we do not advise using these jars. Most of them, relics of the good old days, are no longer reliable because the glass may have weakened and the bailing or wire clamps lost their gimp. If, however, you have on hand jars and lids in perfect condition, here is how to seal them: Fit a hot rubber jar ring on the ledge of the jar just below the rim so that it lies flat. Wipe jar rim and rubber with a moist, hot cloth, put glass lid on the jar so that it rests squarely on the rubber ring. Push the longer of the two wire clamps up on top of the lid so that it is anchored in the notch—don't touch the shorter wire clamp yet. After processing, snap the shorter clamp down against the shoulder of the jar. This completes the seal.

Process as individual recipes or canning instructions direct, that is, in either the water bath or steam pressure canner. The nature of the food, its acid and/or sugar content, determine how it should be processed.

Water Bath Processing

1. *Foods processed in a hot (simmering) water bath (185° F.):*

   Fruit butters   Marmalades
   Fruit conserves   Preserves
   Jams

2. *Foods processed in a boiling water bath (212° F.):*

   Berries and fruits   Pickles
   Berry and fruit juices   Relishes
   Catsups and chili   Rhubarb
      sauces   Sauerkraut
   Mincemeats *(not*   Tomatoes (also tomato
      containing meat   juice, paste, purée
      or suet)   and sauce)

3. *How to process food in a water bath* (The only difference between the hot and the boiling water bath is the temperature of the water—185° F. for the hot water bath, 212° F. for the boiling.):

   Place rack in the bottom of the water bath canner. If you do not have a water bath canner fitted with its own rack, use a very large (2- or 4-gallon) deep kettle and an 8″ or 9″ cake rack. Two-thirds fill the kettle with water, set over high heat and bring to either a simmer (185° F.) or a boil (212° F.).

   Grasp filled, sealed jars, one at a time, with a jar holder or stout tongs and ease into water bath. Jars should stand squarely on the rack and touch neither themselves nor the sides of the kettle. Check water level; it should be 1″ at least above the tops of the jars. There should also be 1″ to 2″ of space above the waterline so that the water won't boil over. If there is insufficient water in the kettle, add *boiling* water, pouring *around* the jars rather than directly upon them. Once the jars are in the kettle, never add cold water. You risk breaking the jars.

   Heat until water in kettle returns to required temperature (185° F. for the hot water bath, 212° F. for the boiling water bath), cover kettle and begin timing the processing. EXCEPTION: The processing of pickles should be timed from the moment all jars are in the kettle, otherwise the pickles may lose their crisp, raw texture.

NOTE: Specific processing times are included with all recipes and directions in this book. They are, however, the times recommended at altitudes from sea

25

level up to 1,000 feet. If you live at a higher altitude, you must increase the processing time to compensate for the fact that water boils at temperatures lower than 212° F. (see Canning at High Altitudes in the Appendix for a table of adjustments).

As soon as processing time is up, lift jars from the water bath with jar holder and stand several inches apart on a rack or dish towel-lined tray or counter to cool. Make sure jars are out of drafts, which may cause them to cool too quickly or unevenly, thus affecting the seal.

Pressure Processing

1. *Foods processed in a steam pressure canner:*

Low-acid vegetables (see list of Low-Acid Foods given earlier in this chapter)	Poultry
	Seafood
	Soups
Meats	Stews (including stewed tomatoes)
Mincemeats (made with meat and/ or suet)	

2. *How to process food in a steam pressure canner:*

Place rack in the bottom of the steam pressure canner, set over a large burner, then add water to a depth of 2″ to 3″.

Arrange filled and sealed jars on the canner rack so that they will not touch or tumble against one another or against the sides of the canner.

Place lid on canner and fasten as manufacturer recommends so that steam will escape only through the petcock or weighted gauge opening. Heat canner until steam has flowed steadily out of the opening for a full 10 minutes (this is to drive air out of the canner so steam pressure can be built up).

Close the petcock or place the weighted pressure gauge on the canner. Pressure will now begin to mount. As soon as it reaches 10 pounds (the equivalent of 240° F. at sea level), begin timing the processing. NOTE: 10 pounds is the pressure recommended for altitudes of less than 2,000 feet. At higher altitudes, the pressure must be increased in order to achieve the necessary temperature inside the canner (see Canning at High Altitudes in the Appendix for a table of adjustments).

Maintain the pressure throughout processing at 10 pounds, raising or lowering the burner heat as needed. *Never try to lower the pressure by opening the petcock* (you risk serious burns).

When the jars have been pressure-processed the required length of time, turn the heat off and let the canner stand undisturbed until 2 minutes *after* the pressure has dropped to zero. Slowly open the petcock or remove the weighted gauge and let canner stand until steam no longer spews out of the opening. Unlock cover, then open the canner using the lid as a shield to protect yourself from any sudden blasts of steam.

With a jar holder, lift jars to a towel-padded tray or counter, spacing them several inches apart so that they will cool evenly.

Complete seals, if necessary. Dome lids are self-sealing and should not be touched after processing (if you try to tighten the screw bands, you may *break* the vacuum seal). Screw tops, used in conjunction with rubber jar rings, must be screwed down tight as soon as the preserving jars are removed from the canner, otherwise the jars will not seal. The old-fashioned bailed or "lightning" jars need a final adjustment, too. Simply snap the shorter wire clamp down firmly against the shoulder of the jar. That completes the seal.

Cool jars for 12 hours. For cooling, jars should be stood on a towel-padded tray or counter or on a rack so that air can circulate freely around them. Make sure there is plenty of space between the jars and that they are not subjected to sudden drafts. Do not cover the jars with towels, simply let them stand in a draft-free spot.

Check the seals. The technique varies according to the particular closure used. Thus:

1. *Dome lids and screw bands:* Remove the screw bands. Tap the dome lid lightly with a spoon. If it gives a clear "pinging" sound, the jar has sealed. Another way to check: Press the dome lid. If it does not budge and its center is slightly concave, the jar has sealed properly. If still in doubt, turn the jar upside down. If there are no signs of leakage, the jar has sealed.

2. *Screw tops and bailed ("lightning") closures:* Slowly turn jar upside down. If no liquid oozes or seeps out, the jar is sealed.

What to do if a jar has not sealed: There are two options. Either refrigerate the jar and serve the contents within 3 to 4 days. Or, begin all over again. Pack the food into a clean, hot preserving jar, seal and process as before.

Label and store jars. The label should include a description of the jar's contents (i.e., Pickled Carrot Sticks Rosemary) and the canning date (August 10, 1976). If you suspect that a particular jar may not have sealed properly, mark that jar as questionable. Then scrutinize it again before using and reject at once if it shows any signs of spoilage.

As for storage, there is a reason why canned foods should be stored in a cool, dark, dry place. Moisture may corrode or rust the jar lids, affecting the seal and inviting spoilage; too much light and / or heat will fade the jar's contents, destroy some of the vitamin content and soften the food. Freezing temperatures, on the other hand, may burst the jar or break the seal. Note: Jars sealed with dome lids should be stored *without* the screw bands.

About Using Home-canned Foods

Perfectly sealed jars of food will remain safe to eat for several years. However, they will lose flavor, color and nutritive value, so it is best to eat home-canned foods within a year of canning. Once a can is opened, store it in the refrigerator.

Always examine a jar of home-canned food (and that includes pickles, relishes, preserves, jams and jellies, too) before using. Reject any jars with bulging or leaking lids, any that are moldy, any that fizz or spurt when opened, any with sour or "off" orders, any that are seriously discolored. If the food is a low-acid vegetable (or meat, fish or poultry), put the contents of the jar into a saucepan and, as a precaution, do not just bring it to serving temperature—you should actually boil it for 15 minutes *before tasting it;* this is the time needed to destroy the deadly botulism toxin. NOTE: When discarding any jar of spoiled or questionable food, do so where neither people nor animals may find it.

FREEZING FOOD

Freezing is so easy, fast and safe a way of preserving food it's a wonder man did not perfect the process until the 20th century. Not that man didn't try. Sir Francis Bacon decided 350 years ago that he could freeze chickens by stuffing them with snow. The chickens didn't freeze, but Sir Francis did—he caught pneumonia and died. Eskimos have, of course, been freezing food for ages, inadvertently because at Arctic temperatures, they had no way to *prevent* their food from freezing. The instant they slice a haunch off a caribou, for example, it freezes as hard as a rock.

It turns out that *quick*-freezing is the secret of preserving the freshness of food, as an American scientist named Clarence Birdseye would learn in 1914 while on expedition to Labrador. Birdseye saw fish freeze solid as soon as fishermen pulled them up through holes in the ice. The fishermen thought nothing of it, but Birdseye did when he tasted the cooked fish. It was every bit as good as fresh fish.

Birdseye returned to the United States, set up a laboratory in Gloucester, Massachusetts, and using refrigerants, began to quick-freeze fish, fruits, vegetables, cakes—all manner of food. He worked on his process throughout the 1920s and, in 1930, first offered packages of frozen food for sale. Birdseye's frozen foods were good but his timing was terrible. America had fallen on the hard times of Depression and his revolutionary new frozen foods were so dear few people could afford them. It wasn't until World War II that the frozen food industry got off the ground.

What Birdseye had learned was that the actual freezing time was critical, that the only way to stop enzymatic action and to retard the growth of bacteria, yeasts and molds was to freeze food as fast as possible. Freezing did not kill the microorganisms or agents of spoilage. But it did stop them cold. Birdseye also determined that frozen foods stored at temperatures of 0° F. or lower would retain their qualities of freshness far longer than those stored at temperatures 10° or 20° higher.

Not All Foods Freeze Well

As excellent as freezing is for conserving some foods, it fails miserably with others. Tomatoes, for instance, are so fragile that the sharp ice crystals formed during freezing cause them to collapse like burst balloons. The foods listed below freeze poorly in the home freezer for one reason or another, so it is time (to say nothing of money) ill spent to try.

Avocados (except when puréed)
Bananas
Cabbage
Carrots (except when puréed)
Cauliflower
Celery
Cream- or egg-thickened sauces or salad
    dressings
Cucumbers
Eggplant
Gelatins
Grapes
Irish potatoes (except when fried)
Lettuce and other salad greens
Mushrooms
Onions
Peppers (hot)
Sauerkraut
Summer squash (except when puréed)
Tomatoes (except as sauce)
Turnips and rutabagas

THE *HOW* OF HASSLE-FREE HOME FREEZING

Get Set:

Plant in your garden those *varieties* of fruits and vegetables particularly suited to freezing. Your county agricultural or home economics agent should be able to advise you.

Buy whatever you need in the way of freezer wraps and cartons well ahead of time so that you won't be caught short at the zero hour. Never try to make do with leftover ice cream cartons or coleslaw containers, which are neither vapor- nor moisture-proof. Unless correctly wrapped, foods will shrivel and dry in the freezer. And never substitute cellophane tape for freezer tape. It will not hold fast at 0°.

Inventory your freezer carefully, making note of how much space is available. As a general rule, you should not attempt to freeze more than 2 to 3 pounds of food per cubic foot of freezer space. (Check the manufacturer's instruction booklet to see what he recommends for your particular freezer; also review his freezing tips.) Make sure that your freezer is working properly and that it registers 0° F. or lower. If it doesn't, have the freezer checked. Not all freezers have a temperature control, but if yours does, turn it to the "coldest" setting 24 hours before you intend to freeze a load of food.

Set aside 1 or 2 days a week for freezing the vegetables and fruits in your garden and keep those days free. It's a good idea to devote a morning to freezing a particular food and an afternoon to another. If you attempt too much at once, both you and the food will suffer.

Prepare and chill ahead of time whatever freezing syrups you will need and add anti-browning agents, if necessary. They are used to keep such fruits as apples, peaches, pears, apricots and plums from turning brown. You will find a thorough discussion of these under Special Ingredients of Food Conservation; see index for page numbers.

Assemble all equipment you will require to get the job done as speedily and efficiently as possible (kettles and blanching baskets, colanders, long-handled forks and spoons, paring and slicing knives, freezer wraps and cartons).

Pick fruits and vegetables when they are at their peak of maturity and do so just before you freeze them. If for some reason you must postpone the freezing, keep the foods refrigerated. And do *not* wash them before putting them into the refrigerator.

Go!

Follow the vegetable-by-vegetable and fruit-by-fruit freezing instructions given elsewhere in this book and don't try to shortcut any of the steps.

Handle all foods as gently and as little as possible. The initial preparation of food for freezing washing, sorting, peeling, slicing, etc. is essentially the same as for canning see in the preceding chapter, The *HOW* of Hassle-Free Canning, Pickling and Preserving .

Try to freeze foods in portions that are apt to be consumed during a meal. Loose vegetables green beans and peas , however, can be frozen in large freezer bags because you can easily reach in and scoop out exactly what you may need. Be careful to reseal the bag carefully each time you open it.

Use sturdy cartons for packing soft or liquid foods, bags for firm ones. Pack all foods snugly, leaving no more head space than is recommended. A certain amount of space should be left at the top of freezer cartons because foods expand as they freeze. When using bags or freezer wraps, smooth all air pockets out before sealing the bag or package. Air trapped inside can cause frozen foods to dry or discolor.

Cool foods to room temperature before setting them in the freezer (placing hot or warm foods in a freezer will raise its temperature, endangering the food stored there).

Label each package using a wax pencil, describing the contents, including the weight or number of servings and the date.

Place each package in the freezer as it is wrapped and place directly on the freezing surface, leaving 1" of space between packages so that the food will freeze as fast as possible. The more quickly a food freezes, the smaller the ice crystals inside it will be and the better the texture.

After the food has been in the freezer for 12 hours, examine the packages. If any seem soft, remove at once to the refrigerator and serve as soon as possible. Also have the freezer checked immediately because it is apparently not working properly.

Once the food is frozen brick-hard, restack in the freezer as compactly as possible. Store the most recently frozen foods at the back or bottom so that older packages will be used first. Freezers work most efficiently, by the way, when kept fully stored.

Update your freezer inventory each time you add food to it—or take food from it—so that you will know exactly what you have on hand. TIP: If you group foods in the freezer according to type (i.e., fruits, vegetables, meats), you will be able to locate them easily.

Check the freezer from time to time to make sure that it is maintaining the necessary 0° F. Food will not spoil as long as it remains frozen, but at temperatures of 10° or 20° it will lose flavor, texture and color. During your freezer check, also look for ripped packages and overwrap immediately to prevent "freezer burn."

What to Do If the Power Fails

First of all, don't panic. Unless the power remains off for an extended period of time, the food in the freezer will not spoil. Freezers are so well insulated that the food inside will remain frozen longer than you think possible, *provided you keep the freezer door shut tight.* In hot weather, for example, the food in a fully loaded freezer will remain frozen for about 2 days. If the freezer is half full, the food will stay frozen about 24 hours. If you discover that the power will be off for more than 2 days, try to transfer your frozen food to a commercial locker plant. Or failing that, pack it with dry ice. With 25 pounds of dry ice, you can keep the food in a fully loaded 10-cubic-foot freezer frozen for 3 to 4 days and the food in a partially loaded freezer frozen for 2 days.

If the food has softened, check the internal temperature by inserting a frozen food thermometer. Fruits and vegetables colder than 40° F., or those still showing ice crystals, may be refrozen. They will have lost quality, true, but they will be fit to eat. (Meats, poultry and fish may be safely refrozen if their internal temperature registers 32° F. or less.) If foods have warmed beyond the point of safe refreezing, there is nothing you can do except cook them and/or eat them straight away. Be especially wary of poultry, seafood and "creamed" mixtures, which spoil more readily than fruits, vegetables and red meats. If in doubt about any food, if it looks or smells "spoiled," discard it *without tasting* where neither people nor animals will find it.

About Using Home-frozen Foods

Frozen vegetables and fruits, if stored at 0° F. or lower, will keep well for about one year. After that, deterioration begins—loss of color, texture, flavor and nutritive value.

With few exceptions (corn on the cob, to name one), frozen vegetables taste fresher if cooked from the solidly frozen state in as little water as possible. Corn on the cob will be sweeter and firmer if unwrapped, thawed about 15 minutes, then boiled 5 to 8 minutes in enough *unsalted* water to cover. Add a teaspoon of sugar to the cooking water, if you like, but never salt. It will toughen the corn.

Thaw frozen fruits only enough to separate them easily before serving, and do so at room temperature or in the refrigerator, never in hot water, which will give the fruits a cooked flavor. At room temperature, a pint of frozen fruit will thaw in about 2 to 3 hours, in the refrigerator in 4 to 6 hours.

Once food has thawed, never refreeze, because you will be flirting with food poisoning. The most critical periods for frozen foods are the actual time it takes them to freeze solid and the time it takes them to thaw. Temperatures inside the food are then higher and the microorganisms of spoilage can develop rapidly.

DRYING FOODS AT HOME

Drying as a means of preserving food dates back to the days of the Old Testament. And yet it remains popular in this age of freezing and canning because many people *like* the texture and flavor of dried foods. Peas, beans and lentils are all dried today as they were in Biblical times. Raisins are nothing more than dried grapes and prunes dried plums. The reason drying works so well is that the molds, yeasts and bacteria that spoil food cannot grow without sufficient moisture.

Drying foods commercially, however, is one thing and drying them at home something else again. If done on a big scale, it requires expensive, cumbersome equipment to say nothing of sheer physical space for spreading the foods out. With few exceptions, drying is not a particularly satisfactory way to conserve foods at home. Canning, pickling, preserving and freezing are all surer, easier and quicker. So in the chapters that follow, we will confine our discussion of drying to those few foods that can be handled easily and effectively in the oven, sun or air. In fact, what I recommend, in most instances, is a combination of parching and freezing. You will find in the vegetable-by-vegetable and fruit-by-fruit preserving directions ways to oven-dry small batches of sweet corn and apples together with recipes for using them once dried (see index for page numbers). I also include directions for sun-drying green beans and air-drying herbs. But with the exception of these few foods, I recommend that you freeze or can, pickle or preserve what you have grown in your garden. Or that you winter them over in cold storage.

WINTERING VEGETABLES AND FRUITS IN COLD STORAGE

Root cellar ... it has such a nostalgic ring. If you have ever spent any time on a farm, or even in a house in the country, you no doubt remember the cold, dark, damp cellar room where boxes of apples and pears, bins of potatoes and carrots were packed away for safekeeping. And you probably remember, too, the mingled smells of vegetables and fruits that filled the air. There were frequent trips to the root cellar—to pick out a dozen apples or so for pie, to gather enough potatoes for supper. Or maybe the trip was a routine inspection one, to see that the vegetables and fruits were wintering over well, that there wasn't one apple going bad or an onion or potato or pear that might spoil the lot.

Root cellars, of course, need not be *in* a cellar. Any spot that is sufficiently and *evenly* cold (usually between 32° and 40° F.), moist (between 70% and 95%

humidity), dark and draft-free will work. But finding such a spot is difficult, if not impossible, in today's super-heated, well-insulated homes, which are much too hot and dry. Sometimes the crawl space in a partial basement can be used for cold storage although it is far from ideal because it is inaccessible and apt to harbor field mice that will feast all winter long upon your carefully packed produce.

Attics, by and large, are a bad choice not only because they collect and hold the heat of the house but also because their temperatures fluctuate wildly depending upon whether sun, rain or sleet has been beating down on the roof all day. Carports are too drafty and cold, garages are filled with fumes of oil and gasoline (which stored fruits and vegetables readily absorb). Companionways linking the garage and house may work provided they are not too light, dry or drafty and provided they do not "run hot and cold." Too many variables, perhaps, to control.

So unless you have a dark, damp, cold cellar corner, your best plan is to winter fresh fruits and vegetables outdoors in metal drums sunk into a hillside or bank. Here, then, are directions for improvising a root cellar, both *in* the cellar and out-of-doors.

How to Prepare a Root Cellar in the Cellar

Find, first of all, an out-of-the-way corner or better yet, a corner room (preferably on the north or east), well away from the furnace, hot water heater, furnace ducts and hot water pipes. Check the room's winter temperature, at night as well as during the day, over a period of several weeks—it should remain in the 32° to 40° F. range. Also check the humidity, which for successful cold storage should be between 70% and 95%. Ideally, the area should contain a small window because an opening to the outside makes it easier to control temperature, humidity, light and ventilation. There should be *slight* circulation of air in a root cellar, but the movement must be *uniform*. Sudden drafts and gusts cause both temperature and humidity to fluctuate sharply; moreover, frequent influxes of fresh air can actually hasten spoilage.

How big should the root cellar be? That depends upon how green your thumb is, but the bare minimum is considered to be 36 square feet, that is, an area measuring 6' × 6'. If the area is enclosed, so much the better. If not, and if you are serious about having a root cellar where you can winter fruits and vegetables year after year, you should wall the area in so that you can more closely control the root cellar environment. If you begin with a corner of the cellar (ideally, it should be a northeast corner where temperatures remain more constant), you have only to build two inside walls at right angles to the corner foundation walls. Anyone relatively handy with hammer and saw can do the job.

Map out first the area you intend to enclose, allowing space for a door in one of the walls. Then secure wooden footings to the floor (by nailing or screwing in place 2 × 4's or 2 × 6's). Nail studs (again 2 × 4's or 2 × 6's) to the footings, spacing about 20″ to 24″ apart and making sure that they extend all the way to the ceiling. Cover the outside of the studs with ½″ plywood or wallboard, then pack fiberglass insulation into the interior walls between the studs. Cover the inside walls, too, with plywood or wallboard, if you like, and seal all the cracks. Frame and hang the door so that it fits snugly, and cover the inside of the door with fiberglass insulation. (For the neatest fit, frame the inside of the door with firring strips, then staple or nail lengths of insulation inside the frame.)

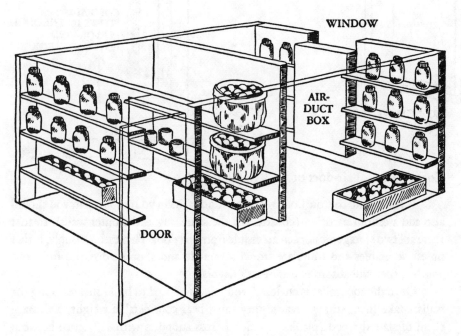

WINDOW

AIR-
DUCT
BOX

DOOR

A simple basement root cellar

If there is a window in the room, cover it with an air duct box which, when the top part of the window is open, will suck fresh air into the room and exhaust stale air. The box should cover the bottom two thirds of the window only and it should extend down the wall below the window for a distance of about 3′. The bottom of the box should be slatted or perforated to allow for air intake, and the back should be left open for air exhaust; the air duct, otherwise, is nothing more than a plain, rectangular plywood box.

35

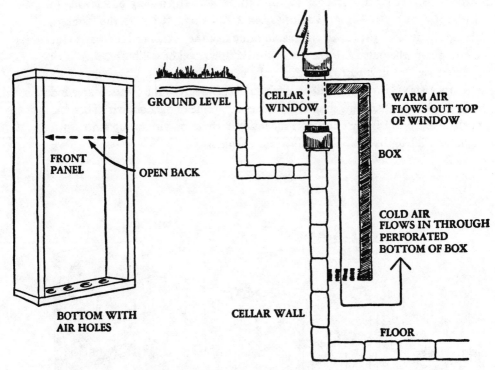

GROUND LEVEL

FRONT PANEL

OPEN BACK

BOTTOM WITH AIR HOLES

CELLAR WINDOW

WARM AIR FLOWS OUT TOP OF WINDOW

BOX

COLD AIR FLOWS IN THROUGH PERFORATED BOTTOM OF BOX

CELLAR WALL

FLOOR

Construction of air-duct box

If you intend to store both vegetables and fruits in your root cellar, you should also add a central partition (constructed the same way as the outer walls), so that there are two storage areas, each accessible from the door. The reason, simply, is that unless vegetables and fruits are stored separately and at some distance from one another, they will absorb one another's flavors.

Once the root cellar is enclosed, you will then need to build shelves along the walls. Make them sturdy because they must bear considerable weight, and make them of slatted wood (planks laid along cross supports with ½" space between them), so that air can circulate. Begin at the bottom, setting the first shelf about 4" off the floor, then add two more shelves, spacing them 24" to 30" apart so that you will have easy access to the stored vegetables and fruits. The highest shelf should be no more than chest- or shoulder-high because you will be hoisting heavy cartons up onto it.

It goes without saying that you will need a light in the root cellar, but it need not be anything more elaborate or expensive than a simple socket, bulb and pull chain. You will also need a hygrometer (humidity gauge) so that you can keep tabs on the humidity of your root cellar. These are available at most hardware stores and usually cost less than $10—a nominal investment considering the value of the food being stored. Some people merely hang a swatch of Spanish moss in their root cellars as an indication of humidity. If the Spanish moss remains fluffy and resilient, the humidity is probably sufficiently high for cold storage; if it becomes withered and brittle, the humidity is too low. Hygrometers, however, are more readily available in most areas of the country than Spanish moss; certainly they provide far more accurate humidity readings. Should you find the humidity in your root cellar dropping well below the recommended percentage, you should also invest in a cool-vapor humidifier (obtainable at most drug stores). A small electric model, about $20, should do the trick. Just make certain that you buy a *cool*-vapor humidifier, not a steam humidifier, which might raise the temperature of the root cellar above the level needed for safekeeping of vegetables and fruits.

For storing food, the best containers are bushel baskets, slatted orange crates or sturdy, perforated cardboard cartons (the kind apples are packed in for shipment). You will also need plenty of tissue paper for cushioning and wrapping food or, if you prefer, clean dry straw or leaves.

How to Prepare a Root Cellar in Metal Drums Out-of-doors

We say drums, plural, because you will need a separate drum for each type of food you intend to store. Apples and potatoes don't mix, for example, nor do onions and cabbage or, for that matter, most different kinds of food. You will want to locate the drums where you can get at them easily without trekking several hundred yards through snow. And you will save yourself hours of hard digging if you can sink the drums into the face of a bank or hill. The ideal would be a good steep bank within a short walk of either the kitchen or cellar door.

How deeply the drums should be sunk in the ground depends upon how cold the winters are in your area. In mild climates where temperatures rarely plunge below 30° F., the drums need only be covered with a thick (12″) layer of straw, hay or dry leaves, then weighted down with a foot or so of soil. In more wintry areas, the drums should be heavily insulated with straw, hay or leaves (a thickness about equal to the diameter of the drum), then covered with about 2′ of soil.

The drums themselves are nothing more than big metal oil drums, open at one end, which have been meticulously scrubbed, rinsed, dried and aired so that no oil smell remains.

To sink the drums in a bank, hollow out tunnels large enough to accommodate the drums and a good thick layer all around of insulating straw, leaves or hay. Remove any rocks from the tunnel because they will cause "cold" spots. Also make

37

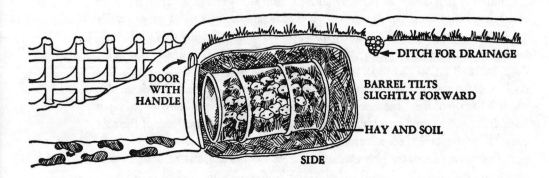

DITCH FOR DRAINAGE

DOOR
WITH
HANDLE

BARREL TILTS
SLIGHTLY FORWARD

HAY AND SOIL

SIDE

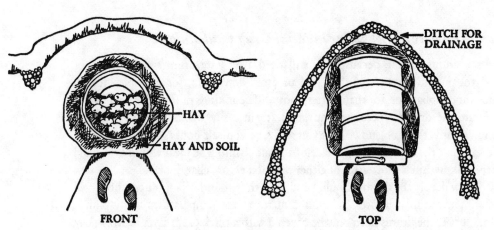

HAY

HAY AND SOIL

FRONT

DITCH FOR
DRAINAGE

TOP

Cross-section showing a properly sunk and filled drum for outdoor cold
storage of vegetables

the back end of the tunnel slightly higher than the front so that the drum will tilt forward allowing for good drainage. Lay a good thick bed of straw, hay or leaves on the tunnel floor, fit the drum in, then blanket it all around with more leaves, hay or straw. Fill in any spaces with soil (again removing rocks) so that the drum is snugly anchored. Then pile more soil on top.

For each drum, you will need a handled cover or "door" so that the vegetables and fruits will be protected and so that you can quickly pull out of cold storage whatever it is that you need. A sturdy wooden cover that will fit tightly over the mouth of the drum is the best choice because wood is a good insulator.

To fill the drums, first lay in the bottom a foot or so of clean dry straw, hay, leaves or corn husks, then fill the drum with one kind of food only, working from back to front, separating individual layers with more insulating material and filling in any spaces so that each vegetable or fruit is well cushioned and protected from the elements. Roll the cover in place, then bury it with more insulating material and soil. As an additional precaution, dig a shallow V-shaped ditch around each drum mound, sloping it from back to front so that rainwater, melting snow and surface moisture will drain off. There's no need to shovel snow off the top of the buried drums because snow is a dandy insulator.

Foods Suited to Cold Storage

Root vegetables, as a rule, weather cold storage the best, although cabbage, winter squash and pumpkins will all keep in a root cellar if the conditions are right. Both fruits and vegetables should be thoroughly cold *before* they go into a root cellar, thus it is advisable to gather them in late fall after the first frost. It is also imperative that the food be firm-ripe and in perfect condition—no blemishes, soft spots, signs of insect damage. One bad apple *can* spoil the whole barrel, or one bad onion, potato or pear. It is important, too, that successive layers of food be well insulated or padded and that they not be piled so high that the weight of the top layers crushes the food on the bottom. Apples and pears must not only be well cushioned, but also individually wrapped in tissue if they are to hold for any length of time.

How long foods will winter over depends upon the particular food (apples keep well for from 4 to 6 months), how cold the winter, and, of course, how well you have dug, insulated and packed your root cellar. (You will find specific packing instructions for various foods in the chapters that follow.)

Here, then, is a list of the vegetables and fruits that you can hold successfully in cold storage either indoors or out. The items marked with an asterisk * are too perishable to keep for more than a few weeks. The others, if properly packed and insulated, will keep well for several months.

Vegetables

Beets
Cabbage
Carrots
Cauliflower
Horseradish
Onions
Parsnips
* Peppers (sweet)

Irish Potatoes
Salsify
Sweet Potatoes and Yams
* Tomatoes
Turnips and Rutabaga
Winter Squash (with the exception of
   * Acorn Squash)

Fruits

Apples
Grapefruit
* Grapes

Oranges
Pears
Pumpkins

The Kitchen Conservatory

What you will need in the way of food conservation equipment depends upon how much food you plan to put by and how you plan to process it. If, for example, you expect to can only a few pints of pickles, or put up an occasional batch of jam, or freeze several quarts of fruits and vegetables, you can make do with kitchen equipment you already have, provided it includes at least two large heavy kettles (the kind you cook pasta in), a set of mixing bowls, a medium-size colander and sieve, measuring cups and spoons, a ladle, and a wire-mesh basket (for blanching vegetables and fruits). These are the barest essentials, but they will get you started.

If, on the other hand, you've planted a garden and the cucumbers and tomatoes and corn are ripening faster than you can eat them, you will want to lay down–as quickly and efficiently as possible–a good store to enjoy throughout the year. Which requires the proper equipment. *Proper,* by the way, needn't mean *expensive.* Most of the implements of canning, freezing, pickling and preserving can be bought reasonably at almost any dime store or hardware store. Many of them, moreover, are handy to have around for everyday cooking, and many of them you no doubt already have in the cupboard.

BASIC EQUIPMENT NEEDED FOR FOOD CONSERVATION

For Measuring:

Measuring spoons   (preferably two sets)
Measuring cups   (1-cup, 1-pint and 1-quart glass measuring cups with pour-

ing spouts for measuring liquids; also two sets of dry measures—nests of metal or plastic measuring cups containing individual ¼-cup, ⅓-cup, ½-cup and 1-cup sizes).

Scale   If you do not already own a kitchen scale, buy one with a large, flat, removable weighing pan and one calibrated in both grams (metric) and pounds. Make sure, too, that the scale will weigh amounts up to 22 pounds (10 kilograms).

For Preparing and Handling Food:

Knives   (paring knives, all-purpose knives, slicing knives and heavy chopping knives—one or two of each)

Swivel-bladed vegetable peeler   (it's the quickest and neatest tool for peeling thin-skinned vegetables and fruits—potatoes, carrots, cucumbers, apples and pears, etc.)

Pitters and corers   (for pitting and coring fruits)

Kitchen shears

Four-sided grater

Food grinder   (for chopping or grinding foods for relishes and chutneys)

Food mill   (for puréeing food; or better yet, an *electric blender)*

Cooking spoons   A well-rounded assortment of sizes is what you need. And be sure you have a good supply of sturdy *long-handled wooden spoons* because they remain cool after hours of stirring boiling-hot chutneys or catsups. Also essential, *long-handled, slotted metal spoons.*

Cooking forks   (again long-handled)

Spatulas   (both small, thin-bladed metal spatulas to help in packing foods in jars and rubber spatulas for bowl and pot scraping)

Tongs   (for handling hot cumbersome foods such as asparagus spears, carrots, broccoli and cauliflowerets)

Saucepans   You'll need small, medium and large saucepans—probably two of each at least. The best for pickling and preserving are those made of inert materials, that is, materials that will not react with the acid of food producing off flavors or colors. Best choices are enameled or porcelain-lined cast-iron pans (although these are uncommonly heavy), heavy-gauge stainless steel saucepans, or flameproof glass. Aluminum pans may also be used although aluminum may react with pickling liquids creating a metallic taste. Make sure that each pan has a snug-fitting lid.

Large heavy kettles   These are for soaking and brining foods, for simmering catsups, chutneys, relishes and marmalades. The sizes you will use most often are the 1½- or 2-gallon kettles. For best results, choose those made of heavy-gauge stainless steel or sturdy enamel. Never use copper, brass or galvanized metal kettles because the acid or alkali in foods may react with the metals to produce poison. Each kettle should have its own close-fitting cover.

Extra-large mixing bowls (for brining and soaking or simply holding food in various stages of preparation)

Large blanching or deep-fat-frying baskets (for blanching foods to be frozen)

Extra-large colander and extra-large fine-mesh strainer (for draining food)

Candy thermometer (for cooking jams and jellies to the exact degree of doneness)

Freezer thermometer (for double-checking temperature inside freezer)

Frozen-food thermometer (for spot-checking internal temperatures of frozen food)

Humidifier (cool-vapor) If needed to increase humidity in your root cellar. These electric appliances can be bought at most pharmacies for about $20 and are simply round containers which, when filled with water and plugged in, send a cool vapor into the air. *The humidifier must be a cool-vapor one,* not a steam-vapor model which would raise the temperature of the root cellar too much for safe cold storage of vegetables and fruits.

Hygrometer Humidity gauge for keeping tabs on root-cellar humidity. These cost about the same as a household thermometer and can be purchased at hardware stores and nurseries.

Jelly bag (a flannel bag for extracting fruit juices for jellies)

Jelmeter (to determine the jelling power of fruit juices and essential only if you want to make jellies the old-fashioned way *without* the commercial liquid or powdered pectins)

Cheesecloth (for countless uses)

Timer-clock (for timing both cooking and processing)

Wide-mouth canning funnel Maybe the most indispensable gadget of all because it makes filling jars so quick, easy and *neat*. The bottom of the funnel rests firmly inside the mouth of the jar and is broad enough for all but large pieces of food to slip through easily. The top flanges out like a cup or small bowl, reducing the risk of spilling. Best of all, the funnel protects the jar from dribbles and spatters, which might prevent a perfect seal.

Large trays or sturdy baking sheets Good ways to protect the counter surface when you're filling jars. Simply stand the jars on towel-lined trays so that they—not the counter or stovetop—catch the spills. Baking sheets and trays are also handy for oven-drying fruits and vegetables.

Clean dish towels and cloths

Pot holders and hot pads

Asbestos flame tamer Particularly useful if you cannot maintain the low burner heat needed for cooking chutneys, catsups and conserves. Flame tamers eliminate "hot spots" in the kettle, make it possible to simmer thick, sweet mixtures without their sticking or scorching.

NOTE: Although the new Cuisinart Food Processor does not belong among such basic pieces of equipment as those listed above, it should nonetheless be mentioned because it can trim food preparation time to seconds. It is a luxury item (retailing at a bit under $200), but if you do much canning or freezing and if you value the time you devote to chopping, mincing, slicing, grinding, grating and shredding, you would do well to splurge and buy one. Consider, for example, the hours you would spend cutting up vegetables for a large batch of pickle relish. This miracle machine will do the job in 30 seconds flat.

For Processing Food:

Preserving jars And plenty of them. Order them well ahead so that you won't be caught short come canning time. They should be spotless and in perfect condition (no cracks, nicks or chips). For each jar, of course, you will need the proper *closure,* also spotless and in perfect condition. Both jars and closures are described later in full detail.

Jar lifter and tongs Hoisting boiling hot jars out of a water bath is difficult (not to mention hazardous) because the jars are heavy, slippery and awkward to grasp. A good, sturdy jar lifter simplifies the job and reduces the risk of dropping a hot jar in midair. You'll need the tongs for fishing closures and empty jars out of the simmering water in which they must remain submerged until you are ready to use them.

Canning basket If you go into canning on a heavy scale, by all means buy a canning basket. It is a large, compartmentalized wire basket with looped handles that allows you to lift an entire canner load (as many as 7 quarts) in and out of a water bath or pressure canner at one fell swoop. Moreover, it holds the jars securely and keeps them from rattling against one another as they process.

The Water Bath Canner and How It Works

This is nothing more than a very large deep kettle with a snugly fitting cover and a rack on which sealed jars of food can rest while being simmered or boiled. You can, of course, make do with a heavy 2- or 4-gallon kettle provided it is deep enough to hold a rack and the jars with plenty of room to spare at the top and provided it has a fairly tight cover. *The water level in the canner should be at least one inch above the tops of the sealed jars. And there should be an additional inch or two of head space above the waterline so that the water in the kettle can circulate freely around the jars without boiling or splashing over.* As for the rack, an 8-inch round cake rack will fit inside most kettles and is large enough to accommodate 4 pint jars or 3 quart jars. In a pinch, you can also improvise a rack by padding the bottom of the kettle with a couple of folded-up dish towels—the idea is simply to keep the jars from touching the metal bottom of the kettle. However, if you intend to put by many quarts of pickles, preserves, chutneys and catsups, the best plan is to invest in a proper water bath. It will come equipped with its own rack and its own cover.

NOTE: *The water bath canner is used for processing high-acid foods only, never for processing canned vegetables, meats or seafood, which must be processed in a steam pressure canner).*

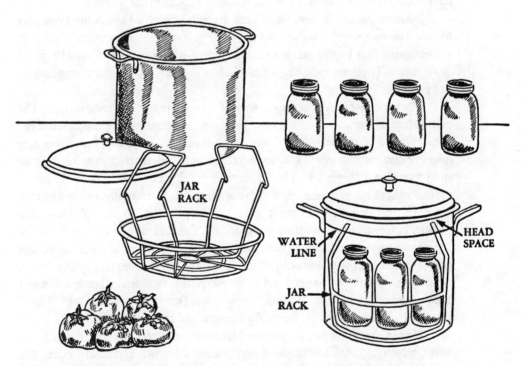

In a water bath canner, food is processed in jars at boiling (212° F.) The canner is a large covered pot or kettle with a rack and deep enough for the water to cover the tops of the jars by one or two inches without boiling over. Use only for acid foods: fruits, tomatoes, and sauerkraut, or for processing pickles, jams, and jellies. It is unsafe for canning low-acid foods.

Depending upon the temperature of the water inside the canner, it becomes either *a hot or simmering water bath* (185°) or *a boiling water bath* (212°). These temperatures, of course, are for altitudes at or near sea level. (You will find elsewhere in the book a table of adjustments that must be made at higher altitudes; see index for the page number.)

The Steam Pressure Canner and How It Works

This is an expensive item and you will need one *only* if you intend to can *low-acid foods* (vegetables, meats, poultry, seafoods, cream soups). I really think most low-acid foods are better frozen than canned. Certainly, freezing is an easier, safer and quicker way of conserving such foods. But if you're fond of canned cream-style corn or canned green beans, you will only be able to process them properly in a steam pressure canner. You cannot achieve in a boiling water bath the high temperature (240° F.) required to kill the microorganisms of spoilage.

What size pressure canner is best? That depends upon how much food you plan to can. The two most popular sizes are the 2-gallon pressure canner (which will accommodate four 1-quart jars at a time) and the 4-gallon (which will hold 7 quarts or 16 pints). There are even larger models, but they are too big for average stoves and needs.

What to look for when buying a pressure canner: First of all, construction. The canner should be made of heavy-gauge metal (cast aluminum, for example), and the surface should be smooth—free of pits, dents or nicks. Check, too, for unnecessary ridges or crevices that might catch and hold bits of food, making cleaning difficult and preventing a proper seal. The lid must be sturdily built, and it must clamp to the canner both air- and steam-tight. It's not a bad idea, incidentally, to buy by brand name. If, for example, you have a pressure saucepan that works well, hunt up a pressure canner made by the same manufacturer. Pressure canners are simply jumbo versions of pressure saucepans. Like them, they have (on the lid) a *steam pressure gauge* (to indicate the pounds of pressure inside the sealed canner), a *petcock* (valve, which when open allows steam and air to escape from inside the kettle and when closed, permits pressure to mount), a *safety valve* (steam release that will "blow" whenever pressure overbuilds inside the canner), and an *interior rack.*

How to care for a pressure canner: Handle gently, very gently, especially the cover, which contains the fragile pressure gauge, petcock and safety valve. The canner and lid should be washed like any fine kettle, that is, they should be sponged with sudsy warm water. Then they should be rinsed well and dried. Do not scour either kettle or lid with metal pads and don't try to brighten them with metal cleaners, which may erode their finish. Keep the sealing edges of both kettle and

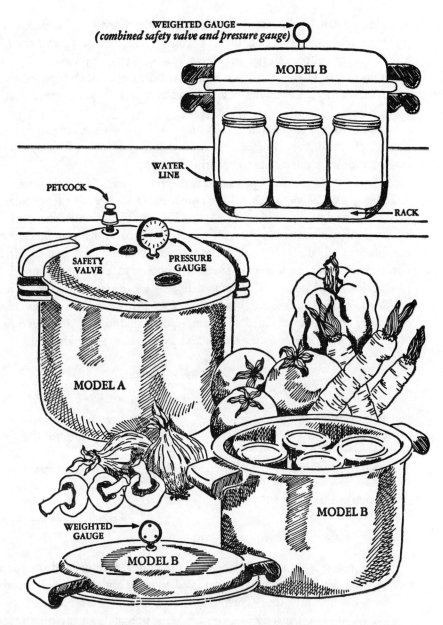

WEIGHTED GAUGE
(combined safety valve and pressure gauge)

MODEL B

WATER LINE

PETCOCK

RACK

SAFETY VALVE

PRESSURE GAUGE

MODEL A

MODEL B

WEIGHTED GAUGE

MODEL B

In a pressure canner, food is processed in jars at 5-lbs. (228° F.) or 10-lbs. (240° F.) pressure. The canner is a steam-tight, covered cooker with a rack and fitted with a pressure control or gauge. Use at 10 lbs. for low-acid foods: meat, poultry, seafood, and all vegetables except tomatoes and sauerkraut. May also be used at 5 lbs. for acid foods like fruits, tomatoes, and sauerkraut.

cover immaculate (check interlocking ridges for bits of food) and make certain the rubber gasket (if your particular model has one) is kept clean and grease-free (grease will soften the rubber and prevent the canner from sealing properly). Pay special attention to the petcock, too, drawing a piece of string through it to dislodge any grit or bits of food. And do the same for the steam pressure gauge opening and the safety valve.

Be careful not to bang the kettle or the lid and do not subject either to abrupt changes of temperature (immersing a hot kettle in cold water, for example); you may crack or warp the metal and ruin the canner.

Finally, *and this is most important, have the pressure gauge checked for accuracy at the beginning of each canning season.* (If the canner manufacturer has a representative in your area, he may be able to help you. Failing that, county extension home economics agents can be of service.) If you should discover that your pressure gauge is as much as 5 pounds off (reading either too high or too low), you should buy a new pressure canner or, if you can obtain it, a new lid for your specific model. If the gauge is less than 5 pounds off, you can still safely use the canner. *But be sure to mark the test results prominently on either the kettle or lid so that you will know precisely how far off the gauge is:* "2 pounds high," for example, or "1 pound low." *If food is to be safely processed, you must then compensate for any discrepancies.* Here's a handy guide:

FOR 10 POUNDS PRESSURE

If gauge reads LOW by	*If gauge reads HIGH by*
1 pound, process at 9 pounds pressure	1 pound, process at 11 pounds pressure
2 pounds, process at 8 pounds pressure	2 pounds, process at 12 pounds pressure
3 pounds, process at 7 pounds pressure	3 pounds, process at 13 pounds pressure
4 pounds, process at 6 pounds pressure	4 pounds, process at 14 pounds pressure

How to store a pressure canner Make sure both the canner and the cover are clean and dry. Stuff the canner with crumpled up paper toweling (it will absorb any off odors, and moisture, too). Then wrap the lid carefully in several thicknesses of paper toweling or soft tissue and set on the kettle upside down and slightly askew. Store the kettle on an out-of-the-way shelf where it is not apt to get banged or knocked about.

How to use a pressure canner: The technique varies somewhat from canner to canner and the best plan is to follow the directions outlined by the manufacturer of your particular model. Keep the instruction booklet handy, and reread it carefully each time you use the pressure canner—especially important at the beginning of each new canning season because you may have forgotten some of the specifics. NOTE: If you live at an altitude of 2,000 feet or more, see the Appendix for adjustments that must be made for pressure canning at high altitudes.

The Different Kinds of Preserving Jars and Closures

There are cans, too, but they require special sealing equipment. Moreover, for canning in moderate quantities, preserving jars are more suitable. They can be recycled and they allow you to show off the fruits of your labors.

In the old days, preserving jars and closures were available in a variety of styles—bailed or "lightning-type" jars with glass lids, metal clamps and rubber rings; glass jars with flat glass lids and screw bands; and the Mason (or screw-top) jars. Many of the old jars are still around, in antique shows, perhaps in your own cellar or attic. And, for nostalgia's sake, manufacturers of decorative kitchenware, many of them European, are again making the old bailed (wire-clamped) jars.

For safe canning, however, we recommend that you use modern preserving jars only, made by one or another of the major preserving jar manufacturers. Keep the old jars as curiosities, if you like. Use them for arranging flowers. Or as kitchen cannisters for sugar, flour, grains and pasta. But do not use them for canning. Jars do not endure forever, the glass may have weakened to the point that it will not stand intense heat (and certainly not the heat generated in a pressure canner). Moreover, the wire on bailed jars may have rusted or corroded or lost its spring. Too much is at stake in canning food to risk using antiquated jars and closures.

Modern preserving jars have been streamlined and perfected so that if you follow the manufacturer's instructions, you should have success every time. The basic types of jars and closures available today are shown on the next page.

How to care for preserving jars and closures: Preserving jars should be washed after they are emptied and then washed again before each use (especially important after long storage). Screw tops and screw bands should also be washed before and after each use. Dome lids and rubber rings should be washed before being used, too, *but they should be used one time only because both lose their sealing power.* For all washing, use hot sudsy water and a soft sponge, never scouring pads or brushes, never abrasive cleansers or washing soda, which may mar the surface of the glass. After washing, rinse well in clear hot water. If jars are to be filled and processed, sterilize if needed (necessary only for foods processed below 212° F. or not processed at all, as in the case of jellies); then

Left: Wide-mouth jars with dome lids and screw bands.
These are the favorites today because the jars are easy to fill and the lids are self-sealing (no completing of seals needed after processing). Sizes: quarts and half-gallons *(although canning in half-gallon quantities is no longer advised).*

Right: Standard jars with screw tops and rubber rings; the same jars also come with dome lids and screw bands.
These are the old Mason jars updated. Sizes: pint, quart, and half-gallon *(the latter no longer recommended for canning,* but they make nifty cannisters for nonperishables).

keep jars immersed in simmering water until you are ready to fill them. *The self-sealing dome lids should never be boiled.* Simply bring a pan of water to a boil, turn the heat off, drop dome lids and screw bands into the water, and let stand immersed until you are ready to use them.

Before using preserving jars, check each one carefully, making sure there are no cracks or nicks in the glass; scrutinize in particular the sealing edge of the rim. Reject any faulty jars and reject, too, any screw tops or screw bands that are misshapen, dented or rusty.

Left: Can-or-freeze jars with dome lids and screw bands.
The newest preserving jars and the most versatile, too, because they can be used for either canning or freezing. They are wide-mouthed, easy to fill. Sizes: half-pint (1 cup), pint, and 1½ pint.

Right: Jelly glasses with metal caps.
Available in plain or textured ("quilted") glass. The 8-ounce (1-cup) size is the most popular today.

To protect preserving jars, handle them gently. And above all, don't subject them to abrupt changes of temperature—plunging a cold jar into a boiling water bath, for example, or dumping cold water into a kettle on top of hot jars. Finally, when processing jars, leave enough room between them so that they don't bang or rattle against one another.

How to sterilize preserving jars and closures: Sterilization is not necessary for foods processed in a pressure canner or in a boiling water bath (212° F.). But it *is* necessary for foods processed below 212° F., that is, in a hot or simmering water bath (185° F.). And it is also necessary for jelly jars because jellies are cooked by the open kettle method and not processed at all. *To sterilize jars,* stand them on a rack in a large kettle, pour in enough boiling water to cover them, then boil rapidly for 10 minutes. Reduce the heat, then let jars stand in the simmering water until you are ready to use them. You can also improvise a sterilizer by using a large deep roasting pan. Lay jars on their sides in the pan, pour in enough boiling water to cover, then boil the prescribed 10 minutes, turn the heat down and keep the jars submerged until you are ready to use them. NOTE: Jelly jars, after being sterilized, can be arranged upside down on a baking sheet and kept hot in a very slow (250°) oven instead of being kept immersed in simmering water. This way, they will be dry and ready to fill.

Closures usually need only to be scalded (follow manufacturer's directions), EXCEPT for reused, porcelain-lined, zinc screw tops. These should be boiled in enough water to cover for 15 minutes, then left submerged in simmering water until you are ready to use them. *The rubber rings, used with the screw tops, should never be reused. Buy a new supply at the start of each canning season.*

How to store empty preserving jars: The best way is upside down in their original cartons, or, if they are jars with screw tops, right side up with the tops loosely screwed on. Screw bands can be strung on a cord and hung in a dry, out-of-the-way spot. Dome lids and rubber rings should be discarded after they have been used.

CAUTION: *Never use anything but preserving jars for canning—*no mayonnaise jars, for example, or pickle jars. They were neither designed nor constructed for home canning. If you must save them, use them for storing such nonperishables as rice, pasta, sugar and flour.

The Different Kinds of Freezer Containers and Wraps

Freezing is such an easy, quick, safe and dependable way of conserving food that we tend to be less particular about packaging than we are when canning, pickling or preserving. It's true that there is less danger of food spoiling in the freezer, but it can nonetheless shrivel, dry, discolor and lose both flavor and nutritive value if sloppily packaged. Moreover, it can absorb disagreeable freezer odors. Packaging is critical, and as in canning, you should never use commercial containers, such as old ice cream cartons or plastic slaw or potato salad containers, when packing food for the freezer.

Use containers that have been designed expressly for freezing food. They are moisture- and vapor-proof to preserve the food's original succulence, flavor, color and vitamin content. The containers themselves are odorless and tasteless (not true of many other plastic containers), they are grease-proof, meaning they can be reused because they will not absorb and hold the flavors of such foods as soups and stews, curries and chilis. Finally, they can be sealed airtight to preserve the food's original quality. Here, then, are the principal types of containers and wraps available and the uses for which each is best suited:

Plastic freezer containers   These have rigid sides and lids that snap on airtight. They may be square (easiest to stack in the freezer) or round. Such containers are best for freezing foods that are soft or liquid at room temperature (soups, stews, purées, fruits packed in syrup, etc.). Sizes: 12-ounce (1½ cups), 1-pint, 1½-pint, 1-quart and 2-quart.

Can-or-freeze jars with dome lids and screw bands   These are described fully under The Different Kinds of Preserving Jars and Closures; see index for page number. Like plastic containers, they are perfect for freezing soft or liquid foods. *Their biggest disadvantages:* They *will* break if dropped or banged roughly, and they cannot be stacked as snugly as square cartons because their sides are rounded. Sizes: half-pint, 1-pint and 1½-pint.

Plastic freezer bags   Because of their flexibility and sturdiness, plastic freezer bags are ideal for packaging irregularly shaped foods such as meats, poultry and fish. They are especially suited, too, to vegetables and to fruits packed dry without added syrup or sugar. The newest bags do not need to be heat sealed. After filling, all you need do is press out as much air as possible, then twist the top tightly, fold over into a gooseneck and secure with a twist-band. Do not use lightweight plastic storage bags in place of bona fide freezing bags; they are not sufficiently sturdy, moisture- or vapor-proof to prevent food from withering or discoloring in the freezer. As for size, plastic freezer bags are available in 1-pint, 1½-pint, 1-quart, and 1-gallon sizes. TIP: The quickest, neatest way to fill a freezer bag is to pile the food first into a container or cup measure the same size as the bag, invert the bag over the container, then turn the two upside down so that the food slides from the container into the bag.

Aluminum foil   Heavy-duty foil is the one to use. It's best for wrapping bulky or irregularly shaped foods such as meats, fish and poultry.

Laminated paper   This, simply, is a two-ply paper, usually foil, plastic or cellophane bonded to heavy paper. Like foil, laminated paper is most suited to wrapping roasts, fowl and fish.

Freezer tape   A sturdy, pliable tape that doesn't lose its grip in sub-zero storage. Use it to seal foil or laminated-paper packages.

How to care for freezer containers: Plastic containers and lids, freezer jars, and screw bands may all be reused. So, too, may the dome lids, *but for freezing only,* not for canning, because a thermetic seal is not necessary when packaging foods for the freezer. Wash plastic containers and lids, freezer jars and their closures as soon as they have been used, sponging with warm, sudsy water. Do not use metal scouring pads, abrasive cleansers or washing soda. Rinse well in very warm water, then stand (containers should drain upside down) on clean towels to dry. Each container should also be well washed and rinsed before each use. And so, too, should the lids and closures.

How to store freezer containers: The jars may be packed upside down in their original cartons and stuck on an out-of-the-way, dry shelf. Screw bands may be threaded on string and hung up (again in a dry spot so that they do not rust). Plastic containers may simply be restacked (tuck lids inside the top container, and cover that one, too, to keep dust, grit and grime out. Plastic freezer bags may also be reused, provided they contain no punctures, rips or tears. Simply wash, rinse, dry, then pack away in a box or drawer. Before using wash and rinse again.

NOTE: It is not necessary to sterilize jars, closures, plastic containers or bags when they are used for freezing foods.

SPECIAL INGREDIENTS OF FOOD CONSERVATION

Alum (ammonium alum) Old-fashioned pickle recipes often call for alum, an astringent that gives pickles an "icicle crispness." Today, however, alum is considered an unnecessary—and possibly harmful—additive, thus modern recipes advise against using it. Brining (soaking in salt water) will also crispen pickles, although not to the degree that alum will.

Anti-browning agents Certain foods (notably apples, peaches, cherries, pears, plums, apricots and nectarines) turn brown when they are peeled, cut open and exposed to the air. The browning will continue inside the preserving jar or freezer carton unless an anti-browning agent is added to check it. The browning does not make the food unsafe to eat, but it does make it unsightly and it destroys some of the vitamin C. *Ascorbic acid* (vitamin C) is the most effective anti-browning agent. Available at drugstores in tablet form, as a powder or as crystals, it can be used alone to prevent darkening. Or it can be used in combination with *citric acid* (another not-quite-so-effective antioxidant extracted from citrus fruits; it is available at drug stores in powder form). You will also find available a commercial, liquid blend of ascorbic and citrus acids. (Use as the manufacturer directs.)

How are anti-browning agents used? First of all, fruits should be dipped into an ascorbic-citric acid solution as soon as they are peeled and cut—1 teaspoon ascorbic *and* 1 tablespoon citric acid to each 1 gallon of cold water. In a pinch, you can substitute ¼ cup lemon juice for the ascorbic and citric acids. And, of course, you may use the commercial blend as the label directs.

To prevent canned fruit from darkening within the jar: Sprinkle ¼ teaspoon pure ascorbic acid into each 1-quart jar of fruit just before it is sealed, or use the commercial blend as directed.

To prevent frozen fruit from darkening in the freezer: If fruit is to be packed in syrup, mix ½ teaspoon ascorbic acid with each 1 quart of syrup. If fruit is to be packed in dry sugar, mix ½ teaspoon powdered or crystalline ascorbic acid with each 1 pound of sugar. Again, the commercial ascorbic-citric acid mixture can be used as the label directs.

Calcium hydroxide (slaked lime)   This is not the garden variety of caustic lime (calcium oxide) but a harmless form used by pharmacists. Like alum, it was used in days past to make pickles super crisp, and like alum, it is scorned by "additive freaks." Certain soft vegetables (asparagus and okra to name two) will become mushy during pickling if they are not first soaked in a solution of slaked lime. There is no other way to keep them crisp. So you will find in the pages that follow, three, perhaps four, recipes that call for slaked lime. The amount used is small (usually 1 teaspoon per quart of water), and the vegetables are thoroughly rinsed—several times—after being soaked in the lime water. If, however, the idea of using slaked lime turns you off, simply skip the recipes that include it. Commercial processors have, by the way, used calcium hydroxide for years to firm up certain foods, among them maraschino cherries.

Pectin   A jelling agent found naturally in certain fruits (apples, grapes and quinces). Commercial pectins in both liquid and powder form have streamlined the once-tedious process of jelly-making. They are quick to use and guarantee an infallible jell when used as directed.

Pickling salt   Table salt should not be used for making pickles and relishes. Iodized salt may turn the pickles black and the adulterants added to make salt free-flowing may cloud the brine. Pickling salt is pure, fine-grained salt. You may also use Kosher or dairy salts—also pure but more coarsely grained. Because of their coarse texture, they should not be substituted measure for measure for pickling salt. Use instead 1½ times as much. Thus, 1 cup pickling salt = 1½ cups Kosher or dairy salt.

Soft water   Whether the water is artificially or naturally soft makes no difference, but for making pickles the water *should be soft.* Hard water throws an ugly scum, and if its iron content is high, it may blacken the pickles. If water in your area is hard and you have no water softening system, here's an easy way to soften it yourself: Boil a large kettle of water for 15 minutes, cover and let stand at room temperature for 24 hours. Carefully skim any scum from the surface, then ladle water into a clean kettle, leaving all sediment behind.

Spices and herbs For most pickles and relishes, whole herbs and spices are preferable to the ground. They impart a more delicate flavor, they do not discolor the pickles or relishes, and they can be bundled up in cheesecloth, boiled in the pickling liquid just long enough to flavor it, then fished out. Certain whole spices (cinnamon, cloves and allspice), if left in jars of pickles may muddy their color and distort their flavor. Preserves, marmalades and chutney recipes, however, often call for ground spices or sometimes for a mixture of the whole and the ground. Always use freshly bought herbs and spices, never those that have been languishing on the kitchen shelf.

Whole herbs and spices commonly used in pickling and preserving: Allspice, bay leaves, celery seeds, chili peppers, cinnamon sticks, cloves, coriander, dill weed and dill seeds, fresh ginger root (as well as crystallized and preserved ginger), mace blades, mint, mustard seeds (both the mild white—actually pale yellow —and the stronger yellow—actually yellow-brown), black peppercorns. Many recipes call simply for *mixed pickling spices,* commercial blends containing mustard seeds, bay leaves, chili peppers, cinnamon, cloves, allspice and ginger.

Ground herbs and spices commonly used in pickling and preserving: Allspice, basil, cinnamon, cloves, ginger, mace, mustard, nutmeg, oregano, rosemary, savory, thyme, and turmeric.

Sugar Plain granulated sugar (either cane or beet sugar) is what you will most often need for canning, freezing, pickling and preserving. Occasionally, however, a recipe will specify light or dark brown sugar, both of which impart mellower flavor and darker color. *What about substituting corn syrup or honey?* When making jams, preserves, butters, marmalades and conserves, you may replace up to ⅓ of the amount of sugar called for with light corn syrup or up to ½ of the amount with honey. Honey, however, has such a pronounced flavor that it is apt to mask the more delicate flavor of fruits. Substitutes are risky in jelly-making (the jelly may not jell) and we do not recommend them.

Sugar syrups Many fruits, whether canned or frozen, must be packed in sugar syrup.

Sugar Syrups for Canning Fruit: Each 1-quart jar of fruit will require from 1 to 1½ cups of syrup. The canning instructions specify which type of syrup is best for each type of fruit.

TYPE OF SYRUP	AMOUNT OF SUGAR	AMOUNT OF WATER	YIELD
Light	2 cups	1 quart	5 cups syrup
	3 cups	1 quart	5 ½ cups syrup
	OR	OR	
Medium	1 ½ cups sugar + 1 cup light corn syrup	3 cups	5 ½ cups syrup
	OR	OR	
	1 cup sugar + 1 cup honey	1 quart	5 ½ cups syrup
Heavy	4 ½ cups	1 quart	6 ½ cups syrup

Method: Heat and stir sugar (or sugar and corn syrup or honey) and water in a heavy saucepan until sugar dissolves. Reduce heat and keep syrup hot but do not allow it to boil down because it will become too heavy. *To prevent browning of fruits:* Sprinkle ¼ teaspoon ascorbic acid into each 1-quart jar filled with fruit and syrup. Or use the commercial ascorbic-citric acid mixture as label recommends. Seal jar and process as directed.

Sugar Syrups for Freezing Fruit: Most fruits require a medium (40%) syrup, but such tart fruits as sour cherries will freeze more successfully in a heavy syrup. The fruit-by-fruit freezing instructions specify which syrup to use, or whether the fruits may be packed dry or in sugar. If syrup is specified, you will need just enough to cover the fruit in the carton—about ½ to ⅔ cup per 1-pint container. Make sure the syrup is *refrigerator cold* before you use it.

TYPE OF SYRUP	AMOUNT OF SUGAR	AMOUNT OF WATER	YIELD
30% *(light)*	2 cups	1 quart	5 cups
40% *(medium)*	3 cups	1 quart	5 ½ cups
50% *(heavy)*	4 ¾ cups	1 quart	6 ½ cups
60% *(very heavy)*	7 cups	1 quart	7 ¾ cups

Method: Bring water to a boil in a heavy saucepan, add sugar, turn heat off, and stir until sugar is completely dissolved. Cover pan and refrigerate until syrup is ice cold. *To prevent browning of fruits:* Mix ½ teaspoon ascorbic acid with each 1 quart of syrup (or use 4 crushed 100-milligram vitamin C tablets or 3 tablespoons lemon juice). If necessary to keep fruits submerged in the syrup in the container, lay a crumpled piece of foil or freezer wrap on top of fruit before snapping on the lid. It will push the fruits underneath the syrup and keep them there.

Vinegar For making pickles, relishes and chutneys you will need clear, fresh vinegar of from 4% to 6% acid strength. The acid strength should be marked on the label; if it isn't, don't use the vinegar. *Cider (brown) vinegar* is the all-purpose pickling vinegar because it has a pleasing, mellow flavor that combines well with other ingredients. It will, however, discolor such light or white foods as cabbage, onions or cauliflower; *white (distilled) vinegar* will not. The disadvantage of white vinegar is its acetic flavor, but the sharpness can easily be toned down by using a somewhat higher proportion of sugar. It is pointless, not to mention extravagant, to use wine or flavored vinegars for making pickles because the pickling spices easily overpower their delicate flavors. So use the plain, inexpensive vinegars–either cider or white. Just make sure the vinegar is sufficiently acid (too weak a vinegar will cause pickles to soften and spoil). Make certain, too, that the vinegar is crystal clear and that there is no sediment in the bottom of the bottle.

Vitriol (copper sulfate) A poisonous additive used years ago to turn pickles bright green. Do not use it–EVER–and do not, as Grandma also did, cook pickles or other acid mixtures in unlined copper kettles. It will "green" the pickles, yes, but it will also make them toxic.

A Mini-Dictionary of Food Conservation

DEFINITIONS OF THE SPECIAL TERMS AND TECHNIQUES

Acid foods For canning, foods are grouped into two large categories, *high-acid foods* and *low-acid foods,* because a food's acid content determines how it should be processed. Acid foods, for example, can be processed safely in a water bath (212° or lower) because their acidity inhibits the growth of certain microorganisms of spoilage and particularly that of dangerous heat-resistant bacteria. Most fruits are high-acid foods, so too are rhubarb and sauerkraut, pickles and relishes, jams, conserves, preserves and marmalades. Meat, poultry, fish and most vegetables, on the other hand, are low-acid foods and as such require processing in a steam pressure canner. You will find high- and low-acid foods listed in the pages that precede; see index for page numbers.

Additive Technically, any "extra" added to food–herbs and spices, for example, even salt and pepper. In modern usage, however, *additive* has come to mean any questionable or possibly harmful adulterant: *alum,* to name one, which our grandmothers used to crispen pickles, and *vitriol,* to name another, which they added to make pickles bright green.

Adjust caps After being processed in a water bath or pressure canner, preserving jars fitted with rubber rings and screw tops must have the tops screwed down tight if they are to vacuum-seal. So whenever the words "adjust caps" appear in a recipe, you can translate them to mean "screw the lids down tight." Sometimes the instruction will read, "complete the seal." It means the same thing.

Antioxidants Another term for *anti-browning agents,* which are discussed fully under Special Ingredients of Food Conservation; see index for page numbers. To give a fast explanation, *oxidation* is what turns certain fruits (apples, peaches, pears) brown when they are cut open and exposed to the air. To prevent the browning, oxidation must be checked and that's where the antioxidant or anti-browning agent comes in. Usually, it is nothing more than ascorbic acid (vitamin C).

Bacteria Without becoming too technical, we can define these simply as one group of the microorganisms that spoil food (yeasts and molds are others). Bacteria exist everywhere—in the soil, in food, water and air—and unless those existing inside jars of canned food are killed by boiling the sealed jars in a water bath or by processing them in a steam pressure canner, they will multiply and ruin the food. Imperfectly sealed jars may become recontaminated, thus the need for a vacuum-seal. Bacteria are a particular menace to low-acid vegetables, meats, fish and poultry.

Blanch To scald raw food in boiling water (or to steam briefly), usually before the food is frozen. Blanching sets the juices in food, stops enzymatic action which may spoil food, reduces the food's bulk and heightens its color. Blanching also makes peeling peaches, apricots, plums and onions a snap. Food should be plunged in ice water to quick-chill immediately after being blanched.

Botulism An often fatal form of food poisoning caused by a heat-resistant bacterium known as *Clostridium botulinum.* It thrives in the absence of air and particularly inside improperly processed or sealed jars of low-acid foods, producing a toxin so powerful that minute quantities of it can kill. Sadly, a contaminated jar may appear perfectly normal. As a precaution, be especially meticulous about the canning and pressure processing of all low-acid foods (vegetables, meats, poultry, seafoods). *And never taste the contents of any can or jar until after they have been boiled vigorously in a saucepan for 15 minutes (the amount of time needed to destroy the toxin).* If in doubt about any can of low-acid food, get rid of it immediately—*without tasting*—and do so where neither people nor animals can get at it. Botulism is rarely a problem in frozen foods (provided they are quick-frozen and stored at 0° F.) because the intense cold prevents the bacterium from growing and producing its toxin.

Brine A strong salt-water solution used in making pickles. For crisping cucumbers or other foods to be pickled, 1 cup of pickling salt to 1 gallon of cold water is the proper strength. For old-fashioned brined pickles, you will need a brine "strong enough to float an egg," or about 1 pound of salt per gallon of cold water. (This is also known as a 10% brine.)

Butter A smooth, thick, sweet spread made by boiling fruit and sugar down to a paste. Apples, peaches, pears and plums make delicious butters.

Chutney   A spicy fruit condiment served as an accompaniment to meats and curries. Most chutneys are made of a combination of fruits apples, raisins and currants, for example), most are tart and peppery. Mangos make a superior chutney. So, too, do pineapples, peaches, apples and pears.

Closure (also known as *Fitting)*   A closure, simply, is whatever is used to seal a jar of food. A screw top and a rubber ring, for example, or a dome lid and a screw band.

Cold pack (see *Pack)*

Cold storage (see *Root cellar)*

Complete seal (see *Adjust caps)*

Conserve   To preserve food (by canning, freezing, pickling, etc.) for future use. Also, a thick, sweet, cooked spread made of fruits and nuts.

Dry   To preserve food by removing most of its moisture. Drying is one of the oldest known methods of conserving food. In the old days, foods were spread in the sun to dry (and in some areas of the world, they still are). Today you can dry apples and corn effectively in the oven. (You will find directions elsewhere in the book; see index for page numbers.)

Enzymes   Chemical substances found in both plants and animals that alter the color, flavor and texture of food. If not destroyed by heat during the processing of canned foods, they may render the food unfit to eat.

Exhaust (also called *Vent)*   To expel steam from a pressure canner after the pressure has dropped to zero. It's done by opening the vent—*slowly,* so that the steam doesn't whoosh out all at once. The reason for exhausting is simply that if most of the steam has been released from the pressure canner, there is little danger of your being scalded by sudden bursts of it when the canner is opened. TIP: As an additional safeguard when opening the canner, use the cover as a shield to direct any remaining wisps of steam away from you.

Extract   To extract juice from fruits for the purpose of making jelly. The technique is to boil the fruit in a small quantity of water until mushy, then to pour the mixture into a jelly bag or into several thicknesses of cheesecloth, to suspend the bag or cheesecloth over a bowl and let the juice trickle out at its own turtle-paced speed. Forcing the juice out makes for a cloudy jelly.

Fermentation   Yeasts are the agents of fermentation, the process by which bread is leavened, beer is brewed and canned food is spoiled. To generalize, yeasts work on the sugars in food, turning them first to alcohol and carbon dioxide, and then to acid (vinegar is an end product of fermentation). Fortunately, yeasts are destroyed by relatively low temperatures (from 140° to 190°), so processing canned food in either a water bath or pressure canner will prevent fermentation (provided, of course, the jars are vacuum-sealed and not recontaminated by airborne yeasts).

Fitting (see *Closure*)

Flat-sour A form of spoilage common in low-acid vegetables. It's easily detected by the pungent sour odor the food gives off.

"Floaters" Pickles that float to the top of the jar. What causes them? Using overripe cucumbers *or* picking the cucumbers too far ahead of pickling time. Occasionally canned fruits will float, too, which means that they were packed in too "heavy" (too sweet) a syrup.

Freezer burn A scorched look on the surface of frozen food that occurs whenever food is exposed directly to zero or sub-zero temperatures. Rips or tears in a package will cause freezer burn as will loose or sloppy packaging.

Head space (also known as *Head room*) The air space left in the top of a jar or freezer container between the level of food and the rim. Head space provides room for the food to expand as it is processed or frozen.

Hot pack (see *Pack*)

Jam A thick, sweet spread made by cooking fruit, sugar and a small amount of water until thick enough to jell.

Jell To thicken, after long cooking, into a quivery mass stiff enough to "stand" without collapsing or running at room temperature.

Jelmeter A calibrated glass tube used to measure the amount of pectin present in fruit juice, which in turn indicates how much sugar is needed for making jelly. The higher the pectin content, the more slowly the juice will drain through the tube. Jelmeters can be bought in housewares sections of many department stores and come equipped with complete how-to instructions.

Jelly A sparkling, quivery-soft spread made by boiling pectin-rich fruit juice and sugar down until thick enough to jell (usually at a temperature of about 220°). Pectin is the vital ingredient, the jelling agent. Without it, a fruit juice will not "set up" (jell), no matter how long it is boiled. Fortunately, however, the commercial pectins available today (in both liquid and powder form) make it possible to jell almost any juice at all.

Jelly bag A large flannel or fine-weave cloth bag used to filter the juice out of fruit. Jelly bags can be bought at specialty kitchen shops and in housewares sections of some department stores. Most come equipped with metal stands from which they can be suspended.

Marmalade A clear, sweet, jelly-like spread usually made from citrus fruits and usually containing fine shreds of rind.

Mason jar A high-shouldered glass preserving jar fitted with an airtight screw top. It is named for John L. Mason, an American who patented the design in 1857.

Microorganism A microscopic animal or plant. In conserving food, three are of particular concern: bacteria, yeasts and molds, any one of which can cause food to spoil.

Mold Microscopic fungi which grow in long filaments. These mat and intertwine forming the wooly or downy masses we recognize as mold. Molds are particularly troublesome when it comes to preserving food. Like bacteria, they exist everywhere, producing airborne spores (dormant germ cells or "seeds") that alight and, when conditions are right, begin growing. Mold spores can withstand strongly acid mixtures (a jar of pickles or pickle relish, for example) but they *are* destroyed by heat. For this reason, modern pickle recipes call for processing pickles in a boiling water bath (212°). In our grandmother's day, pickles were packed in jars, covered with a strong vinegar pickling syrup, then sealed. They were not processed, and a good number of jars did mold.

Open kettle A method of cooking jams, fruit butters, jellies, preserves and chutneys in a large uncovered kettle until the desired consistency is reached. Jellies are poured boiling hot into hot sterilized jars and sealed straightaway without further processing. But jams, fruit butters and preserves should all be processed in a hot water bath (185°). The recipes included in later chapters all specify how long the processing should be.

Pack To fill preserving jars or freezer containers with food. *For canning,* there are two methods: *Cold (or raw) pack,* which means arranging cold or raw foods in hot jars and *hot pack* (filling hot jars with hot foods).

Pectin Discussed under Special Ingredients of Food Conservation; see index for page number.

pH Chemical shorthand which refers to the acid strength of a substance. The pH scale runs from 1 to 14 with 1 being the strongest acid reading, 7 the neutral point, and 14 the most alkaline reading. Strongly acid foods such as plums and gooseberries have a pH of about 2.75. Low-acid ones like green peas have a pH approaching 7, which means they are very nearly neutral. As we have stressed, in canning the acidity of food determines how it should be processed. Acid foods may be processed in a boiling water bath, *but all low-acid foods must be pressure processed.*

Pickle To preserve in brine or vinegar. A *relish* is a pickle, too, merely a more finely cut-up one.

Preserves Fruit cooked in sugar syrup until thick and clear. The fruit may be left whole or cut up.

Pressure canner (Discussed in The Kitchen Conservatory; see index for page number.)

Process To subject sealed jars of food to intense heat in order to kill the microorganisms of spoilage. There are two methods: in a *water bath*—either hot (185° F.) or boiling water (212° F.)—and in a *steam pressure canner.* Water bath processing is for high-acid foods only (fruits, pickles, preserves, etc.), steam pressure processing for low-acid vegetables, meats, poultry and seafood.

Put food by An old-fashioned, all-encompassing phrase that means to conserve today's harvest to enjoy later on during the lean winter months.

Relish (see *Pickle*)

Remove air or air bubbles To run a knife or narrow spatula around the inside of a filled jar to release the air bubbles trapped inside. If not removed, the air in the jar may cause the food to discolor.

Root cellar A storage place (not necessarily in the cellar) where such root vegetables as potatoes, turnips, onions, beets, etc., and some fruits can winter over without spoiling. It must be moist, warm enough to keep the foods from freezing but cold enough to prevent them from decomposing.

Scald (see *Blanch*)

Seal To screw the closures (lids and fittings) on preserving jars airtight.

Sheet The term used to describe jelly cooked to the correct degree of doneness. When a little of the hot jelly is taken up on a metal spoon, then tilted, the drops will run together forming a single "jelly-like sheet." If you use a candy thermometer, sheeting will occur at a temperature 8° to 9° F. above the boiling point of water in your area (at sea level, then, sheeting will occur at 220° to 221° F.).

Sterilize To boil preserving jars 10 minutes in sufficient water to cover them. The jars should then be kept immersed in simmering water (simply lower the heat under the kettle) until they are filled. Jars need not be sterilized for foods processed in a boiling water bath (212° F.) or for those processed in a steam pressure canner. But they *must* be sterilized when foods are processed in a hot water bath (185° F.) or, as in the case of jellies, not processed at all.

Vacuum-seal After food has been processed and begins to cool, a partial vacuum forms inside the preserving jar. The atmospheric pressure, now greater outside the jar than inside, forces the lid down against the jar rim airtight. This, then, is a vacuum-seal, which prevents air, moisture or microorganisms from entering the jar and spoiling the food.

Vent (see *Exhaust*)

Water bath Discussed in The Kitchen Conservatory; see index for page number.

Yeast Microscopic plants that can spoil canned food by fermentation.

part
TWO

DOING

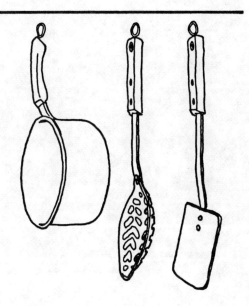

Home-grown Vegetables: How to Conserve Them

You won't find offbeat vegetables here because we are concerned only with those vegetables home gardeners can grow successfully throughout most of the United States. We'll take up the vegetables alphabetically, one at a time, then describe how best to conserve each one. If, for example, you have a bumper crop of corn, corn is what you are going to want to know how to can or freeze or whatever. So, simply flip through the pages that follow as you would through a dictionary. Under *CORN* you will find detailed directions for putting corn by but *only,* I should add, directions for those methods that do the corn credit. No point in wasting space now—or your time and money later—with instructions for canning a vegetable that cans poorly (broccoli, to name one), and I say so straight out. The policy, then, will be to discuss the very best ways of conserving each home-grown vegetable. And those ways only.

The time to think about conserving vegetables is not when you're bringing your crop in. Or even when you're setting the seeds in the ground. It is in the dead of winter when you're poring over seed catalogues. If your intent in gardening is to grow enough vegetables to enjoy throughout the year, you should order those varieties especially suited to canning, freezing, pickling or preserving. And, it goes without saying, you should also buy those varieties that grow well in your part of the country. Most seed catalogues spell this information out. But if you are still in doubt, ask your county agricultural agent or home economics agent for advice. They will know not only the latest recommendations of your state agricultural extension service but also of the U.S. Department of Agriculture. (You can reach them through your county government offices headquartered in the county seat.)

NOTE: All processing times and pounds of pressure given in the recipes and canning instructions that follow are for altitudes at or near sea level. If you live at an elevation of 1,000 feet or more, see the Appendix for tables of adjustments that must be made in water bath and steam pressure processing.

Altitude must also be considered when you are making jams, jellies, preserves, catsups, marmalades and butters. To make certain they are the proper consistency, use a candy thermometer and cook them until they are 8° to 9° F. above the boiling point of water in your particular area.

ASPARAGUS

TO CAN: Forget it. Canning so completely alters the color, flavor and crispness of fresh asparagus that you are better off giving your surplus asparagus away. Or freezing it.

TO FREEZE: Frozen asparagus is the next best thing to freshly cut asparagus—*if* you freeze it properly. *Amount of fresh asparagus needed to fill a 1-pint freezer container:* 1 to 1½ pounds.

1. Choose only young, tender stalks and cut them just before you're ready to freeze them. Then work fast because once asparagus has been cut, it quickly shrivels and toughens.

2. Group stalks together according to size—slim ones together, medium-size ones, chunky ones (but avoid using any that measure more than 1″ in diameter at the base; they will be tough). Break off woody stems so that the stalks are all approximately the same length, then even up the rough edges with a sharp knife. TIP: Don't throw the woody stems out. Save them to make a purée, which you can freeze, then use as a base for making asparagus soup or soufflé (recipes follow).

3. Wash stalks first in cold water, then in tepid water, then once again in cold water. The triple bath is to float out all grit and dirt embedded in the buds and spines.

4. Blanch stalks in boiling water, allowing 3 minutes for those measuring ¾″ in diameter or less, 4 minutes for those measuring ¾″ to 1″. TIP: If you have a large, open roasting pan fitted with a rack, use it for blanching the asparagus. Set it over two burners, pour in enough water to two-thirds fill the pan and bring it to a fast rolling boil. Lay the asparagus stalks flat on the rack, then lower slowly into the boiling water. Just make sure that the water completely covers the asparagus.

5. Quick-chill the blanched asparagus by plunging in ice water. Lift the rack of asparagus from the boiling water and lower into a second large pan (even a dishpan or the sink) filled with water and ice (2 to 3 trays of ice cubes should be sufficient). Keep asparagus in the ice water until completely chilled—about 5 minutes.

6.   Lift rack of asparagus from ice water and pack stalks flat in one-pint plastic containers or in freezer bags. You'll get more asparagus into each container or bag if you place the stalks parallel to one another but with tips pointing alternately in opposite directions. Fill container to the brim, snap on lid, label and freeze. Or if using the freezer bag, fill, smooth out air pockets, twist neck of bag into a gooseneck and secure with a twist-band.

KEEPING TIME: One year at 0° F., but the asparagus will taste fresher if used within 6 months.

TO PICKLE: Pickled asparagus? Try it before you pass judgment. It's crisp, scented with dill, a delicious, low-calorie cocktail snack. An excellent way to use up those skimpy last cuttings (see the recipe for Pickled Asparagus Tips that follows).

What about DRYING or STORING IN A ROOT CELLAR? Neither one works for asparagus.

FROZEN ASPARAGUS PURÉE
Makes 3 Cups

9 cups peeled, 1" chunks of asparagus stems (use all but the woodiest portions of the stalk; for this amount, you will need stem ends of about 8 pounds of asparagus)

1½ cups boiling water mixed with 2 teaspoons salt

2 teaspoons butter

Cook the asparagus in a large, heavy, covered pan in the boiling salted water 12 to 15 minutes until tender. Drain well, then purée in an electric blender at high speed. Return purée to saucepan, add butter, then simmer uncovered, stirring frequently, until about the consistency of thick applesauce (this will take about 1 hour, perhaps slightly longer).

Pack into two (1½ cup) freezer containers filling to within ½" of the tops, cool to room temperature, then cover, label and quick-freeze at 0° F. Use the purée to make asparagus soup or soufflé.

CREAM OF ASPARAGUS SOUP
Makes 4 Servings

3 tablespoons unsalted butter
3 tablespoons all-purpose flour
2 cups chicken broth
1½ cups milk or light cream
1½ cups Frozen Asparagus Purée, completely thawed (recipe precedes)

⅛ teaspoon dried leaf thyme, crumbled
⅛ teaspoon ground mace
¾ teaspoon salt
⅛ teaspoon white pepper
3 tablespoons dry white wine

Melt the butter in a large heavy saucepan over moderate heat and blend in the flour. Add the chicken broth and milk and heat, stirring constantly, until thickened and smooth—about 3 minutes. Mix in the thawed asparagus purée, the thyme, mace, salt and pepper, and heat and stir about 5 minutes or until the flavors are well mingled. Stir in the wine, heat and stir about 1 minute longer (do not allow to boil or the soup may curdle) and serve at once.

ASPARAGUS SOUFFLÉ WITH DILL AND PARMESAN
Makes 4 Servings

The single most common cause of collapsed soufflés is overbeating the egg whites. They should not be beaten "to dry peaks" because if they are, the egg whites will break down when you mix them with the basic soufflé mixture. When properly beaten, the egg whites should be billowing and soft with peaks that curl over when the beater is withdrawn. Do not beat the egg whites in an electric mixer but do them by hand, because only then will you be able to control the consistency. This soufflé, made of the tough ends of asparagus that have been puréed and frozen, is surprisingly delicate. It is best served with seafood (especially broiled or poached lean white fish) or with broiled chicken.

3 tablespoons unsalted butter
2 teaspoons minced fresh dill or ¼ teaspoon dill weed
5 tablespoons all-purpose flour
¾ cup milk or light cream
1½ cups Frozen Asparagus Purée (recipe precedes), completely thawed

1 teaspoon salt
⅛ teaspoon white pepper
3 tablespoons freshly grated parmesan cheese
4 egg yolks, lightly beaten (use large eggs)
5 egg whites (use large eggs)
Pinch of cream of tartar

Melt the butter in a medium-size saucepan over moderate heat, then let it brown until a pale topaz color (this is important for flavor). Add the dill, remove from heat and let mellow in the browned butter 2 to 3 minutes. Blend in the flour, return to heat and stir 1 to 2 minutes. Stir in the milk and thawed asparagus purée and heat, stirring constantly, until thickened and smooth—about 3 minutes. Mix in the salt, pepper and parmesan, and heat and stir another 2 to 3 minutes until cheese is melted. Briskly mix a little of the hot sauce into the beaten egg yolks, then stir back into pan and heat and stir about ½ minute. Remove sauce from heat at once and continue stirring for about 1 minute. Cool 15 to 20 minutes until lukewarm, stirring often to prevent a "skin" from forming on the top of the sauce.

Place the egg whites in a large bowl and add the cream of tartar. Using a rotary egg beater or a balloon whip, beat until the egg whites are foamy and white and form peaks that curl over when the beater is withdrawn. Quickly mix about 1 cup of the egg whites into the cooled sauce, then pour over beaten egg whites and fold in gently using a rubber spatula and an over and over motion. Handle the mixture carefully so as not to break down the volume.

Pour into an ungreased 6-cup soufflé dish and bake in a moderate oven (350° F.) until soufflé is puffed, lightly browned and still quivers when you nudge the dish—about 30 minutes. Rush to the table and serve.

PICKLED ASPARAGUS TIPS
Makes 2 Half-Pints

A "something-different" pickle to try if you have worlds of asparagus in the garden—more than you can enjoy fresh, more than you can freeze or share with neighbors. The pickles are fairly crisp, slightly sweet, slightly sour and delicately scented with dill. You need asparagus tips only, so save the stalks and make into a purée. Freeze the purée, then use as a base for making soups and soufflés.

30 medium-size asparagus spears	1 teaspoon white mustard seeds
2 quarts cold water mixed with 2 teaspoons	1 teaspoon dill seeds
slaked lime (calcium hydroxide)	1 small white onion, peeled, sliced tissue
1½ cups white vinegar	thin, and separated into rings
¾ cup sugar	2 small hot red chili peppers (fresh or
1 teaspoon salt	dried)

Break off the tough ends of asparagus spears, then cut each spear so that it measures 3¾" in length. Peel the scales from the stalks of the tips. Place the asparagus tips in a large enamel or stainless steel kettle, pour in lime-water mixture and let stand, uncovered, at room temperature for 2 hours. Drain asparagus tips well, then rinse several times in cool, clear water. Drain well again.

Wash and rinse 2 half-pint preserving jars, and their closures, then keep jars and closures immersed in simmering water until ready to use.

Mix vinegar, sugar, salt, mustard and dill seeds in a large, heavy enamel or stainless steel saucepan, add onion rings and bring to a boil. Boil 1 minute, then add asparagus spears and chili peppers and boil, covered, for 1 minute exactly.

Pack hot asparagus, tips down, in hot jars—the easiest way to do this is to make a ring of tips around the inner edge of the jar, then to fill in the center. Use a thin-bladed small spatula or table knife to help you in arranging the asparagus tips as neatly as possible. There should be about ½" of head room at the top of the jar. Tuck a hot red pepper into each jar, then pour hot pickling liquid into jars, filling to within ¼" of the tops. Make sure that asparagus is fully covered.

Wipe jar rims and seal. Process in boiling water bath (212° F.) for 10 minutes. Lift jars from water bath, complete seals if necessary, and cool to room temperature; check seals, then label and store on a cool, dark, dry shelf.

BEANS (GREEN AND WAX)

TO CAN: Next to corn, green beans are America's favorite canned vegetable, so much so, in fact, that thousands of people actually prefer their flavor over that of fresh or frozen beans. Though less popular, wax beans can equally well. Both varieties are prepared and processed the same way. You may pack the beans *hot* or *raw* (a method that is maybe five minutes faster). The pack you use, however, makes no difference in the end product. The beans will look, taste and "chew" the same. *Amount of fresh beans needed to fill a 1-quart jar: 2 to 2½ pounds.*

Cold (Raw) Pack:

1. Pick the beans just before you are ready to can them and select tender, young pods with plenty of "snap" that have not yet reached the "shell out" stage (ready to burst at the side seams). Wash the beans well in several changes of cool water. Tip the beans, remove any strings (modern varieties have few), then snap into 2″ lengths.

2. Pack the beans tightly in hot 1-pint or 1-quart preserving jars, filling to within 1″ of the tops. Add ½ teaspoon salt to each pint or 1 teaspoon salt to each quart. Pour enough boiling water into jars to cover beans, at the same time leaving 1″ head space at the top of each jar.

3. Wipe jar rims, seal jars, then PRESSURE PROCESS pints for 20 minutes at 10 pounds pressure and quarts for 25 minutes at 10 pounds pressure.

4. Remove jars from pressure canner (after pressure has dropped to 0°, of course), then complete seals, if necessary. Cool jars for 12 hours, check seals, then label and store on a cool, dark, dry shelf.

Hot Pack:

1. Follow directions for Step 1 in COLD PACK (above).

2. Boil beans for 3 minutes in enough water to cover, then using a large slotted spoon, lift beans from kettle and pack tightly in hot preserving jars (either the pint or quart size), filling to within 1″ of the tops. Add ½ teaspoon salt to each pint jar of beans and 1 teaspoon salt to each quart jar. Pour in enough clear boiling water to cover the beans, but allow 1″ head space.

3. & 4. Follow steps 3 and 4 for COLD PACK (above).

NOTE: If at the end of the season you find you have a good number of mature beans left in the garden, you may can them, using either the cold or hot pack. You must, however, PRESSURE PROCESS them longer than you would young beans: process pint jars for 35 minutes at 10 pounds pressure and quart jars for 45 minutes at 10 pounds pressure.

KEEPING TIME: One year, although the beans will be more flavorful if eaten within 6 to 8 months.

TO FREEZE: Green and wax beans both freeze best if cut into lengths of about 4″. They may be Frenched, but frankly Frenched beans, when frozen, lose their fresh "snap." Frenching (slicing the beans tissue-thin lengthwise) is tedious and as far as we're concerned, a waste of time. *Amount of fresh beans needed to fill a 1-pint freezer container:* ¾ to 1 pound.

1. Gather the beans just before you are ready to freeze them and choose those that are very young and tender (the inner beans should just be discernible in the pods). Wash the beans thoroughly in several changes of cool water, then tip, string (if necessary) and cut into 4″ lengths.

2. Allowing 1 gallon of boiling water for each 1 pound of beans, blanch the beans for 3 minutes (begin timing as soon as you immerse the beans in the boiling water). The most efficient way to blanch beans is to pile them in a blanching basket, then plunge into rapidly boiling water.

3. Lift beans (basket and all) from boiling water and empty into a colander set in a large pan of ice water. Chill beans 3 minutes.

4. Lift colander from ice bath and shake so that all excess water drains off beans. Pack beans tightly in 1- or 1½-pint freezer bags, pressing out all air pockets. Twist the top of each bag into a tight gooseneck, bend over, secure with a twist-band, then quick-freeze.

KEEPING TIME: One year at 0° F.

TO PICKLE: By all means put up some of your green beans using the recipe for Dilled Green Bean Pickles that follows. These have plenty of crunch and are a virtually calorie-free cocktail snack.

TO DRY: Dried green beans are known in the South as "Leather Britches Beans." They are an acquired taste—like olives or anchovies—and they *are* leathery, which no doubt accounts for the name. Drying is the way Indians in Virginia and the Carolinas conserved their excess green beans and it is from them that early colonists learned the trick. Not everyone likes Leather Britches Beans; in fact, many who have tried them consider them as fit to eat as shoe leather. But they get an argument from Southerners who look forward to nothing so much as a mess o'

Leather Britches Beans simmered most of the morning with a meaty ham bone. If you want to dry green beans, we suggest that you begin on a modest scale, stringing up a few pounds only. If you like them, you can be more ambitious next year. *Amount of fresh green beans needed to produce 1 pound Leather Britches Beans:* about 3 pounds.

Wash 3 pounds young green beans well, snap off the tips, then string up loosely (the beans should barely touch one another) on heavy white thread, using a heavy-gauge needle. Hang the string of beans clothesline fashion indoors in a sunny spot and let dry for about 2 months. Check the beans occasionally for signs of mold and discard them should they begin to soften or mold. If the spot is sufficiently dry and sunny (an east or south exposure is best), the beans will wither gradually, turn a sort of khaki color, then as they give up more and more of their moisture, become lightweight and leathery. They are now ready to cook (see the recipe for Leather Britches Beans that follows).

TO STORE IN A ROOT CELLAR: Don't bother. The beans will only mold and/or decompose.

DILLED GREEN BEAN PICKLES
Makes About 4 Pints
Crisp, ultra-low-calorie cocktail "sticks."

2 pounds tender young green beans, tipped and cut in 4" lengths	*3 cups white vinegar*
4 garlic cloves, peeled	*¼ cup sugar*
4 teaspoons dill weed	*2 tablespoons pickling salt*
1 cup water	*½ teaspoon crushed dried red chili peppers*

Wash and rinse four 1-pint preserving jars and their closures, then immerse jars and closures 3 minutes in two separate pans of simmering water. Remove one jar from the water and pack tightly with green beans, standing them on end. Pack the remaining jars the same way. Tuck a garlic clove down into each jar, then spoon 1 teaspoon dill weed into each jar.

While you are packing the beans in the jars, bring water, vinegar, sugar, salt and chili peppers to a boil, reduce heat and simmer, uncovered, for 5 minutes. When all jars are packed, pour in simmering hot pickling liquid, filling each jar to within ¼" of the top. Wipe jar rims, seal jars, then process for 10 minutes in a boiling water bath (212° F.).

Lift jars from water bath, cool thoroughly, then check seals, label and store on a cool, dark, dry shelf. Let the pickles mellow for about 1 month before serving. *Approximately 1 calorie per green bean.*

LEATHER BRITCHES BEANS
Makes About 4 Servings
The old Southern way to cook dried green beans.

1 pound dried green beans (see directions
    for drying that precede)
2 quarts cold water

1 large meaty ham bone
1 teaspoon salt (or more, if needed, to taste)
Pinch of black pepper

Place the beans in a heavy, medium-size kettle, pour in the water, cover and let the beans soak for about 2 hours. Add the ham bone, set the kettle over moderate heat and bring to a boil. Reduce heat so that water barely ripples, then simmer slowly, uncovered, about 3 hours or until beans have plumped and softened and meat falls away from the bone. Watch the pot closely toward the end of cooking and add more water if beans threaten to boil dry. There should be quite a bit of liquid in the kettle at serving time (about 2 cups). Taste for salt and add more, if needed. Also add pepper to taste. Spoon into soup bowls and serve, making sure that each person gets a nice chunk of ham and plenty of "pot likker." The traditional Southern accompaniment is fresh-baked corn bread, which is used for sopping up the pot likker after the beans have been eaten.

BEANS (LIMA)

TO CAN: Limas (or butterbeans as they're sometimes called) are one of the few vegetables that must be packed loosely in preserving jars. The reason, briefly, is that starch soaks up moisture and that limas, being highly starchy, absorb considerable canning liquid as they process and therefore swell. If packed too tightly within the jar, they'll burst and you'll end up not with beans but with sludge. So spoon the beans lightly into the jars and do not shake them down. Limas may be packed hot, or if you want to save a few minutes of preparation time, they may be packed raw. As far as the end product is concerned, it makes no difference how you pack them. *Amount of fresh* unshelled *limas needed to fill a 1-quart jar:* 3 to 5 pounds.

Cold (Raw) Pack:

1. Pick the limas on the day that you will can them and be choosy about the ones you use. For best results, the pods should be young and tender and the inner beans pale green. Wash the beans in the shell in cool water, drain, shell, then wash again.

2. Pack beans loosely in hot preserving jars (either the pint or quart size), filling to within 1" of the tops. Add ½ teaspoon of salt to each 1-pint jar or 1 teaspoon salt to each 1-quart jar. Pour enough clear boiling water into jars to cover beans, but allow 1″ head space at the top.

3. Wipe jar rims, seal jars, then PRESSURE PROCESS pints for 40 minutes at 10 pounds pressure and quarts for 50 minutes at 10 pounds pressure. NOTE: If beans are large, pressure process 10 minutes longer.

4. Remove jars from canner, complete seals, if necessary, then cool thoroughly, away from drafts. Check seals, label jars, then store on a cool, dark, dry shelf.

Hot Pack:

1. The same as for COLD PACK above.

2. Boil the limas 3 minutes in enough water to cover. Drain, then pack loosely in hot pint or quart preserving jars, filling to within 1″ of the tops. To each 1-pint jar add ½ teaspoon salt or to each 1-quart jar add 1 teaspoon salt. Pour enough fresh boiling water into jars to cover beans, at the same time leaving 1″ head space.

3. & 4. The same as for COLD PACK above.

KEEPING TIME: One year, although the limas will have better color, texture and flavor if eaten within 6 to 8 months.

TO FREEZE: Amount of unshelled limas needed to fill a 1-pint freezer container: 2 to 2½ pounds.

1. Pick the limas just before you are ready to freeze them, selecting the youngest, tenderest pods only. Wash the unshelled beans in cool water and drain. Shell the limas, then wash once again in cool water and drain.

2. Sort the beans, grouping all small ones together, all medium-size, and all large—the size of the bean determines how long it should be blanched.

3. Pile beans of uniform size into a blanching basket and scald in boiling water, allowing 1 minute for small beans, 2 minutes for medium-size beans, and 3 minutes for large beans.

4. Quick-chill beans by dumping into a colander submerged in ice water, again allowing about 1 minute for small beans, 2 minutes for medium-size ones, and 3 minutes for the large. Drain well.

5. Pack beans loosely, once again according to size, in 1-pint or 1½-pint freezer cartons, filling to within ½″ of the tops; snap on lids. Or, if you prefer, freeze in freezer bags, pressing out all air, twisting the top of each into a gooseneck, bending over and securing with a twist-band. Label each container or bag and quick-freeze.

KEEPING TIME: One year at 0° F.

TO PICKLE: Limas are too soft and starchy to pickle well.

TO DRY: Without special racks and an electric dryer that will maintain very low temperatures, you cannot dry limas successfully at home. Even the lowest oven temperatures are too high, so for small-scale conserving, you are better off canning or freezing your limas.

TO STORE IN A ROOT CELLAR: Fresh limas don't take to cold storage. They're much too perishable.

BEET GREENS
See Spinach and Other Greens
BEETS

TO CAN: Beets can exceptionally well (whole, sliced or diced) because they retain their flavor, texture and color. Indeed, their color seems to brighten with canning. Because they must be cooked before they are canned, beets are packed hot only. *Amount of fresh beets needed to fill a 1-quart jar:* about 2 pounds (weighed with all but 2" of the tops cut off) if the beets are packed whole, 3 to 3½ pounds if they are sliced or diced.

Hot Pack (Cold pack is not recommended):

1. Pull the beets shortly before you are ready to can them, choosing those of small- to medium-size and those that are free of blemishes.

2. Remove all but 2" of the beet greens, but do not trim off the root ends (so that as little red color as possible will leech out into the cooking water). Scrub the beets well in cool water, but do not peel. Boil the beets in enough *un*salted water to cover for 30 to 35 minutes or until their skins will slip off easily. Drain the beets, peel, trim off stems and root ends, then leave whole, slice or dice. Whichever you prefer.

3. Pack the hot beets into hot preserving jars (either the pint or quart size), filling to within 1" of the tops. To each pint jar add ½ teaspoon salt and to each quart jar, 1 teaspoon salt. Pour enough fresh boiling water into jars to cover beets, leaving 1" head space.

4. Wipe jar rims, seal jars, then PRESSURE PROCESS pints for 30 minutes at 10 pounds pressure and quarts for 35 minutes at 10 pounds pressure. These times, by the way, are for whole, sliced and diced beets.

5. Remove jars from canner, complete seals if necessary, then cool to room temperature. Check seals, label jars and store on a cool, dark, dry shelf.

   KEEPING TIME: One year, although the beets may begin to fade and lose flavor after about 8 months.

TO FREEZE: Because beets can and pickle so much better than they freeze, you'd be wise to reserve your freezer space for those fruits and vegetables that can be conserved only by freezing or for those that freeze better than they can.

TO PICKLE: Beets make superb pickles and relishes (see the recipes that follow).

TO DRY: Don't even try.

TO STORE IN A ROOT CELLAR: If the conditions are right *(slight* ventilation, temperatures ranging between 32° and 40° F. and humidity between 90% and 95%) beets will hold well in either a basement root cellar or properly insulated metal drum sunk into the ground outdoors (directions for building both types of cold storage are included elsewhere in the book; consult the index for page numbers).

If you intend to put beets in cold storage, you must pull them in late fall, *after* night temperatures have dropped to 30° F. but before snows and rains have turned your garden to mud. Ideally, the soil should still be fairly dry when the beets are pulled (if too wet, the beets may rot in cold storage). Do not wash the beets after you have pulled them, do not trim off the root ends, but *do* slice off all but ½" of the tops. *For root cellar storage,* pack the beets in perforated cartons or slatted boxes between layers of moist (not wet) sand or peat (the bottom layer should be bedded on moist sand or peat, too). *For outdoor metal drum storage,* layer the beets on a thick bed of clean dry straw, hay or leaves, separating subsequent layers and filling in spaces with more straw, hay or leaves.

KEEPING TIME: 4 to 5 months.

PICKLED BEETS
Makes 4 Quarts

1 gallon uniformly small beets (do not peel)   2 cups sugar
1 cinnamon stick, broken in several pieces   3½ cups cider vinegar
1 tablespoon whole allspice   1½ cups water
1 teaspoon whole cloves

Scrub beets well in cool water; trim off all but 2 inches of the tops; leave the root ends untouched. Place in a large kettle, add just enough water to cover, and boil, covered, until firm-tender (about 30 minutes).

While beets cook, wash and rinse four 1-quart preserving jars and their closures (or if you prefer, eight 1-pint preserving jars and their closures).

Drain beets, cover with ice water and let stand 1 to 2 minutes. Drain again. Trim off tops and root ends and slip off skins. Place beets in a very large, heavy enamel or stainless steel kettle. Tie cinnamon, allspice and cloves in several thicknesses of cheesecloth and drop into kettle. Mix sugar with vinegar and water and pour into kettle. Bring to a boil, then reduce heat and simmer uncovered for 15 minutes. Remove spice bag.

Pack hot beets into hot jars, then pour in boiling pickling liquid, filling to within ¼″ of the tops. Run a thin-blade spatula or table knife around inside edge of jars to release air bubbles. Wipe jar rims and seal jars. Process in a boiling water bath (212° F.) for 10 minutes. Remove jars from water bath, complete seals, if necessary, and cool to room temperature. Check seals, then label and store on a cool, dark, dry shelf.

RUBY BEET RELISH
Makes 4 to 5 Pints

To make this relish as sparkling and red as possible, use firm, medium-size, freshly pulled beets. Scrub the beets well but do not peel. Leave both the roots and about one inch of the tops on the beets, and cook in just enough water to cover—this prevents much of the red color from fading out of the beets. Cook the beets only until they are firm-tender (for about 20 minutes), then plunge in ice water, drain, slip off the skins and chop or shred coarsely.

1 quart coarsely chopped or shredded peeled, cooked beets (for this quantity, you will need 14 to 16 medium-size beets)

1 quart coarsely shredded red cabbage (about ½ medium-size head)

1¾ cups finely diced celery

1 cup coarsely chopped yellow onion

1 cup cranberry juice

1½ cups white vinegar

1⅔ cups sugar

2 tablespoons finely grated fresh horseradish or prepared horseradish

½ teaspoon finely grated orange rind

1 teaspoon salt

¼ teaspoon white pepper

⅛ teaspoon cayenne pepper

Wash and rinse five 1-pint preserving jars and their closures; keep jars and closures immersed in separate kettles of simmering water until you are ready to use them.

Place all relish ingredients in a large, heavy enamel or stainless-steel kettle, set uncovered over moderately high heat, and bring to a boil, stirring occasionally. Boil, uncovered and stirring frequently, for 5 minutes. Ladle hot relish into hot jars, filling to within ¼″ of the tops. Run a thin-blade spatula or knife around inside edges of jars to free air bubbles. Wipe jar rims and seal jars. Process for 15 minutes in a boiling water bath (212° F.). Remove jars from water bath, complete seals if necessary and cool completely. Check seals, label jars and store on a cool, dark, dry shelf. Let the relish mellow for about a month before serving.

BROCCOLI

Freezing is the only way you can conserve broccoli with any measure of success and even frozen broccoli runs fresh broccoli a poor second because it tends to be mushy. Canned broccoli is wretched (brown, strong-flavored and soft). Broccoli can't be pickled or dried or held in cold storage, so if you have more than you can eat fresh or share with friends, your only choice is to freeze it. As quickly and carefully as possible.

TO FREEZE: If broccoli is to retain a degree of its original crispness, you must rush it from the garden to the freezer. *Amount of fresh broccoli needed to fill a 1-pint container:* 1 pound.

1. Choose bright-green young broccoli with tightly budded heads that show no sign of blossoming or yellowing. Cut the broccoli just before you are ready to freeze it and lose no time getting it into the freezer. Slice off the woody stalk ends, remove coarse leaves, any discolored buds or wormy stalks. Divide the broccoli into stalks about 5" long and ½" in diameter. Wash well in several changes of cool water, handling as gently as possible so as not to bruise the fragile heads. Using 1 cup of pickling salt to 1 gallon of water, soak the broccoli for ½ hour in enough brine to cover (the salt-water bath is to float out any insects that may have embedded themselves in the heads). Rinse broccoli well and drain.

2. Lay broccoli stalks flat in a blanching basket and scald 3 minutes in boiling water. Lift the blanching basket from the kettle and plunge directly in a large pan of ice water. Let the broccoli chill for 3 minutes. Drain well.

3. Pack the broccoli in 1- or 1½-pint freezer containers, laying the stalks flat and alternating the direction of their heads so that you can pack more into each container. Fill the containers to within ¼" of the brim and snap on the lids. If you prefer, pack the stalks in freezer bags, press out all air pockets, twist the top of each into a tight gooseneck, bend over and secure with a twist-band. Label packages and quick-freeze.

KEEPING TIME: About 1 year at 0° F., although the broccoli will have fresher flavor and more crunch if eaten within 4 to 6 months.

CABBAGE

Cabbage cannot be canned satisfactorily except as sauerkraut (more of which later). It freezes poorly and dries not at all. The best ways, then, to conserve cabbage are to pickle it or winter it over in cold storage.

TO PICKLE: Two methods of pickling cabbage follow: Sauerkraut, which is nothing more than cabbage fermented in strong brine, and Shredded Pickled Cabbage, a crisp, sweet-sour relish pickled in vinegar.

TO STORE IN A METAL DRUM BURIED OUTDOORS: Cabbage will hold perfectly well in a basement root cellar, but it sends such disagreeable fumes throughout the house that we don't recommend storing it there. You cannot control the temperature and humidity in a buried drum as well as you can in a basement root cellar, it's true. However, if you prepare and pack the cabbage carefully, it should weather the winter well out-of-doors.

Gather the cabbages in late fall after "first frost" (frost won't harm cabbage, nor will a hard freeze; if the cabbages themselves freeze, bury in moist sand and let thaw slowly in a cool spot—a glassed-in porch or a companionway.) Don't let the cabbages refreeze, however, or they won't be fit to eat. Once the cabbages have thawed, prepare them for cold storage as you would cabbages that have not frozen in the field.

Cut roots off the cabbages, then peel away all outer leaves and any inner ones that are blemished, withered or insect-damaged. Lay down a good insulating bed of dry leaves, hay or straw in the metal drum, then a thick layer of moist (not wet) sand on which you will arrange the cabbages. Space the heads, not touching, in the sand, cover well with more moist sand, filling spaces between the heads so that they are completely buried. Top with another thick insulating layer of dry leaves, hay or straw and finally, with another heavy layer of moist sand or soil. Roll the drum's door in place and pad thickly with straw or leaves. The optimum "keeping" conditions for cabbage in cold storage are *slight* circulation of air, a temperature of 32° F. and a humidity that ranges between 85% and 90%.

KEEPING TIME: 4 to 6 months.

PICKLED SHREDDED CABBAGE
Makes 4 to 5 Pints

This particular recipe is sweet-sour and crisp and according to the quantity of chili peppers used, "lukewarm" or "hot." It is delicious with pork, ham and chicken.

4 quarts coarsely shredded cabbage (you will need about 2 medium-size heads)

2 quarts thinly sliced yellow onions (you will need about 14 to 16 medium-size onions)

½ cup pickling salt

½ to 1 teaspoon crushed dried red chili peppers (depending upon how "hot" you like things)

1 quart white vinegar

4 cups sugar

2 tablespoons ground turmeric

81

2 teaspoons ground mace	*3 tablespoons white mustard seeds*
1 teaspoon freshly ground black pepper	*1 tablespoon celery seeds*

Layer cabbage and onions into a very large bowl, sprinkle with pickling salt and let stand, uncovered, at room temperature for 20 minutes.

Meanwhile, wash and rinse five 1-pint preserving jars and their closures; keep jars and closures immersed in separate kettles of simmering water until you are ready to use them.

Rinse the brined vegetables in cool water and drain well, pressing very dry. Place chili peppers, vinegar, sugar, all spices and seeds in a very large heavy enamel or stainless-steel kettle and stir to mix. Set uncovered over moderate heat and bring to a boil. Add cabbage and onions and when mixture returns to the boil, boil uncovered for 5 minutes exactly.

Ladle boiling hot pickled cabbage into hot jars, using a slotted spoon and packing firmly. Fill jars to within ⅛" of the tops, making sure that pickling liquid covers the cabbage. Run a thin-blade spatula or table knife around inside edges of jars to release trapped air bubbles. Wipe jar rims and seal jars.

Process for 10 minutes in a boiling water bath (212° F.). Remove jars from water bath, complete seals if necessary, and cool completely. Check seals, then label jars and store on a cool, dark, dry shelf. Let "season" about a month before serving.

VARIATION: *Curried Pickled Cabbage.* Prepare as directed but reduce amount of ground turmeric to 1 tablespoon and add 2 tablespoons of curry powder. Also add, if you like, 1 peeled and minced clove of garlic at the same time that you add the chili peppers.

Although we think of sauerkraut as a German innovation, Germans came late into the art of souring *Kraut* (greens). The first sauerkraut was made, quite by accident, some 2,000 years ago in China during the building of The Great Wall. Cabbage was one of the staples fed to coolies building the wall and someone, in an effort to keep the cabbage from spoiling, cut it up and mixed it with rice wine. The cabbage bubbled and soured, and from then on pickled cabbage was a great Chinese delicacy. The Tartars, about 1,000 years later, traveled with kegs of sauerkraut (which they fermented in salt instead of wine), and it was they who carried the recipe across Mongolia into Russia, Poland and Austria. Austrians first called the fermented cabbage *sauerkraut,* and the name stuck. Sauerkraut is not difficult to make at home, but it does take time—about 4 to 6 weeks. Because cabbage does not ferment well in small quantities, you might as well be prepared to make a big batch of it. You'll need, for best results, a deep, heavy stoneware crock (4 gallons is a good size). You will also need a heavy plate slightly smaller than the diameter of the crock with which to weight the fermenting cabbage down and a yard or two of clean, bleached muslin.

SAUERKRAUT
Makes About 2 Gallons

25 pounds cabbage (about 5 to 6 large heads), trimmed of coarse outer leaves, cored, and sliced or shredded moderately fine
½ pound pickling salt

Mix about 5 pounds of the shredded cabbage with 3 tablespoons pickling salt in a large mixing bowl and let stand uncovered about 5 minutes until juices begin to run out of the cabbage. Transfer all to a heavy 4-gallon crock and pack in firmly. Repeat, mixing each time about 5 pounds of shredded cabbage with 3 tablespoons salt, until all cabbage and salt have been used up. Each time you add a batch of cabbage to the crock, pack it down well.

Lay a clean piece of bleached muslin flat on top of the cabbage and tuck the edges underneath. Place a clean heavy plate upside down on top of the muslin and weight down by standing a 1-quart or ½-gallon preserving jar, filled with water and sealed, in the center of the plate. The juices from the cabbage will ooze up over the plate but that is as it should be. The point is to keep the cabbage well submerged in brine. Lay several thicknesses of clean cheesecloth loosely over the top of the crock—it should not fall into the brine.

Set the crock in a dry, coolish, out-of-the-way spot (ideally, the temperature should remain between 68° and 72° F.). As a precaution, set the crock on a large metal tray, because once the fermentation gets going, the juices may bubble over.

After about a day, you'll notice bubbles in the brine. This means that fermentation has begun. It will continue for 4 to 6 weeks, depending upon whether the temperature stays around 68° or 72° F. (the higher the temperature, the faster the fermentation).

Every day or so, skim off any scum that has collected in the top of the crock, then re-cover, using a fresh piece of muslin if the original one becomes heavily encrusted with scum.

After 4 weeks, check to see if the cabbage is still bubbling. If not, nudge the crock. If no bubbles rise to the surface, the fermentation has stopped and the sauerkraut is ready to eat.

You can, if you like, store the crock of sauerkraut in a cool cellar, but the temperature must remain, at all times, at 55° or less. And make certain that the sauerkraut is submerged in the brine and that the crock is covered. A safer way to conserve the kraut, in these days of superheated houses, is to can it. Here's how.

TO CAN SAUERKRAUT: The preceding recipe makes enough sauerkraut to fill eight to nine 1-quart preserving jars. Wash and rinse nine 1-quart preserving jars and their closures, then keep jars and closures immersed in separate kettles of simmering water until you are ready to use them.

Empty about half of the sauerkraut (do not drain it) into a 4-gallon, heavy enamel or stainless steel kettle set over moderate heat, and bring just to the simmering point (between 185° and 210° F.). Do not allow the sauerkraut to boil. Using a slotted spoon and a wide-mouth canning funnel to make the jar-filling both quicker and neater, pack the sauerkraut into the jars, shaking it down as you go and filling each jar with brine to cover the sauerkraut, at the same time leaving ½" head space. Wipe jar rims and seal jars. Repeat with remaining sauerkraut.

Process the quarts of sauerkraut in a boiling water bath (212° F.) for 20 minutes. (If you should pack the sauerkraut in pint jars, process them for 15 minutes.) Remove jars from the water bath, complete seals, if necessary, then cool to room temperature. Check seals, label jars and store on a cool, dark, dry shelf.

KEEPING TIME: About one year.

CARROTS

TO CAN: Amount of fresh carrots needed to fill a 1-quart jar: 2 pounds (weighed without tops) if the carrots are to be packed whole, 2½ to 3 pounds if they are to be sliced or diced. NOTE: If you want to pack the carrots whole, choose small ones because you can pack them more easily and uniformly in the jars.

Cold (Raw) Pack:

1. Pull the carrots shortly before you will can them and remove the tops. Wash the carrots well, peel and wash well again. Leave whole or if carrots are large, slice or dice.

2. Pack raw carrots tightly in hot 1-pint or 1-quart preserving jars, filling to within 1" of the tops. Add ½ teaspoon salt to each pint jar and 1 teaspoon salt to each quart jar. Pour enough clear boiling water into jars to cover carrots, at the same time leaving 1" head space.

3. Wipe jar rims, seal jars, then PRESSURE PROCESS pints for 25 minutes at 10 pounds pressure and quarts for 30 minutes at 10 pounds pressure (these times are for whole, sliced and diced carrots).

4. Remove jars from canner, adjust seals, if necessary, and cool to room temperature. Check seals, then label jars and store on a cool, dark, dry shelf.

Hot Pack:

1. The same as for COLD PACK (above).

2. Boil the carrots for 3 minutes (whether whole, sliced or diced) in just enough water to cover them, then drain and pack tightly into hot 1-pint or 1-quart preserving jars, filling to within 1" of the tops. To each 1-pint jar add ½ teaspoon salt and to each 1-quart jar add 1 teaspoon salt. Pour enough clear boiling water into jars to cover carrots, but leave 1" head space.

3. & 4. The same as for COLD PACK (above).

KEEPING TIME: About one year.

TO FREEZE: Unfortunately, whole, diced or sliced carrots don't freeze very well because they become watery and, after being cooked, have an unpleasant soggy texture. You can, however, cook them, season them, purée them and *then* freeze them. The frozen purée makes an excellent base for both soups and soufflés (see recipes that follow).

TO PICKLE AND PRESERVE: You can turn carrots into delicious, crunchy pickles. And you can cook them down with orange, lemon and fresh ginger into a nippy marmalade (recipes follow).

TO DRY: No way.

TO STORE IN A ROOT CELLAR: Being hardy, carrots winter over well in either a basement root cellar or in a metal drum buried outdoors. They will hold best if the temperature is kept between 32° F. and 40° F., the humidity between 90% and 95% and the circulation of air at a minimum.

Dig the carrots in late fall after the first several frosts but while the garden soil is still dry (if it is wet or muddy, the carrots may rot). Do not wash the carrots and do not trim off the root ends. But do slice off all but about ½" of the tops. *For storing in the basement root cellar,* pack the carrots in well-perforated cartons or slatted boxes between layers of moist (not wet) peat or sand, making sure that the top layer is well covered. *For storing outdoors in a buried metal drum,* line the bottom of the drum with a thick insulating layer of dry straw, hay or leaves, add about 2" of moist sand or peat, then bed the carrots down. Cover with more moist sand or peat, filling in all spaces between the carrots. Build up successive layers the same way, then top the final layer of carrots with moist sand or peat and a good thick blanket of dry leaves, straw or hay. Weight down with more moist sand or soil.

KEEPING TIME: About 6 months.

FROZEN CARROT PURÉE
Makes 4 Pints

So that your carrot purée will be thick, cut the carrots in large chunks before you cook them. If the carrots are cut too fine, they will absorb unwanted cooking water and the purée will be too thin to freeze well.

> 4 dozen medium-size carrots
> 3 tablespoons unsalted butter
> ¼ teaspoon ground mace

Trim the carrots of tops and root ends, wash in cool water, then peel and cut in 2" chunks. Place in a medium-size heavy kettle, add just enough cold water to cover the carrots, then cover the kettle and boil about 20 minutes or until carrots are very tender. Drain well, return kettle to heat and shake about a minute to drive off excess moisture.

Purée the carrots by buzzing a few chunks at a time in an electric blender at high speed, or by putting through a food mill or forcing through a fine sieve. Place carrot purée in a heavy saucepan, add butter and mace and set uncovered over low heat. Cook and stir 2 to 3 minutes, just until butter melts.

Cool the purée to room temperature, then pack tightly into 1-pint freezer containers, filling to within ½" of the tops. Snap on lids, label containers and quick-freeze.

GOLDEN CREAM OF CARROT SOUP
Makes 4 to 6 Servings

2 tablespoons butter
1 small yellow onion, peeled and finely grated
⅛ teaspoon crumbled leaf rosemary
⅛ teaspoon ground nutmeg
2 tablespoons all-purpose flour
2 cups chicken broth
1 cup milk
1 cup light cream
1 pint Frozen Carrot Purée, completely thawed (recipe precedes)
1 teaspoon salt
⅛ teaspoon white pepper

Melt the butter in a large heavy saucepan over moderate heat, add onion, rosemary and nutmeg and heat, stirring, 3 to 4 minutes until onion is golden. Blend in flour, then add chicken broth and milk and heat, stirring constantly, until thickened and smooth—about 3 minutes. Stir in cream, carrot purée, salt and pepper and continue heating, stirring now and then, 5 to 10 minutes to blend the flavors. Do not allow soup to boil because it may curdle. Ladle into soup bowls and serve. For a fragrant garnish, top each serving with a scattering of chopped fresh chervil, dill or parsley.

CARROT SOUFFLÉ WITH ORANGE AND ROSEMARY
Makes 4 Servings
Delicious with broiled chicken or fish.

3 tablespoons unsalted butter
2 tablespoons finely grated yellow onion
⅛ teaspoon crumbled leaf rosemary
½ teaspoon finely grated orange rind
Pinch of ground nutmeg
4 tablespoons all-purpose flour
1 cup milk

1 pint Frozen Carrot Purée, completely thawed (recipe precedes)
1 teaspoon salt
⅛ teaspoon white pepper
4 egg yolks, lightly beaten (use large eggs)
5 egg whites (use large eggs)
Pinch of cream of tartar

Melt the butter in a large heavy saucepan over moderate heat, add onion, rosemary, orange rind and nutmeg and heat and stir about 5 minutes until onion is limp and golden. Blend in the flour and warm 2 to 3 minutes. Add the milk and thawed carrot purée and heat, stirring constantly, until thickened and smooth–3 to 4 minutes. Stir in the salt and pepper. Briskly mix a little of the hot sauce into the egg yolks, then stir back into pan. Heat, stirring constantly, for 1 minute–do not allow to boil. Remove from heat at once and cool to room temperature, stirring often to prevent a skin from forming on the surface of the sauce.

Beat the egg whites with the cream of tartar in a large bowl until soft peaks form (they should curl over when the beater is withdrawn). Stir about 1 cup of the beaten whites into the sauce (this is to lighten the sauce and make it easier to fold into the beaten whites). Pour sauce gently over beaten egg whites, then fold in using a rubber spatula and a light over and over motion until no streaks of white or yellow show.

Pour into an ungreased 6-cup soufflé dish and bake uncovered in a moderate oven (350° F.) about 30 minutes or until puffy and touched with brown (nudge the soufflé lightly on the oven shelf–it should quiver in the center). Remove from the oven, rush to the table and serve.

PICKLED CARROT STICKS ROSEMARY
Makes About 4 Pints

Serve these with cocktails. They're crisp and tart. Low-calorie, too. The carrot sticks will be more fragrant if made with fresh rosemary; however, you can substitute dried leaf rosemary if you add just enough to each jar to flavor the carrots (¼ teaspoon is about right). Too much rosemary will make the carrots bitter.

2 pounds carrots (weighed without tops), peeled and cut in uniform sticks about 4" long and ⅜" thick	1 pint water
	1 pint white vinegar
	3 tablespoons sugar
4 small garlic cloves, peeled	3 tablespoons pickling salt
1 teaspoon dried leaf rosemary or better yet, 4 small, tender sprigs of fresh rosemary (they should be 1½" to 2" long)	¼ teaspoon liquid hot red pepper seasoning

Wash and rinse four 1-pint preserving jars and their closures, then immerse in simmering water for about 3 minutes to heat through (pull the jars and closures from the hot water one at a time as you are ready to use them). Pack the hot jars tightly with carrot sticks, standing the sticks on end. Tuck a clove of garlic into each jar, also add ¼ teaspoon dried leaf rosemary to each jar or 1 sprig of fresh rosemary, pushing it down among the carrot sticks.

While you are packing the jars, bring water, vinegar, sugar, salt and liquid hot red pepper seasoning to a boil, reduce heat and simmer, uncovered, for 5 minutes. When all jars are packed, pour in simmering pickling liquid, filling each jar to within ¼" of the top. Wipe jar rims, seal jars, then process for 10 minutes in a boiling water bath (212° F.).

Lift jars from water bath, cool thoroughly, then check seals, label and store on a cool, dark, dry shelf. Let the pickles "age" for about a month before you serve them. *Approximately 2 calories per carrot stick.*

OLD SOUTH CARROT AND CUCUMBER RELISH
Makes 3 Pints

One of the best ways we know to use up the last of the carrot crop, this relish is particularly good with roast chicken or turkey, or baked ham, and tastes best if chilled slightly before being served.

12 medium-size carrots, peeled and coarsely grated	cumbers, washed, halved lengthwise, seeded and cut in fine dice
10 small to medium-size unpeeled cu-	3 large yellow onions, peeled and

        moderately coarsely chopped   3 cups white vinegar
¼ cup pickling salt   1 tablespoon white mustard seeds
2 cups sugar   1½ teaspoons celery seeds

Place carrots, cucumbers and onions in a large mixing bowl, sprinkle with pickling salt and toss well to mix. Let stand uncovered at room temperature for 4 hours. Line a large colander with several thicknesses of cheesecloth, pour in vegetables, rinse well in cool water, then bundle cheesecloth up around vegetables and squeeze out as much liquid as possible.

Wash and rinse three 1-pint preserving jars and their closures; keep jars and closures immersed in separate kettles of simmering liquid until you are ready to use them.

In a medium-size heavy enamel or stainless-steel kettle, bring sugar and vinegar to a boil, stirring until sugar dissolves; boil uncovered for 10 minutes, add mustard and celery seeds and boil uncovered 5 minutes longer. Add drained vegetables, let mixture return to the boil, then boil uncovered for 2 minutes. Using a wide-mouth canning funnel, pack hot relish into hot jars, filling each to within ⅛" of the tops. Run a thin-blade spatula around inside edge of each jar to free air bubbles. Wipe jar rims and seal jars.

Process in a boiling water bath (212° F.) for 10 minutes. Remove jars from water bath, complete seals if necessary, and cool to room temperature. Check seals, label jars and store on a cool, dark, dry shelf. Allow relish to season for about a month before serving.

CARROT MARMALADE
Makes 8 to 10 Half-Pints

Such a good way to conserve carrots that even carrot-loathing children will like it. Delicious on fresh-baked muffins, biscuits or bread, especially raisin bread.

Coarsely grated rind of 1 orange   Juice of 4 lemons
Coarsely grated rind of 2 lemons   Sugar (you will need ⅔ cup for each 1 cup
6 cups water   of carrot mixture)
1 quart peeled, coarsely grated carrots (you   2 tablespoons finely minced crystallized
    will need about 8 medium-size   ginger
    carrots)   ¼ teaspoon ground mace
Juice of 2 oranges   ⅛ teaspoon ground cardamom

Place orange and lemon rinds and 3 cups water in a medium-size heavy kettle (preferably an enameled cast-iron kettle) and simmer uncovered for ½ hour. Add the carrots and remaining 3 cups water and simmer uncovered 20 to 25 minutes until carrots are tender. Stir in orange and lemon juices; measure mixture carefully and for each 1 cup, add ⅔ cup sugar. Return to kettle and mix in ginger, mace and cardamom. Boil slowly, uncovered, until very thick and the consistency of marmalade (220° to 222° F. on a candy thermometer).

Meanwhile, wash and sterilize 10 half-pint preserving jars and their closures; keep jars and closures immersed in separate kettles of simmering water until you are ready to use them.

Pour boiling hot marmalade into hot jars, filling to within ¼" of the tops. Wipe jar rims and seal. Process for 10 minutes in a simmering water bath (185° F.). Remove jars from water bath, complete seals if necessary, and cool to room temperature. Check seals, then label jars and store on a cool, dark, dry shelf.

CAULIFLOWER

"Cabbage with a college education," that's how Mark Twain described cauliflower. Cauliflower *is* a member of the cabbage family and for that reason has many of the shortcomings of cabbage when it comes to canning and freezing. Canning not only intensifies the cabbagey flavor of cauliflower but also yellows and softens the flowerets. Freezing preserves the delicate flavor better, but it breaks down the fragile tissues and makes the cauliflower so watery that none of the crispness we prize about fresh cauliflower remains. Neither canning nor freezing, then, is a satisfactory way to conserve cauliflower. And drying is out of the question. Which leaves pickling and root cellaring. Of the two, pickling is preferable because, under the best of conditions, you can hold cauliflower in cold storage only for about eight weeks. If you're fond of cauliflower, your best plan would be to grow only what you can enjoy fresh with perhaps some few extra heads to pickle or tuck briefly into cold storage.

TO PICKLE: See the recipe for mustard pickles that follows.

TO STORE IN A ROOT CELLAR: Cauliflower is far more perishable than most vegetables that can be kept in cold storage and requires precisely the right amount of humidity (from 80% to 90%), a temperature of 32° F. and the merest circulation of air. You cannot control these conditions sufficiently well in a metal drum buried out-of-doors to store cauliflower, so you will have to settle for the basement root cellar where you can to some extent regulate the temperature, ventilation and humidity (by opening or closing the window).

The cauliflower must be thoroughly chilled before it goes into the root cellar, so gather it after "first frost." Cut off the roots and remove the outermost leaves only (there should be plenty of green leaves encasing the head if the cauliflower is to store well). Pack the heads one layer deep in perforated cartons or slatted crates on a thick, soft bed of moist (not wet) sand, spacing the heads 3″ to 4″ apart. Sprinkle enough additional moist sand over the heads to cover them and fill in all spaces around them. Let the sand lie as it falls, don't pack it down. Check the cauliflower every week or so to see how it is faring and remove at once any heads that show signs of decay.

KEEPING TIME: 6 to 8 weeks.

FARM-STYLE MUSTARD PICKLES
Makes About 8 Pints

Cauliflower neither cans nor freezes well, but it does pickle superbly when combined with cucumbers, sweet and hot peppers, onions and mustard.

2 small heads of cauliflower, washed, trimmed and divided into very small (about ½″) flowerets

3 medium-size cucumbers, peeled, seeded and cut in ¼″ cubes

4 medium-size sweet green peppers, cored, seeded and coarsely chopped

2 medium-size sweet red peppers, cored, seeded and coarsely chopped

2 hot red chili peppers, cored, seeded and minced

3 cups tiny white (pearl) onions, peeled (an easy way to peel them is to blanch in boiling water, quick-chill in ice water, then slip off the skins)

8 cups ice water combined with ½ cup pickling salt (brine)

⅔ cup unsifted all-purpose flour

2 cups sugar

¼ cup powdered mustard

2 teaspoons ground turmeric

¼ teaspoon ground cloves

6 cups white vinegar

Layer cauliflowerets, cucumbers, sweet and hot peppers and onions in a very large bowl; pour in brine, cover and let stand 12 hours or overnight in the refrigerator.

Next day, wash and rinse eight 1-pint preserving jars and their closures; keep jars and closures immersed in separate kettles of simmering water until you are ready to use them.

Transfer vegetables and brine to a large, heavy enamel or stainless steel kettle, set over high heat and bring to a rolling boil; cover and boil for 1 minute exactly. Drain vegetables in a colander and rinse; drain again. Rinse kettle and dry. Add flour to kettle, then blend in sugar, mustard, turmeric and cloves until no lumps remain. Slowly mix in vinegar, stirring until smooth. Set over moderate heat and cook and stir until thickened and smooth—about 3 minutes. Add drained vegetables, cover and heat, stirring now and then, 10 to 12 minutes until mixture boils vigorously.

Using a wide-mouth canning funnel to make things neater, ladle boiling hot into hot jars, filling to within ⅛″ of the tops. Run a thin-blade spatula or table knife around inside edges of jars to release trapped air bubbles. Wipe jar rims and seal jars.

Process for 10 minutes in a boiling water bath (212° F.). Lift jars from water bath, complete seals if necessary and cool completely. Check seals, label jars and store on a cool, dark, dry shelf. Let the pickles "season" for about a month before serving them.

CORN

Corn, in this case, is sweet corn, to my mind the only corn worth growing. It cans, pickles, freezes and dries well. But if you would preserve its original sweetness, you must work fast, because once corn has been picked, its natural sugars turn to starch. Two hours, it has been said, is the maximum time that should elapse between picking and processing. If you can do the job faster, so much the better.

TO CAN: Corn is America's favorite canned vegetable, perhaps because the high temperatures of pressure processing give it a faintly caramel flavor. Corn is a very low-acid vegetable and as such must be processed for long periods at 10 pounds pressure if it is to be safe to eat. Cream-style corn, because of its thick, sauce-like consistency, should not be packed in preserving jars larger than 1 pint and even these must be processed for well over 1 hour at 10 pounds pressure. Whole-kernel corn may be packed in either quarts or pints. *Amount of fresh corn needed to fill a 1-pint preserving jar:* About 5 to 6 medium-size ears, if the corn is prepared cream-style, 4 to 5 medium-size ears if it is canned as whole kernels.

CREAM-STYLE CORN

INITIAL PREPARATION (FOR BOTH COLD AND HOT PACK): Have everything at the ready—preserving jars and closures, steam pressure canner, wide-mouth funnel, jar holders, ladles, tongs, etc.—*before* you gather the corn so that you will waste no time packing and processing it. Gather the corn quickly, selecting young but mature ears (the kernels should be shiny-plump and bursting with milk). Husk the corn, remove silks, wash well in cool water, then cut the kernels from the cob cream-style. The easiest way to do this is to cut down the center of each row with a sharp knife, then to scrape the pulp and kernels directly into a large mixing bowl.

Cold (Raw) Pack (pack in 1-pint preserving jars, not in quarts):

1. Spoon the corn pulp *loosely* in hot 1-pint preserving jars, filling to within 1" of the tops. Do not shake the corn down in the jars and do not pack. Add ½ teaspoon salt to each 1-pint jar, then pour in enough clear boiling water to cover the corn, at the same time leaving 1" head space.

2. Wipe jar rims and seal jars. PRESSURE PROCESS the pints for 1 hour and 35 minutes at 10 pounds pressure.

3. Remove jars from canner, complete seals if necessary, then cool to room temperature. Check seals, label and store on a cool, dark, dry shelf.

Hot Pack (pack in 1-pint preserving jars only, not in quarts):

1. Measure the corn and pulp and for each quart of it, add 1 teaspoon salt and 2½ cups boiling water. Place in a large kettle and boil uncovered for 3 minutes. Pour boiling hot into hot 1-pint preserving jars, filling to within 1" of the tops. Do not shake or pack the corn down.

2. Wipe jar rims and seal jars. PRESSURE PROCESS pints for 1 hour and 25 minutes at 10 pounds pressure.

3. The same as for COLD PACK (above).
KEEPING TIME: About one year.

WHOLE-KERNEL CORN

INITIAL PREPARATION (FOR BOTH COLD AND HOT PACK): Choose plump young ears and gather minutes before you will can them. Husk the corn, remove silks, then wash in cool water. Cut the whole kernels from the cobs with a sharp knife (simply cut down along the cob, freeing 3 to 4 rows of kernels at a time). *Do not scrape the cobs or you will cloud the jars of corn.*

Cold (Raw) Pack:

1. Pack the kernels *loosely* into hot 1-pint or 1-quart preserving jars, filling to within 1" of the tops. Do not shake or pack the corn down. To each 1-pint jar, add ½ teaspoon salt and to each 1-quart jar, 1 teaspoon salt. Pour enough clear boiling water into jars to cover corn, leaving 1" head space.

2. Wipe jar rims and seal jars. PRESSURE PROCESS pints for 55 minutes at 10 pounds pressure and quarts for 1 hour and 25 minutes at 10 pounds pressure.

3. Remove jars from canner, complete seals if necessary, then cool to room temperature. Check seals, label and store on a cool, dark, dry shelf.

Hot Pack:

1. Measure the whole-kernel corn and to each 1 quart of it, add 1 teaspoon salt and 2 cups boiling water. Bring to a boil in a large heavy kettle, then pour boiling hot into hot pint or quart preserving jars, packing *loosely* and filling to within 1" of the tops.

2. & 3. The same as for COLD PACK (under Whole-Kernel corn above).
KEEPING TIME: About 1 year.

TO FREEZE: Sweet corn does "water down" somewhat in freezing, yet if carefully and quickly frozen, it can be surprisingly good indeed, whether on the cob or off.

CORN ON THE COB

1. Pick plump but young and tender ears just before you are ready to freeze them (and it's a good idea to put a big kettle of water on to boil before you go into the garden so that you can pop the husked corn straight into the blanching water). For best results, reject any ears that are less than 1" in diameter, also any that are more than 2½". Husk the corn quickly, desilk and break off pointed tips. Group the ears by size: all ears measuring 1½" or less in diameter together, all measuring between 1½" and 2" together, and all measuring more than 2" together (the size of the ear determines how long it should be blanched and chilled).

2. Blanch the corn in enough boiling water to cover allowing 6 minutes for ears measuring 1" to 1½" in diameter, 8 minutes for ears between 1½" and 2" in diameter, and 10 minutes for those between 2" and 2½". Quick-chill the ears in a large pan or sink of ice water, allowing the same times for cooling that you did for blanching, that is, 6 minutes for the ears measuring 1" to 1½" in diameter and so on.

3. Drain ears well, then wrap individually in freezer wrap, smoothing out all air and sealing with freezer tape. Label and quick-freeze. Once the ears are solidly frozen, you may bundle the ears up, 4 to 6 of uniform size together, in large freezer bags so that they won't get lost in the freezer. Don't unwrap the frozen ears, however, simply overwrap them in freezer bags, pressing out all air, twisting the top of each bag into a tight gooseneck, bending over and securing with a twist-band. Label each bag and return to freezer.

KEEPING TIME: About one year, although if you want a "fresh-picked" flavor, you'd better serve the corn within 4 to 6 months.

WHOLE-KERNEL CORN
("Miss Essie's" Method)

"Miss Essie" Williams, who lives in a small town in eastern North Carolina, grows, according to friends, the most beautiful corn in the world. And her way of freezing it, somehow, preserves all of the corn's original beauty. "It tastes exactly like fresh corn," her friends insist. "You cannot tell the difference." Miss Essie's secret? Quite simple, really. She uses fresh-pulled corn only and she gets it into the freezer lickity-split. *Amount of fresh corn needed to fill a 1-pint freezer container:* 4 to 5 medium-size ears.

Ask family and friends to help you gather and husk the corn (a share of the frozen corn will be reward enough). Choose ears just when they are chunky and sweet and full of milk (they should measure about 2″ to 2½″ in diameter). Husk and desilk them as fast as you can, then wash in cool water. Drop ears into a great big kettle of water, then boil for 3 minutes exactly. Using tongs, fish the ears from the blanching water and plunge at once into a huge pan filled with ice cubes and water. The corn will cool even faster if you swish it around in the ice bath. After 3 minutes—and no more than 3 minutes or the corn will begin to absorb water—take the ears from the ice water and shake them dry. Slice the kernels off the cobs (do not scrape the cobs because you want the whole kernels only). Pack into 1-pint freezer containers, shaking kernels down lightly and filling almost to the brim. Snap on the lids, label and quick-freeze by setting the containers directly on the freezing surface of your freezer. You can, if you prefer, freeze the corn in 1- or 1½-pint freezer bags (don't use giant bags because the corn will not freeze as fast as it should). Press all air pockets out of the bags, twist tops tightly, fold over and secure with twist-bands. Label and quick-freeze.

KEEPING TIME: One year at 0° F., although if you value the field-fresh flavor of corn, you'd better eat up your frozen supply within 4 to 6 months.

CREAM-STYLE CORN

NOTE: Be sure to try Mrs. Peter Dohanos's Frozen Corn Pudding recipe that follows, which is maybe the best of all ways to freeze cream-style corn. *Amount of fresh corn needed to fill a 1-pint freezer container:* 5 to 6 medium-size ears.

1.   Gather, husk and desilk young-ripe ears as quickly as possible. Wash in cool water, again wasting no time. Boil the ears 3 minutes in enough water to cover, cool 3 minutes in ice water and drain well.

2.   Cut down the center of each row of kernels with a sharp knife, then scrape the corn pulp into a large mixing bowl.

3.　Pack into 1-pint freezer containers, shaking corn pulp down lightly and filling to within ¼″ of the tops. Snap on lids, label and quick freeze.

KEEPING TIME: About one year at 0° F., although again, the corn will seem fresher if eaten within 6 months.

TO DRY CORN: You can parch corn easily in the oven, but because you cannot dry it there as thoroughly as you can in a specially built electric dryer, bundle up the parched corn in small freezer bags and store in the freezer so that there is no risk of spoilage. Parched corn has a flavor quite unique. It is nutlike and makes delicious soups and stews (see recipes that follow). *Amount of fresh corn needed to make 2 cups dried corn:* 8 to 10 medium-size ears.

1.　Gather medium-size ears that are sugary and plump (the kernels should look shiny and filled to bursting, showing neither dimples nor "dents," which indicate that the sugar is already turning to starch). Husk the ears, desilk, then boil, covered, for 5 minutes in a large kettle of water.

2.　Drain the ears, then roll on paper toweling to remove all traces of moisture. Cut the kernels from the cob. You want only whole kernels, so do not scrape the cobs.

3.　Spread the kernels out in a thin, single layer on a baking sheet, set uncovered in a very slow oven (175° F.), and let dry for 12 to 15 hours. Stir occasionally. When the corn is amber brown, hard and brittle, it is properly dried.

4.　Bundle the corn into 1-pint freezer bags, pressing out all air, twist the tops into tight goosenecks, bend over and secure with twist-bands. Store in the freezer.

KEEPING TIME: About one year.

TO PICKLE: Yes, corn pickles well and is particularly suited, because of the size of the kernels, to making relish (see the Old-Timey Corn Relish recipe).

TO STORE IN A ROOT CELLAR: No point in trying. Corn simply won't hold in cold storage.

MRS. PETER DOHANOS'S FROZEN CORN PUDDING
Makes 4 (9″) Corn Puddings, Each Enough to Serve 4 Persons

From friends we heard about an uncommonly good corn pudding that Mrs. Peter Dohanos of East Hampton, Long Island, prepares and freezes in late summer, then gift-wraps and presents to friends at Christmas. We called Mrs. Dohanos at Whimseys, the gift shop she operates in East Hampton, to inquire about the recipe, and she was good enough to share it with us. You will not find the recipe complicated, although you will find it slow-going ("all that scratching of corn off the cob," a friend remarked). Draft what volunteers you can to help husk the corn and cut the kernels off the cob. You must work fast, because once the corn is picked, its natural sugars speedily turn to starch. The easiest way to cut corn from the cob cream-style is to slit each row of kernels down the middle with a sharp knife, then to scrape all the pulp and milk into a large shallow pan.

10 cups (2½ quarts) fresh, cream-style sweet corn (for this amount you will need about 20 large ripe ears; you do not, by the way, blanch the corn before cutting it off the cob)

3 to 4 tablespoons sugar (depending upon how sweet the corn—and your own sweet tooth)

2 tablespoons cornstarch (this helps soak up the water that will ooze out of the corn after it is frozen and thawed)

2 teaspoons salt

¼ teaspoon freshly ground black pepper

Mix all ingredients thoroughly, then pack firmly into 4 well-buttered 9″ × 1⅛″ foil pie pans, dividing the total amount evenly and smoothing the surface as flat as possible. Over-wrap each pie pan snugly in heavy-duty aluminum foil and quick-freeze.

To Serve: Thaw the corn pudding completely, unwrap, sprinkle the top lightly with sugar, if you like, then bake uncovered in a hot oven (400° F.) for about 40 to 45 minutes or until crusty and golden brown on top.

OLD-TIMEY CORN RELISH
Makes 8 to 10 Pints

For a sparklingly clear corn relish, cut the kernels from the cob carefully and do *not* scrape the cob—the "milk" will cloud the relish. This particular relish is good with roast fowl, pork and baked ham.   ¼ Rec, = 5 c,   Reg rec, = 5 qts.

16 medium-size ears fresh sweet corn, husked and stripped of silks

1 quart finely diced celery

1 pint finely diced sweet green peppers

1 pint finely diced sweet red peppers

1 cup moderately coarsely chopped yellow onion

1 quart cider vinegar

1 cup sugar

2 tablespoons salt

2 teaspoons celery seeds

4 tablespoons all-purpose flour

2 tablespoons powdered mustard

1 teaspoon ground turmeric

⅓ cup cold water

Boil ears of corn 10 minutes in unsalted water; drain, plunge ears in ice water and when easy to handle, drain and cut the kernels from the cobs using a very sharp knife (the easiest way is to hold the cob at a slight angle to the cutting board, then to cut straight down the rows of kernels, doing about 3 rows at a time). Do not scrape the cobs–you want whole kernels only, not the pulp. Measure out and reserve 2 quarts of the whole-kernel corn.

Wash and rinse ten 1-pint preserving jars and their closures; keep closures and jars immersed in separate pans of simmering water until you are ready to use them.

In a very large enamel or stainless steel kettle, mix together the celery, green and red peppers, onion, vinegar, sugar, salt and celery seeds. Bring to a boil, then boil gently, uncovered, for 5 minutes. Blend flour with mustard and turmeric, then mix with cold water to form a paste. Ladle a little of the hot pickling liquid into flour paste, stirring rapidly to blend, then mix paste into kettle and boil, stirring constantly, until slightly thickened–about 2 to 3 minutes. Add the whole-kernel corn, cover and boil 5 minutes, stirring once or twice.

Using a wide-mouth funnel, pack hot relish into hot jars, filling to within ¼″ of the tops. Wipe jar rims and seal jars. Process for 15 minutes in a boiling water bath (212° F.). Remove jars from water bath, complete seals if necessary and cool completely. Check seals. Label jars and store on a cool, dark, dry shelf. Let the relish "mellow" for about three weeks before serving.

DRIED CORN CHOWDER
Makes About 6 Servings

¼ *pound bacon or salt pork, in one piece,*	1 *tablespoon sugar*
cut in fine dice	¾ *teaspoon paprika*
2 *large yellow onions, peeled and coarsely*	1 *pint light cream*
chopped	2 *tablespoons minced parsley*
2 *celery stalks, finely diced*	1 *teaspoon salt (or more to taste)*
1½ *cups dried corn*	⅛ *teaspoon freshly ground black pepper*
1 *quart water*	

Brown the bacon or salt pork over moderately high heat in a very large heavy saucepan until all the drippings have cooked out and only crisp brown bits remain. With a slotted spoon, scoop up the browned bits and drain on paper toweling. Pour all but 3 tablespoons of drippings from the saucepan. Add onions and celery, reduce heat to moderate, and fry, stirring occasionally, about 10 minutes until golden and touched with brown. Add dried corn, water, sugar and paprika, cover and simmer slowly about 1 hour until corn is tender. Uncover and simmer 10 to 15 minutes longer until mixture reduces slightly–the broth should not be watery, but it should not be gravy-thick either. Return the browned bacon or salt pork to the pan, mix in all remaining ingredients, adjusting the amount of salt and pepper to suit your taste, then simmer slowly, uncovered, 10 to 15 minutes longer–just enough to mellow the flavors. Do not allow to boil or the cream may curdle. Ladle into soup bowls and serve.

LAMB AND INDIAN CORN STEW
Makes About 6 Servings

Corn was the food most cherished by American Indians. It could be eaten fresh in summer, but most important, it could be dried, then used in winter for making breads or bolstering meat-skimpy soups and stews. The recipe here is essentially Indian although we have added rather more seasonings than early Indian women would have used.

1½ pounds lean boneless lamb shoulder, cut in ¾" chunks
2 tablespoons meat or bacon drippings
2 medium-size yellow onions, peeled and coarsely chopped
1 small garlic clove, peeled and minced
½ cup minced sweet green or red pepper or, if you prefer, a half-and-half mixture of each

2 tablespoons minced parsley
6 cups water
1½ cups dried corn
1 teaspoon salt (or more to taste)
¼ teaspoon crushed dried hot red chili peppers (½ teaspoon if you like things peppery)
Pinch of black pepper

Brown the lamb well on all sides in the drippings in a medium-size heavy kettle set over high heat. Push meat to one side, add onions, garlic, and sweet pepper, lower heat to moderate and stir-fry 8 to 10 minutes until limp and touched with brown. Add parsley and water, cover and simmer 1 hour. Add dried corn and all remaining ingredients, cover and simmer 1 hour longer or until both the lamb and the corn are tender. Ladle into soup bowls and serve.

CUCUMBERS

You can pickle cucumbers—in either brine or vinegar. And that, frankly, is it. Here, then, are some of the very best pickle recipes I have ever tried.

OLD-FASHIONED "PICKLE BARREL" PICKLES
Makes 8 to 10 Quarts

Here's the way our great-grandmothers made pickles—by fermenting them in brine for several weeks. Do not attempt to use the large salad-type cucumbers for this recipe because they are too watery and soft to pickle well. Choose instead the small, firm pickling cucumbers. For best results, you should brine the cucumbers in a very large stoneware crock—the five-gallon size is about right. But you can also use a very large deep enamel kettle.

20 *pounds firm pickling cucumbers of uniform size (they should be about 4" long)*
⅔ cup mixed pickling spices
18 *umbels of fresh dill (umbels are the rounded bud clusters)*
6 *cloves of garlic, peeled*
2½ *cups white vinegar*
1¾ *cups pickling salt mixed with 2½ gallons cold water (brine)*

Scrub the cucumbers well in cool water with a vegetable brush, but handle gently lest you bruise them or rip their skins. Rinse well, spread out and let dry thoroughly.

Set a 5-gallon crock or enamel kettle on a metal tray in an out-of-the-way corner. Spread ⅓ cup of the mixed pickling spices, 9 umbels of dill and 3 cloves of garlic over the bottom of the crock. Layer the cucumbers in the crock, filling to within 3" of the top, then spread the remaining pickling spices, dill and garlic on top. Mix the vinegar with the brine and pour into the crock, making sure that it covers the cucumbers. Set a heavy plate on top of the cucumbers and weight down by standing a water-filled and sealed 1-quart jar in the center of the plate. The cucumbers must be completely submerged in the brine. Cover the crock loosely with several thicknesses of clean cheesecloth.

Check the crock each day and skim off the scum as it forms—it may not begin to form until after the fourth or fifth day. Do not stir the pickles, but do make certain that they are covered and weighted down in the brine at all times. If necessary, add additional brine, using the proportions of 6 tablespoons of pickling salt for each 1 quart of cold water.

After 3 to 4 weeks, you will find that the pickles have turned an even olive drab and that their texture is soft-crisp. They should also be uniformly translucent—cut one open to check. The pickles are now ready to be canned.

TO CAN: Drain the brine from the cucumbers and reserve. If it is not objectionably cloudy, you can use it for packing the pickles. But first, strain it through several thicknesses cheesecloth to remove all traces of scum. If, however, the brine is very cloudy, you should make a fresh brine in which to pack the pickles: Mix ½ cup pickling salt with 1 quart white vinegar and 1 gallon cold water. Place the brine (either the fresh brine or the strained brine) in a very large heavy enamel or stainless steel kettle and bring slowly to a boil.

Wash and rinse ten 1-quart preserving jars and their closures; keep jars and closures immersed in separate kettles of simmering water until you are ready to use them.

Pack the cold pickles, not too snugly, in the hot jars, filling to within ½" of the tops. Also tuck an umbel of dill into each jar and, if you like, a fresh peeled clove of garlic. Pour enough boiling brine into each jar to cover the pickles, at the same time leaving ½″ head space. Run a thin-blade spatula or table knife around inside edges of jars to free air bubbles. Wipe jar rims and seal jars.

Process pickles for 15 minutes in a boiling water bath (212° F.), timing from the moment that all jars are in the water bath. Remove jars from water bath, complete seals if necessary and cool completely. Label jars and store on a cool, dark, dry shelf. Let the pickles season for about a month before serving.

DILL PICKLES
Makes About 7 Quarts

A much quicker way to make dill pickles. They are brined, but only overnight.

6 dozen firm pickling cucumbers of uniform size (they should be about 4″ long)

2 gallons cold water mixed with 1½ cups pickling salt (brine)

6 cups white vinegar

⅔ cup pickling salt

⅓ cup sugar

9 cups cold water

2 tablespoons mixed pickling spices, tied loosely in several thicknesses of cheesecloth

⅓ cup (about) white mustard seeds (you will need 2 teaspoons for each 1-quart jar)

21 umbels of fresh dill (umbels are the rounded bud clusters)

7 cloves of garlic, peeled

Scrub the cucumbers well in cool water with a vegetable brush, then rinse and drain. Place the cucumbers in a very large (about 5-gallon) enamel or stainless steel kettle, pour in the brine, cover and let stand overnight at room temperature.

Next day, wash and rinse seven 1-quart preserving jars and their closures. Keep jars and closures immersed in separate kettles of simmering water until you are ready to use them.

Drain the cucumbers, rinse and drain again. Also rinse and dry the kettle. Combine the vinegar, salt, sugar and water in the kettle; drop in the spice bag. Set uncovered over moderate heat and bring slowly to a boil.

Meanwhile, pack the cold cucumbers in the hot jars, filling to within ½″ of the tops. To each jar add 2 teaspoons of mustard seeds, then tuck into each 3 umbels of dill and 1 garlic clove. Pour enough boiling pickling liquid into jars to cover cucumbers, at the same time leaving ½″ head space. Run a thin-blade spatula or table knife around inside edges of each jar to remove air bubbles. Wipe jar rims and seal jars.

Process jars for 20 minutes in a boiling water bath (212° F.), timing the processing from the minute all jars are in the water bath. Remove jars from water bath, complete seals if necessary and cool completely. Check seals, label jars and store on a cool, dark, dry shelf. Let the pickles season for about a month before serving.

SOUR SANDWICH PICKLES
Makes 4 Quarts

Slip these crisp, pickled cucumber slices into sandwiches or serve as a condiment with roast chicken, turkey, pork or baked ham. Make them sour or make them sweet—the only adjustment needed is in the quantity of sugar used.

1 gallon sliced unpeeled cucumbers (make the slices about ¼" thick)
¾ cup pickling salt
1 gallon ice water (with ice cubes in it)
1 cup sugar
1 quart white vinegar
1 tablespoon whole allspice

1 tablespoon whole cloves
2 cinnamon sticks, each broken in several places
2 bay leaves, crumbled
2 tablespoons white mustard seeds
1 tablespoon celery seeds

Place cucumber slices in a very large enamel or stainless steel kettle, sprinkle with salt and add ice water to cover; let stand at room temperature 3 hours, replenishing ice cubes as they melt. Drain thoroughly. Rinse out kettle.

Meanwhile, wash and rinse four 1-quart preserving jars and their closures; keep jars and closures immersed in separate kettles of simmering water until you are ready to use them.

Mix sugar and vinegar in the kettle in which you soaked the cucumber slices and stir until sugar dissolves. Tie allspice, cloves, cinnamon sticks and bay leaves in cheesecloth and add to kettle along with mustard and celery seeds. Cover and simmer 15 minutes. Add cucumber slices and heat uncovered just until mixture returns to the boil.

Ladle cucumber slices into hot jars, filling to within ⅛" of the tops (a wide-mouth canning funnel will make the packing both quicker and neater). Pour enough boiling pickling liquid (including some mustard and celery seeds) into jars to cover cucumbers, at the same time leaving ⅛" head space. Wipe jar rims and seal jars. Process jars for 10 minutes in a boiling water bath (212° F.). Remove jars from water bath, complete seals if necessary, and cool thoroughly. Check seals, then label jars and store in a cool, dark, dry spot. Let the pickles "season" for about 6 weeks before serving them.

VARIATION: *Sweet Sandwich Pickles.* Prepare as directed for Sour Sandwich Pickles but increase the quantity of sugar to 4 cups.

GRANDMOTHER JOHNSON'S BREAD AND BUTTER PICKLES
Makes 8 to 10 Pints

This old Illinois farm recipe provides an excellent way to use up those extra-large cucumbers. Just make certain that they are good and firm throughout, not soft or pithy. If you want to make this recipe with store-bought cucumbers, hunt up those that have not been waxed. If the cucumbers have been waxed (and most are nowadays), they will have to be peeled before you use them and the pickles, in the end, will be softer than they should be.

12 large but firm cucumbers, sliced ⅛″ thick (do not peel)
6 medium-size yellow onions, peeled and sliced thin
1 gallon cold water mixed with ½ cup pickling salt (brine)

3 cups cider vinegar
2 cups sugar
1 teaspoon ground turmeric
1 teaspoon celery seeds
2 teaspoons white mustard seeds

Layer cucumber and onion slices in a large enamel or stainless steel kettle, pour in brine, cover and let stand overnight in a cool spot. Next day, drain, rinse in cool water and drain very dry. It is important that you press as much liquid from the cucumbers and onions as possible so that they will not become overly soft in processing. Also rinse and dry the kettle.

Wash and rinse ten 1-pint preserving jars and their closures; keep jars and closures immersed in separate kettles of simmering water until ready to use.

Place vinegar, sugar, turmeric, celery and mustard seeds in kettle and stir to mix. Set over moderate heat and bring to a boil. Add cucumber and onion slices and when mixture returns to the boil, boil uncovered for 1 minute.

Using a slotted spoon, pack the pickles in hot preserving jars, arranging as snugly and attractively as possible and filling each jar to within ⅛″ of the top. Pour enough boiling pickling liquid into jars to cover pickles, at the same time leaving ⅛″ head space. Run a thin-blade spatula or table knife around inside edges of jars to release trapped air bubbles. Wipe jar rims and seal jars.

Process for 10 minutes in a boiling water bath (212° F.). Remove jars from water bath, complete seals if necessary, and cool completely. Check seals, label jars and store on a cool, dark, dry shelf. Let the pickles season for about a month before you serve them.

EGGPLANT

There's very little you can do to conserve eggplant attractively unless you can it as Caponata, a tart and salty Italian cooked vegetable salad filled with olives, tomatoes, onions, garlic and capers (see recipe). If canned by itself, eggplant not only turns brown but also cooks down to mush during processing in the steam pressure canner. Freezing does little better by eggplant because it is so fragile, porous and water-saturated a vegetable that the ice crystals formed in freezing break down its structure. Moreover, once the ice melts, it soaks into the eggplant as water would into a sponge. You can't pickle or dry eggplant with success either. And you can't hold it in cold storage. So grow only what eggplant you will be able to enjoy fresh, then clean up the garden at the end of the season by putting up a few pints of Caponata.

CAPONATA
Makes About 3 Pints

In Italy Caponata is made with a combination of vegetables and fish (usually anchovies). It is served both as a salad, mounded on crisp greens, and as an integral part of antipasto. Americans, however, seem to prefer Caponata as a cocktail spread. The following recipe is made of vegetables only—no fish—and is the most appetizing way we know to conserve eggplant at home.

½ cup olive oil
2 medium-size young eggplants, cut in 1" cubes (do not peel, but do wash well)
2 large Spanish onions, peeled and coarsely chopped
1 large garlic clove, peeled and crushed
¾ cup finely diced celery
2 cups tomato purée or sauce (not paste)
⅓ cup coarsely chopped pitted green olives
⅓ cup coarsely chopped pitted ripe olives (preferably Greek olives)

¼ cup drained capers
¼ cup red or white wine vinegar
2 tablespoons brown sugar
½ teaspoon salt
½ teaspoon freshly ground black pepper
1 tablespoon minced fresh oregano or marjoram or ½ teaspoon crumbled leaf oregano or marjoram
2 teaspoons minced fresh thyme or ¼ teaspoon crumbled leaf thyme
3 tablespoons minced parsley

Heat 5 tablespoons of the olive oil in a very large heavy enamel or stainless steel kettle over moderately high heat; add eggplant cubes and stir-fry 10 to 12 minutes until golden and touched with brown. Add remaining oil, onions, garlic and celery and stir-fry about 10 minutes longer until golden. Mix in all remaining ingredients, cover, reduce heat to moderately low and simmer 1 hour, stirring now and then.

Uncover and continue cooking until mixture is quite thick, about the consistency of chutney.

Meanwhile, wash and rinse three 1-pint preserving jars and their closures; keep hot in separate kettles of simmering water until you are ready to use them.

When caponata has cooked down to a thick, spreadable consistency, ladle into hot jars, filling to within 1″ of the tops. Wipe jar rims and seal, then process at 10 pounds pressure for 30 minutes. Remove jars from canner, adjust seals if necessary, then cool to room temperature. Check seals, then label jars and store in a cool, dark, dry place.

HERBS

Most herbs can be dried, many can be frozen, and a few can be made into herbal butters, jellies and vinegars (see recipes that follow). The time to gather herbs is when they have budded but not yet blossomed because this is when they reach their peak of flavor. You should pick them midmorning of a sunny day—after the dew has dried (herbs gathered wet are more likely to mold) but before the sun has warmed or wilted them.

TO FREEZE: Tender-leafed herbs are the most suitable for freezing: Basil, chervil, chives, coriander, dill, fennel, mint, parsley, summer savory and tarragon.

1. Gather the herbs when they are at their most fragrant. Wash gently in cool water and drain on paper toweling. For freezing, choose only the most tender young leaves (do not use flower buds). Pluck the leaves from the stalks and chop them fairly coarsely.

2. Spoon 1 tablespoon chopped herb into each compartment of an ice cube tray, add about 1″ of water to each and freeze solid. TIP: To avoid mixing herb flavors, freeze one kind of herb only in each ice cube tray.

3. Remove herb ice cubes from trays and bundle all of a kind in plastic freezer bags. Twist tops of bags into tight goosenecks, bend over and secure with twist-bands. Label bags and store in the freezer.

KEEPING TIME: About one year at 0° F. TO USE: Frozen herb cubes are ideal for flavoring soups, sauces, gravies, stews and casseroles—simply add at the point the particular recipe specifies. The ice will melt and evaporate during cooking, leaving the herb to flavor the dish. One frozen herb cube is the equivalent of 1 tablespoon chopped fresh herb or about ¾ to 1 teaspoon of dried herb.

TO DRY: Dried parsley and chives are about as flavorful as dried grass, so freeze those herbs instead of drying them. Tarragon, although aromatic when dried, bears little resemblance to fresh tarragon, so you are really better off freezing it, too. The herbs that dry most successfully are: Basil, chervil, coriander, dill, fennel, lavender, lemon verbena, marjoram, mint, oregano, rosemary, sage, summer and winter savory, and thyme. For drying herbs you will need a sheet of aluminum window screening. Do not use copper or galvanized metal screening because these may react with the herbs to produce toxins. Cut the screen so that it is about 1" smaller all around than the rack in your oven.

1.   Choose a dry, sunny day for drying herbs so that they will not absorb moisture from the air. Gather the herbs just before they blossom, wash them tenderly in cool water and spread out on several thicknesses of paper toweling. Let air-dry until all drops of wash water have evaporated.

2.   Spread the herbs out (one variety at a time) on the aluminum screen. Turn oven to lowest possible setting (150° F. is best, but herbs can be dried at 175° F. or 200° F.). Place the oven rack in the middle position, lay the screen of herbs on the rack, and leave the oven door open. Let the herbs dry until they are shattery-crisp—this will take from 2 to 4 hours depending upon the size and the succulence of the leaves. To test, crumble a leaf between your fingers. When properly dry it should crumble at the lightest touch into flakes or powder.

3.   Remove the screen of herbs from the oven and cool to room temperature. Separate leaves from the stalks (also discard any buds), then crumble the leaves as coarsely or finely as you like. Pack loosely into clean, dry, small jars and let stand uncovered at room temperature for 24 hours. Inspect each jar closely for signs of moisture. If there are none, cap the jars airtight, label and store on a cool, dark, dry shelf.

4.   If there are signs of moisture in any jar, you will have to oven-dry the herb again, but more briefly this time. Spread one thickness of paper toweling over the wire screen. Empty the herb onto the paper (again work with only one flavor at a time), and return to the oven set at the lowest possible temperature. Dry 30 minutes with the oven door open, test for dryness, and if not yet crumbly, dry about 30 minutes longer. When the herb passes the finger-crumble test, pack loosely in a clean dry jar and let stand uncovered at room temperature for another 24 hours. It should, by now, be dry and ready for capping, but if not, return to the oven and dry as before. The point, simply, is to drive as much moisture out of an herb as possible so that it will not mold in storage.

KEEPING TIME: 4 to 6 months, although the sooner you use dried herbs the more fragrant they will be.

FROZEN HERB BUTTERS
Makes 1 Pound

One of the most successful ways to preserve the bouquet of fresh herbs is to mince them and mix them with butter. The butter can then be shaped into sticks or logs, wrapped and frozen (the herbal butters will keep fragrant and fresh for about 4 months at 0° F.). To use, slice off ¼" pats (one to two for each person being served), allow to soften slightly, then plop down on top of sizzling broiled fish, steaks or chops. The butter will melt at once, releasing its flavor. The herb butters may also be softened, spread on slices of French or Italian bread and toasted *à la* garlic bread. And they may also be used in place of plain butter to season vegetables. Chives butter is particularly compatible with boiled or baked potatoes, with broiled steaks and chops. Dill, parsley and tarragon butters are all equally delicious over broiled fish, chicken, steaks or lamb chops. These three may also be used to season boiled carrots or green beans.

1 pound lightly salted butter, softened slightly   *3 tablespoons finely minced fresh chives, dill, parsley or tarragon*

Cream the butter until fluffy-soft, add herb and blend well. Cover and chill until firm enough to mold. Shape into 4 logs or sticks, about 1" thick, wrap each in heavy-duty aluminum foil, label and quick-freeze.

FROZEN MAÎTRE D'HÔTEL BUTTER
Makes 1 Pound

Use this parsley-lemon butter to season grilled or steamed fish, broiled steaks, chops and chicken. It's quick to mix and keeps well in the freezer for several months. To use, slice off the amount you will need from a frozen stick, let soften slightly, cut into ¼" pats, then top each serving of meat or fish with a pat or two.

1 pound lightly salted butter, softened slightly   *¼ cup lemon juice*
¼ cup very finely minced fresh parsley

Cream butter, lemon juice and parsley until well blended, chill until firm enough to mold, then shape into 4 sticks or logs about 1" in diameter. Wrap each stick or log individually in heavy-duty aluminum foil, label and quick-freeze.

TARRAGON VINEGAR
Makes About 2 Quarts

Tarragon vinegar makes a wonderfully aromatic salad, especially if you bottle the vinegar using tarragon you have grown. Pick the tarragon on a sunny morning just before it is ready to bloom so that it will be at the peak of flavor. Tarragon vinegar will keep well for several months if stored on a cool, dark, dry shelf.

> *20 large, leafy, tender stalks of tarragon*
> *1 quart white- or red-wine vinegar*
> *3¼ cups cider vinegar*

Wash the tarragon tenderly in cool water, then sort, removing any flower buds, coarse stem ends and withered leaves. Pat dry on paper toweling but take care not to bruise the tarragon because it will lose flavor.

Wash and sterilize two 1-quart preserving jars and their closures (or, if you prefer, four 1-pint preserving jars and their closures). Pack the tarragon into each jar, dividing the total amount evenly.

Bring wine and cider vinegars to a simmer (do not boil), then pour into jars, covering the tarragon branches. Wipe jar rims and seal jars. Cool to room temperature, label and store on a cool, dark, dry shelf. That's all there is to it—no processing needed.

DILLED WINE VINEGAR
Makes About 2 Quarts

Another fragrant herbal vinegar to use in dressing salads or vegetables. Good, too, drizzled over cooked crab meat or shrimp.

3 dozen umbels of fresh dill (umbels are the rounded bud clusters)
2½ cups dry white wine (Sauternes, Chablis or Rhine wine are particularly good)
3 cups white wine vinegar
1 cup cider vinegar

Gather the dill when it has budded but not yet blossomed. Sort carefully, removing any withered buds or coarse branches, then wash gently in cool water. Pat dry on paper toweling.

Wash and sterilize two 1-quart preserving jars and their closures (or, if you prefer, four 1-pint preserving jars and their closures). Pack the dill into the jars, dividing the total amount evenly.

Bring wine, wine and cider vinegars to a simmer (do not boil), then pour into jars, covering the dill. Wipe jar rims and seal. Cool to room temperature, then let mellow for three weeks on a cool, dark, dry shelf. To prevent the vinegar from clouding, strain it through cheesecloth after it has mellowed for three weeks, then pour into clean sterilized jars, label and store on a cool, dark, dry shelf. The vinegar should keep well for several months.

GARDEN MINT JELLY
Makes Enough to Fill Four (8-ounce) Jelly Jars

For a particularly fragrant mint jelly, gather the mint just as it is ready to blossom. Tint the jelly a pale spring green, if you like; or leave plain—the jelly will be a pale honey color.

2 cups coarsely chopped, washed fresh mint leaves
1⅓ cups boiling water

3 cups sugar
½ cup bottled liquid pectin
1–2 drops green food coloring (optional)

Wash and sterilize four (8-ounce) jelly jars, stand upside down on a baking sheet, and keep warm in a very slow oven (250°) until you are ready to use them.

Steep the mint in the boiling water 15 minutes, strain the liquid through 4 thicknesses of cheesecloth and reserve; discard the mint. Place the mint liquid and sugar in a large, heavy enamel or stainless steel saucepan, set uncovered over high heat, and bring to a boil without stirring. Mix in remaining ingredients and boil precisely 30 seconds. Remove from heat, skim off froth and fill jelly jars to within ½″ of tops; seal with ⅛″ of melted paraffin. Cool, cover the jars with their caps, then label. Store in a cool, dark, dry place.

VARIATIONS:

Tart Mint Jelly. Steep the 2 cups chopped mint leaves 15 minutes in 1¼ cups boiling water; strain the liquid through 4 thicknesses of cheesecloth and reserve; discard the mint. Place the mint liquid, 2 tablespoons cider vinegar or lemon juice, and the 3 cups sugar in a large, heavy enamel or stainless steel saucepan, set uncovered over high heat, and bring to a boil as directed. Mix in ½ cup liquid pectin and, if you like, just enough green food coloring to tint a pale green. Boil hard for 30 seconds, then remove from heat and proceed as directed.

Wine-Mint Jelly. Steep the 2 cups chopped mint leaves 15 minutes in 1 cup boiling water; strain the liquid through 4 thicknesses of cheesecloth and reserve; discard the mint. Place the mint liquid, ⅓ cup dry white wine (Chablis or Sauternes) and the 3 cups sugar in a large, heavy enamel or stainless steel saucepan, set uncovered over high heat, and bring to a boil. Mix in ½ cup liquid pectin and, if you wish, just enough green food coloring to tint a pastel green. Boil hard for 30 seconds, then remove from heat and proceed as directed.

FRESH ROSEMARY JELLY
Makes Enough to Fill Four (8-ounce) Jelly Jars

If you grow rosemary in your garden (or in pots indoors), try this delicate jelly. It is delicious with roast pork, lamb, fowl or game. The jelly will be prettier if you tint it ever so lightly with green and yellow food coloring. But if you have an aversion to using food colors, leave the jelly plain. It will be a pale khaki color.

2 cups tender young rosemary sprigs, washed
1 cup boiling water
Juice of 2 limes plus enough lemon juice to total ⅓ cup (strain the juices through a fine sieve)

3 cups sugar
½ cup bottled liquid pectin
1 drop yellow food coloring (optional)
1 drop green food coloring (optional)

Wash and sterilize four (8-ounce) jelly jars, stand upside down on a baking sheet and keep warm in a very slow oven (250°) until you are ready to use them.

Steep the rosemary in the boiling water 15 minutes, strain the liquid through 4 thicknesses of cheesecloth and reserve; discard the rosemary. Place the rosemary liquid, the lime-lemon juice mixture and sugar in a large, heavy enamel or stainless steel saucepan, set uncovered over high heat, and bring to a boil without stirring. Mix in remaining ingredients and boil exactly 30 seconds. Remove from heat, skim off froth, and fill jelly jars to within ½" of tops; seal with ⅛" of melted paraffin. Cool, cover the jars with their caps, then label. Store in a cool, dark, dry place.

HORSERADISH

Horseradish is not something you will want to grow much of because a little of it goes such a long way. It is difficult, moreover, to work with fresh horseradish because its biting fumes fill the air, to say nothing of your eyes and nose. Chopping, shredding, even peeling fresh horseradish is a tearful task.

How can you conserve it? The easiest way is simply to leave the plants in the ground. They will winter over well, weathering hard frosts and snows, if you mulch them well.

You can also make a pungent relish of fresh horseradish to serve with roasts and game that will keep well for several months in the refrigerator. The relish is not processed and for that reason must be kept well chilled.

REFRIGERATOR HORSERADISH RELISH
Makes About 1½ Cups

1 large horseradish root (you will need   ¾ cup white vinegar
    1½ cups moderately coarsely grated   ¼ teaspoon salt
    horseradish)

Wash the horseradish well, then peel off all brown skin using a vegetable peeler. Grate or chop enough of the horseradish to equal 1½ cups. Mix with the vinegar and salt, then pack into a clean one-pint preserving jar (or, if you prefer, 2 half-pint jars), screw on the lid (or lids) and store in the refrigerator. Let mellow about 2 weeks before serving. If kept refrigerated, the relish will keep well for several months. To use, simply spoon out the amount you need, recover the jar and return to the refrigerator.

LETTUCE AND OTHER SALAD GREENS

Enjoy them fresh! There is no way you can conserve or store them successfully.

OKRA

TO CAN: To be honest, canning brings out the worst in okra, most especially its icky, mucilage-like texture. Canning also destroys the fresh green color of okra, so you will be happier if you freeze what you cannot eat fresh.

TO FREEZE: The best way to freeze okra is as a cooked gumbo base (see recipe) because all the stickiness and sliminess of raw okra disappear in the long slow cooking. Astonishingly, however, a good deal of the original crunch remains. You can also freeze raw okra if you choose the youngest, tenderest pods in the garden and pack them whole. *Amount of fresh okra needed to fill a 1-pint freezer bag:* about ¾ pound.

1.   Gather bright green, baby pods about the size of your little finger just before you are ready to freeze them. Wash gently in several changes of cool water, trim off the stems but leave the crowns intact. Be very careful not to break or bruise the pods (the frozen okra will be mushy if you do).

2.   Place okra in a large blanching basket and scald for 4 minutes in enough boiling water to cover. Plunge immediately into ice water and chill for 4 minutes.

111

3. Drain the okra, then pack *loosely* in 1- or 1½-pint freezer bags, pressing out all air pockets. Twist the tops of the bags into tight goosenecks, bend over and secure with twist-bands. Label and quick-freeze.

KEEPING TIME: About one year at 0° F., although the okra will be better if eaten within 6 months.

TO PICKLE: Cajuns like pickled okra as do more than a few other Southerners. They, however, like okra prepared almost any way, while most Americans decidedly do not. Try the recipe for Pickled Okra that follows, if you wish, but we're not guaranteeing you'll think as much of it as Cajuns do.

TO DRY: Impossible.

TO STORE IN A ROOT CELLAR: Also impossible.

GUMBO BASE
Makes 6 Half-Pints

Gumbo can be thickened either with filé powder or with okra, but not with both. The Cajun way is to use okra, but *cooked* okra, which thickens the gumbo without making it slimy. Gumbo base can be cooked in season, then frozen in half-pint freezer jars. A half-pint (1 cup) is exactly what's needed to thicken the Crab and Okra Gumbo recipe that follows (enough to serve 8 people amply). The okra must cook slowly for about three hours, but miraculously it retains a certain crunchiness. The gumbo base can also be served as a vegetable. Simply bring to serving temperature. Three half-pints should serve four.

4 pounds fresh okra
6 tablespoons lard (hog lard, not vegetable
  shortening)

2 cans (8 ounces each) tomato sauce (not
  tomato paste)

Wash 6 half-pint freezer jars and their closures in hot soapy water, rinse well in hot water, then stand upside down on a clean towel and cool thoroughly before filling.

Wash okra well in cool water, remove and discard caps, then slice okra tissue thin. Place lard in a very large heavy kettle (not cast iron because iron will turn okra black), melt over moderately high heat, then add okra. Stir-fry about 5 minutes, then reduce heat to lowest point and let okra cook 1 hour, uncovered, stirring now and then. Mix in tomato sauce and cook over lowest heat, stirring occasionally, about 2 hours longer until okra seems dry and as a Cajun cook described it, "just comes together in a great big ball."

Pack into half-pint freezer jars, using a wide-mouth funnel to make the job neater, and filling to within ¼" of the tops. Screw on closures, cool gumbo base to room temperature, label and date, then freeze in a 0° F. freezer.

CRAB AND OKRA GUMBO
Makes 8 Hearty Servings

This gumbo can be made with almost any shellfish—crab, shrimp or crawfish. You want the shellfish meat only, and it should be no more than blanched. Shrimp and crawfish should be boiled for 1 minute exactly in lightly salted water, then shelled and deveined—they will cook for 15 minutes in the gumbo and if fully cooked beforehand, will toughen and dry. Crab and Okra Gumbo is a good choice for a party buffet because it requires only boiled rice to accompany plus a crisp green salad, because it can be stretched to serve 10, perhaps 12, by increasing the amount of rice per serving, and, finally because it can be neatly served and eaten (no unmanageable chunks of food). The gumbo will be better if made a day ahead, cooled to room temperature, then covered and refrigerated until shortly before serving. You have only to heat it up at the last minute.

Roux:
3 tablespoon: lard (hog lard, not vegetable shortening)
⅓ cup unsifted all-purpose flour (do not substitute the new instant-type flour or self-rising flour—neither will make a proper roux)

Gumbo:
3 medium-size yellow onions, peeled and finely chopped
1 large sweet green pepper, cored, seeded and finely chopped
4 medium-size celery ribs, finely diced
2 cloves garlic, peeled and crushed
2½ quarts cold water

2 to 3 teaspoons salt (or to taste)
½ teaspoon cayenne pepper
⅛ teaspoon freshly ground black pepper
1 half-pint frozen Gumbo Base (do not thaw)
2 pounds cooked lump or backfin crab-meat, picked over for bits of shell and cartilage (or, if you prefer, 1½ pounds medium-size shrimp or crawfish, boiled 1 minute in lightly salted water, then shelled and deveined)
¼ cup finely sliced scallion tops (green part only)
2 tablespoons minced parsley

The secret of a good gumbo is to work the roux properly, and this means for 30 minutes at least until it turns a rich russet brown (*roux* is the French word for "russet"). Melt the lard in a very heavy large kettle (an enameled cast-iron kettle is particularly suitable because it distributes the heat slowly and evenly). Blend in the flour, then heat and stir until the roux is a rich rust-brown and has a nice gloss to it ("halo," is the way Cajuns describe this sheen). You'll have to raise and lower the heat under the kettle so that the roux browns slowly, turning first a pale ivory color, then blond, then butterscotch, then russet.

Stir in the onions, green pepper, celery and garlic, turn heat off under kettle, clap the lid on and let stand 15 minutes. Blend in 1 quart of the cold water, turn heat under kettle to moderate, and cook and stir until mixture thickens slightly—4 to 5 minutes. Add the remaining 1½ quarts water, 2 teaspoons of the salt, the cayenne and black pepper, then boil slowly, uncovered, about ¾ of an hour to 1 hour or until mixture has reduced by about one-third. Stir in the Gumbo Base and continue to stir until it thaws; simmer uncovered, stirring now and then, for 1 to 1¼ hours, until fairly thick.

Add the crab (or shrimp or crawfish) and simmer uncovered for 5 minutes. Mix in the scallion tops and simmer uncovered for another 5 minutes. Stir in the parsley and simmer uncovered for 5 minutes more. Taste, and add more salt, if needed. Serve over fluffy boiled rice.

PICKLED OKRA
Makes About 8 Pints

Here's another old Cajun recipe from Southwestern Louisiana and a surprisingly good way to conserve okra. Cajuns like pickled okra as a hot-weather snack, washed down with plenty of well-chilled beer.

4 pounds uniformly small young okra pods (each should be about the size of your little finger)	4 teaspoons pickling salt
	2 tablespoons white mustard seeds
	4 teaspoons celery seeds
1 gallon cold water mixed with 4 teaspoons slaked lime (calcium hydroxide)	1 tablespoon ground turmeric
	4 small white onions, peeled, sliced paper thin and separated into rings
2 quarts white vinegar	
6 cups sugar	8 fresh small green chili peppers (optional)

Wash okra well in cool water but do not stem or slice. Soak okra for 2 hours in a large, uncovered, enamel kettle in the mixture of cold water and slaked lime (this is to make the okra crisp). Drain okra well, then rinse several times in cool, clear water.

Wash and rinse eight 1-pint preserving jars and their closures, then keep immersed in separate kettles of simmering water until you are ready to use them.

Bring vinegar, sugar, salt, mustard and celery seeds, turmeric and onion rings to a boil in a very large heavy enamel kettle. Add okra and the minute mixture returns to a boil, boil uncovered for 1 minute exactly (no longer or okra will overcook). Pack okra and onion slices into hot jars, tuck a green chili pepper into each, if you like, then pour in enough boiling pickling liquid to cover the okra, at the same time leaving ¼" head space.

Wipe jar rims, seal jars, then process 10 minutes in a boiling water bath (212°

F.). Remove jars from water bath, complete seals if necessary, then cool to room temperature. Check seals, label jars and store on a cool, dark, dry shelf.

ONIONS

Although onions are canned and frozen commercially, you will not find either of these methods a satisfactory way of conserving them at home (commercial processors, remember, use specialized equipment and preservatives unavailable to you).

Onions are, of course, called for in dozens of pickle and relish recipes and pickling is perhaps the best way to use up your surplus. You can also air-dry yellow, white and red onions, then keep them in cold storage. (Scallions and spring onions are too perishable for cold storage.)

TO DRY ONIONS AND HOLD IN COLD STORAGE: First of all, if you intend to grow onions for cold storage, you should grow them from seeds or seedlings, not from sets (small sprouting onions grown the year before) because these onions will not hold well. Second, the onions must be thoroughly mature and dry *before* they go into cold storage. Do not pull the onions until after the tops have yellowed, withered and bent over touching the ground. And do not pull them unless the ground itself is good and dry.

Once you have pulled the onions, spread them out (with the tops still on) one-layer deep on wire netting or wooden slats and let air-dry in a cool, dry spot, turning them often so that they will dry evenly. If they are to dry properly, the humidity in your drying area should not exceed 70%.

Once the onions are thoroughly dry (the outer skins should feel like parchment and the onions themselves should be hard), cut off the tops. Bundle the onions in mesh bags (the kind oranges and grapefruits are sold in), but only half-fill each bag so that there will be plenty of air circulating around the onions. Hang the bags from the rafters or crossbeams in a dry, cold (ideally, 32° F.) spot. The basement root cellar is not a good place to store onions for two reasons: (1) It is too humid, and (2) the onions will send their odor throughout the house. Choose instead a cold, dry companionway, spare room or attic (if the attic temperature is sufficiently and uniformly cold).

KEEPING TIME: All winter long.

ONION RELISH
Makes About 6 Half-Pints

For a strong, crisp relish, use white (silverskin) onions, for a softer, mellower one, yellow or Spanish onions.

1 quart coarsely chopped onions (you will need about 20 white onions, 8 to 10 medium-size yellow onions, and 2 to 3 large Spanish onions)
1 pint moderately finely diced sweet red peppers

1 pint moderately finely diced sweet green peppers
1 cup sugar
1 cup white vinegar (about)
4 teaspoons salt
1 teaspoon cayenne pepper

Wash and rinse 6 half-pint preserving jars and their closures; keep jars and closures immersed in separate kettles of simmering water until you are ready to use them.

Place all ingredients in a large heavy enamel or stainless steel kettle, stir to mix, then bring slowly to a boil, uncovered. Relish should seem quite juicy but if not, add about ¼ cup additional white vinegar. Using a slotted spoon and a wide-mouth canning funnel, pack hot relish into hot jars, filling to within ⅛″ of the tops. Run a thin-blade spatula around inside edge of each jar to free trapped air bubbles. Wipe jar rims and seal jars. Process for 10 minutes in a boiling water bath (212° F.).

Lift jars from water bath, complete seals if necessary and cool thoroughly. Check seals, then label jars and store on a cool, dark, dry shelf. Let relish mellow for about three weeks before serving.

PARSNIPS AND SALSIFY

The surest way to conserve these two root vegetables is also the easiest and most economical: simply leave them right where they are—in the ground in the garden. Hard freezes don't faze parsnips or salsify although alternate freezes and thaws do. You must protect them, then, for some few weeks between the end of the growing season and the onset of winter. But that's easily enough done. All you have to do is cover the plants with a thin layer of mulch.

Once temperatures drop below freezing—and stay there—push the mulch aside so that the parsnips and salsify will freeze in the ground. Then re-cover them with mulch, using a thicker layer this time, so that they will remain frozen throughout the winter. To use? Simply go out and dig up however much you need, thaw in a cool spot, then cook as you normally would.

KEEPING TIME: All winter long.

PEAS (BLACK-EYED)

TO CAN: Amount of unshelled *black-eyed peas needed to fill a 1-quart jar:* approximately 3½ to 4 pounds.

Cold (Raw) Pack:

1. Gather succulent young pods shortly before you will can the peas. Wash and rinse the unshelled peas in cool water, shell and wash well again.

2. Pack the raw peas *loosely* in hot pint or quart preserving jars, filling to within 1″ of the tops. Do not shake or pack the peas down. To each pint jar add ½ teaspoon salt and to each quart jar, 1 teaspoon salt. Pour enough clear boiling water into jars to cover peas, but leave 1″ head space.

3. Wipe jar rims and seal jars. PRESSURE PROCESS pints for 35 minutes at 10 pounds pressure and quarts for 40 minutes at 10 pounds pressure.

4. Remove jars from pressure canner, complete seals if necessary, then cool to room temperature. Check seals, label jars, and store on a cool, dark, dry shelf.

Hot Pack:

1. The same as for COLD PACK (above).

2. Boil the peas for 3 minutes in just enough water to cover. Using a slotted spoon, pack *loosely* into hot pint or quart preserving jars filling to within 1″ of the tops. The filling will be faster and neater if you use a wide-mouth canning funnel. Don't pack the peas in the jars and don't shake them down either (being starchy, they need plenty of room to expand during processing). To each pint jar add ½ teaspoon salt and to each quart jar 1 teaspoon salt. Pour enough fresh boiling water into jars to cover the peas, at the same time leaving 1″ head space.

3. & 4. The same as for COLD PACK (above).

KEEPING TIME: About one year.

TO FREEZE: Like corn, black-eyed peas must be moved from field to freezer as fast as possible. Draft whatever assistance you can to help with the shelling because black-eyed peas are not nearly so neatly or quickly shelled as green peas. It's best, in fact, to set up a sort of assembly line with two to three people shelling the peas, a fourth manning the blanching water and ice bath, and a fifth packing the peas and popping them into the freezer. If you have to do the job solo, don't try to cope with more than 6 to 8 pounds of unshelled peas at one session. You'll be exhausted and the peas will be a bit time-worn, too. *Amount of* unshelled *black-eyed peas needed to fill a 1-pint freezer container:* about 2 pounds.

1. Select mature-but-young peas. The pods should still be green and tender. Wash the unshelled peas in cool water, shell, then wash well again and rinse.

2. Pile the shelled peas in a blanching basket, filling no more than two-thirds, then scald 2 minutes in enough boiling water to cover. Whisk the basket of peas from the blanching kettle to a large kettle of ice water. Chill for 2 minutes, then drain.

3. Pack the peas loosely in 1- or 1½-pint freezer bags, pressing out all air pockets, then twisting the tops into tight goosenecks, bending over and securing with twist-bands. Label each bag and quick-freeze.

KEEPING TIME: About one year at 0° F.

TO PICKLE: Don't bother. Black-eyed peas are not suited to pickling.

TO DRY: Black-eyed peas are dried commercially, but without expensive drying equipment you cannot do the job effectively at home.

TO STORE IN A ROOT CELLAR: Forget it.

PEAS (GREEN)

TO CAN: In my view, canned peas are as tasteless as a chip, but in deference to those who do like them, I include canning directions. *Amount of* unshelled *peas needed to fill a 1-quart jar:* 4 to 6 pounds.

Cold (Raw) Pack:

1. Have ready whatever equipment and utensils you will need for canning the peas before you go into the garden (and it's a good idea to have a couple of willing pea-shellers on hand, too). When picking, choose bright green, well-filled pods that seem moist and crisp. Wash the unshelled peas well in cool water, shell, wash well again and drain.

2. Pack the raw peas *loosely* into hot 1-pint or 1-quart preserving jars, filling them to within 1″ of the tops. Do not pack the peas or shake them down in the jars. To each 1-pint jar add ½ teaspoon salt and 1 teaspoon sugar, and to each 1-quart jar, add 1 teaspoon salt and 2 teaspoons sugar. Pour enough clear boiling water into each jar to cover the peas, at the same time leaving 1″ head space.

3. Wipe jar rims and seal jars. PRESSURE PROCESS both pints and quarts for 40 minutes at 10 pounds pressure. NOTE: If peas are extralarge, process for 10 minutes longer.

4. Remove jars from canner, complete seals if necessary, and cool to room temperature. Check seals, then label jars and store on a cool, dark, dry shelf.

Hot Pack:

1. The same as for COLD PACK (above).

2. Group the peas together by size—small and medium-size ones together, large and extra-large ones together. Then boil the two batches separately in enough water to cover, allowing 3 minutes for small and medium-size peas and 4 minutes for large ones. Ladle peas into hot pint or quart preserving jars, using a wide-mouth funnel to facilitate filling and leaving 1" of head space at the tops. Don't pack the peas firmly and don't shake them down. To each 1-pint jar add ½ teaspoon salt and 1 teaspoon sugar and to each 1-quart jar, add 1 teaspoon salt and 2 teaspoons sugar. Pour enough of the cooking water into each jar to cover the peas, but allow 1" head space. If there is insufficient cooking water, simply add clear boiling water.

3. & 4. The same as for COLD PACK (above).

KEEPING TIME: About one year.

TO FREEZE: The faster you can get the peas into the freezer, the more nearly like garden-fresh peas they will be. Peas need not, by the way, always be frozen whole. They may be cooked, pressed through a food mill or buzzed in an electric blender, then frozen as purée. Pea purée can be heated and served as is or it can be used in making Potage Saint-Germain (French green pea soup; recipes follow). NOTE: If you intend to freeze the peas you grow, you must plant varieties that freeze well—not all of them do. Your county agricultural extension agent (reachable through the county government offices) can advise you. *Amount of unshelled green peas needed to fill a 1-pint freezer container:* about 2½ pounds.

1. Gather the peas in the cool of the morning, selecting young, plumply filled pods and picking no more peas than you will be able to freeze within 2 hours. Wash the unshelled peas in cool water, shell, wash again and drain.

2. Place shelled peas in a blanching basket (no more than half-filling it), then scald 2 minutes in enough boiling water to cover.

3. Rush the basket of peas from the blanching kettle to a large pan or sink full of ice water. Chill 2 minutes. Drain.

4. Pack the peas loosely in 1- or 1½-pint freezer bags, smooth out all air pockets, twist the tops tightly, bend over and secure with twist-bands. Label each package and quick-freeze.

KEEPING TIME: About one year at 0° F., although the peas will taste more freshly picked if served within 4 to 6 months.

TO DRY: You cannot dry green peas successfully at home without special low-heat dryers.

TO PICKLE: Pickling ruins green peas.

TO STORE IN A ROOT CELLAR: It can't be done.

FROZEN GREEN PEA PURÉE
Makes About 2 Pints

An excellent way to conserve *not*-so-young-and-tender green peas. The purée may be heated, seasoned to taste with salt, butter and pepper, and served; it may be mounded into cooked artichoke bottoms or large sautéed mushroom caps and used to garnish a roast platter. Or it may be made into Potage Saint-Germain (recipe follows).

2 quarts shelled, fresh green peas
2 tablespoons butter

Place the peas in a large heavy kettle and add water almost to cover them. Cover and boil 10 to 15 minutes until peas are very soft. Drain the peas, then purée in a food mill (you will only be able to purée a small amount of peas at a time and it's a slow, tedious job).

Place the purée in a large heavy saucepan and if it seems very stiff and dry, add a tablespoon or so of water (the consistency should be about the same as soft mashed potatoes). Add the butter and heat and stir over low heat until the butter is melted.

Cool the purée to room temperature, then pack tightly in 1-pint freezer cartons, filling to within ½″ of the tops. Snap on lids, label cartons and quick-freeze.

POTAGE SAINT-GERMAIN
Makes 4 Servings

1 pint Frozen Green Pea Purée, completely thawed (recipe precedes)
3 cups veal stock or chicken broth or 1½ cups each beef broth and water
1 tablespoon butter
1 teaspoon minced fresh chervil or ¼ teaspoon crumbled leaf chervil
1 teaspoon salt
⅛ teaspoon white pepper
¼ cup small butter-browned croutons

Place the pea purée and stock in a large heavy saucepan and heat, uncovered, over moderately low heat 5 minutes, stirring frequently. Drain through fine sieve, pressing out as much liquid and pulp as possible. Rinse out the saucepan and return sieved mixture to pan. Set over moderate heat, add butter, chervil, salt and pepper and heat and stir about 5 minutes or of a good serving temperature. Taste for salt and pepper and add more if needed to suit your taste. Ladle into large flat soup plates and scatter a few croutons on top of each portion.

PEPPERS (HOT)

Chili peppers, like sweet peppers, turn scarlet as they ripen, and how you should conserve them depends upon whether you pick them green or red. Green chilis pickle well (as Mexicans have long known) because they are firm enough to hold their shape (you'll find a recipe for Pickled Green Chili Peppers further on). Green chilis don't, however, can or freeze satisfactorily so you might as well not waste time trying either method.

As for red chilis, far and away the best way to conserve them is to dry them. CAUTION: Handle chilis (whether red or green) carefully, trying not to break or bruise the pods. And do not, under any circumstances, rub your face (especially yours eyes) while working with them because the pain will be excruciating. Wash your hands several times in warm sudsy water after working with chilis, paying particular attention to any bits that may have become lodged under your nails. You won't feel the fire of the peppers on your hands (unless you have a cut), but you will most definitely feel it the minute you rub your face or neck or arms.

TO DRY HOT RED PEPPERS: There are two ways, both of them easy. First of all, the peppers should be red—or well on their way to becoming red. The quickest way to dry them is to uproot the plants, peppers and all, then to hang them upside down in a cool dry attic or spare room. A basement root cellar is too humid so don't attempt to dry peppers there; they will mold.

The second method of drying red peppers is the Pueblo Indian way: Pick the peppers when red, then string on stout cord or thread, running the needle through the green stems or crowns, *not* through the pepper pods. String the peppers loosely, making certain there is sufficient air space between them to discourage mold. If you live in a dry sunny climate, hang the peppers out-of-doors (Indians traditionally suspend garlands of chilis from the eaves of their adobe houses). Otherwise, hang the chilis indoors from the rafters of a cool dry attic or unheated spare room (again, not in a basement root cellar).

KEEPING TIME: About one year.

How do you use dried peppers? In dozens of ways. They are the soul of Tex-Mex cooking, an integral ingredient in barbecue, stew, chili and guacamole.

PICKLED GREEN CHILI PEPPERS
Makes 3 to 4 Pints

These are torrid, so if you do not have an appetite for fiery foods, you might as well skip this recipe.

2 pounds large green chili peppers (they should be about the size of your ring finger)

2 quarts cold water mixed with 2 teaspoons slaked lime (calcium hydroxide)

1 quart white vinegar

2 cups sugar

2 teaspoons pickling salt

2 teaspoons white mustard seeds

2 teaspoons celery seeds

Wash chili peppers well in cool water and drain but do not stem or slice. Soak the chili peppers for 2 hours in a large, uncovered, enamel kettle in the mixture of cold water and slaked lime (this is to make the pickles crisp). Drain chili peppers well, then rinse in several changes of cool water and drain well again.

Wash and rinse four 1-pint preserving jars and their closures; keep jars and closures immersed in separate kettles of simmering water until you are ready to use them.

Bring vinegar, sugar, pickling salt, mustard and celery seeds to a boil in a large heavy enamel or stainless steel kettle. Add chili peppers and the minute the mixture returns to a boil, boil uncovered for 30 seconds (no longer or the peppers will overcook). Pack the chili peppers into hot jars, arranging as snugly and attractively as possible to within ¼" of the jar tops. Pour in enough boiling pickling liquid to cover the peppers, at the same time leaving ¼" head space. Run a thin-blade spatula or table knife around inside edges of jars to free air bubbles. Wipe jar rims and seal jars.

Process for 10 minutes in a boiling water bath (212° F.). Remove jars from water bath, complete seals if necessary and cool completely. Check seals, label jars and store on a cool, dark, dry shelf.

PEPPERS (SWEET)

TO CAN: Sweet peppers can be canned, but they are so soft and unappetizing that we do not recommend doing so.

TO FREEZE: If you want to freeze peppers, mince them first. Frozen whole or half peppers, once thawed, virtually collapse because the ice crystals formed in freezing shatter their delicate structure. Minced or diced peppers lose their crispness, too, but they are ideal for making soups, stews and casseroles where flavor, not texture, is the object. *Amount of fresh peppers, minced, needed to fill a 1-pint freezer container:* 2 to 3 medium-size.

1. Gather peppers shortly before you will freeze them, choosing only those that are crisp and tender and bright green or red. Wash well in cool water, core, remove seeds and any soft pith around the seeds. Dice or mince peppers fairly fine. *Do not blanch.*

2. Pack the diced peppers loosely in 1- to 1½-pint freezer bags, press out all air pockets, twist tops of bags into tight goosenecks, bend over and secure with twist-bands. Label each bag and quick-freeze.

KEEPING TIME: About 6 months at 0° F.

TO PICKLE: Sweet peppers are used to add color, crunch and flavor to many pickles and relishes. See recipes throughout the book; also the Sweet Pepper Relish below.

TO DRY: Not practical.

TO STORE IN A ROOT CELLAR: Sweet peppers are too perishable to store for long periods of time in a root cellar. However, you can, in a pinch, hold them for a month or so, all conditions being right (temperature between 45° and 50° F., humidity between 80% and 90% and slight circulation of air). You cannot control conditions closely enough in a drum buried outdoors to store peppers there, but you may be able to in a basement root cellar.

Pick the peppers *before* "first frost" and wipe any dew or moisture from them, taking care not to bruise them. Sort the peppers carefully and reject any that show blemishes, soft spots or mold about the crown. Pack the peppers one-layer deep in a slatted wooden box lined with a sheet of polyethylene in which you have cut about a dozen evenly spaced holes (the holes should be about the diameter of a pencil). Cover the peppers loosely with a second sheet of plastic (again perforated with about a dozen evenly spaced holes).

KEEPING TIME: 4 to 6 weeks.

SWEET PEPPER RELISH
Makes About 4 Half-Pints

6 cups diced sweet red peppers (you'll need about 6 large sweet red peppers)	3 tablespoons pickling salt
	2 cups sugar
6 cups diced sweet green peppers (you'll need about 6 large sweet green peppers)	3 cups white vinegar
	1 tablespoon white mustard seeds
	1 cinnamon stick

Place the red and green peppers in a large bowl, sprinkle with pickling salt, toss to mix, then let stand uncovered at room temperature for 3 hours. Rinse the peppers in a colander under cool water and drain very dry.

Place sugar, vinegar, mustard seeds and cinnamon stick in a large heavy enamel or stainless steel kettle, set uncovered over moderate heat and bring to the boil, stirring until sugar dissolves. Boil uncovered for 20 minutes to form a clear syrup.

Meanwhile, wash and rinse 4 half-pint preserving jars and their closures. Keep jars and closures immersed in separate kettles of simmering water until you are ready to use them.

Add the drained peppers to the syrup, let come to the boil, stirring occasionally, then boil uncovered for 3 minutes. Remove cinnamon stick and discard. Ladle hot relish into hot jars, using a slotted spoon and a wide-mouth canning funnel to facilitate filling. Pack jars to within ¼" of the tops, making sure there is enough pickling syrup in the jars to ooze up over the pepper relish. Run a thin-blade spatula or table knife around inside edges of jars to release trapped air bubbles. Wipe jar rims and seal jars. Process for 10 minutes in a boiling water bath (212° F.). Remove jars from water bath, complete seals if necessary and cool completely. Check seals, label jars and store on a cool, dark, dry shelf.

POTATOES (IRISH)

TO CAN: The best potatoes for canning are fairly firm or waxy ones (Maine or Eastern varieties). Small potatoes, obviously, will pack more easily and uniformly into preserving jars than large ones and whole potatoes will hold their shape better under pressure processing than quartered, sliced or diced potatoes. *Amount of fresh (2") potatoes needed to fill a 1-quart preserving jar:* About 1½ to 2 pounds.

Hot Pack (cold pack is not recommended):

1. Wash the potatoes well in cool water, peel and cut out all "eyes." Wash peeled potatoes well in cool water.
2. Boil potatoes for 10 minutes in enough water to cover. With a slotted spoon, pack hot potatoes into hot 1-quart preserving jars, filling to within 1" of the tops. To each jar add 1 teaspoon salt, then pour in enough fresh boiling water to cover the potatoes, leaving 1" head space. NOTE: It is not practical to pack potatoes in pint jars because you can get so few of them into each jar.
3. Wipe jar rims and seal jars. PRESSURE PROCESS quarts for 40 minutes at 10 pounds pressure.
4. Remove jars from canner, complete seals if necessary, and cool to room temperature. Check seals, then label jars and store on a cool, dark, dry shelf.

KEEPING TIME: About one year.

TO FREEZE: Not a good way to conserve potatoes because they become watery.

TO PICKLE: Don't.

TO DRY: Don't.

TO STORE IN A ROOT CELLAR: Late-crop potatoes are a better choice for cold storage than those harvested early because, before potatoes go into a root cellar, they must be cured at cool temperatures (between 60° and 75° F.). You will have no difficulty maintaining such temperatures with potatoes dug in the fall, but you will with early-crop potatoes harvested in warm weather. So, if you intend to root cellar potatoes, plant varieties you can harvest in late fall.

Dig the potatoes carefully so that you don't hack into them with your shovel. As soon as they are dug, get them into a *dark,* cool room indoors so that they will be neither wind-dried nor light-struck. (Exposure to either sunlight or artificial light will turn potatoes green.) These green patches are not only bitter, they are also an indication of high concentrations of solanine, which can be converted by the body into a poison known as solanidine. Spread the potatoes out (without washing them) in a dark, moist, cool area (ideally, the humidity should be about 85% and the temperature between 60° and 75° F.).

After the potatoes have cured for about two weeks, pile them several layers deep in slatted crates, cover (to keep all light out), and store in the basement root cellar, trying as nearly as possible to maintain the temperature between 35° and 40° F. and the humidity between 80% and 90%. Do not store apples near the potatoes, for they will absorb the earthy-musty aroma of the potatoes.

KEEPING TIME: All winter long.

NOTE: If you pull potatoes from cold storage and cook them straight away, you will find them unusually sweet because at low temperatures potato starch is converted to sugar. Happily, the process is reversible. So for potatoes that taste as you like them to taste, remove from cold storage and hold at 70° F. for about two weeks before cooking. If the potatoes show any green spots or sprouts, remove sprouts and peel before cooking, removing all green areas. There will be no danger then of making anyone sick.

POTATOES (SWEET) AND YAMS

TO CAN: Because sweet potatoes and yams are partially cooked before they are canned, they are packed hot only. They may, however, be packed dry (with no liquid at all) or wet (with boiling water or syrup added). Here, then, are the two hot pack methods. *Amount of fresh sweet potatoes or yams needed to fill a 1-quart preserving jar:* About 1½ to 2 pounds.

Dry Pack:

1.   Group the potatoes together by size. Small potatoes can be canned whole, but large ones should be halved or quartered *after* they have been washed, boiled and peeled. Scrub the unpeeled potatoes well in cool water, then rinse. Boil in enough water to cover just until the skins loosen–this will take 25 to 30 minutes. Do not test for doneness by jabbing the potatoes with a fork. Drain the potatoes, slip off the skins and, if the potatoes are large, halve or quarter them.

2.   Pack the hot potatoes firmly into hot 1-pint or 1-quart preserving jars, pressing them down as you go and filling to within 1″ of the jar tops. Do not add water and do not add salt.

3.   Wipe the jar rims and seal jars. PRESSURE PROCESS the pints for 1 hour and 5 minutes at 10 pounds pressure and the quarts for 1 hour and 35 minutes at 10 pounds pressure.

4.   Remove jars from canner, complete seals if necessary and cool to room temperature. Check seals, label jars and store on a cool, dark, dry shelf.

Wet Pack:

1.   The same as for DRY PACK (above).

2.   Pack the hot potatoes, not too firmly, into hot 1-pint or 1-quart preserving jars, filling to within 1″ of the tops. Pour in enough fresh boiling water to cover potatoes or, if you prefer, boiling syrup made using the proportion of 3 cups sugar to each 1 quart of water. Leave 1″ head space.

3.   Wipe jar rims and seal jars. PRESSURE PROCESS pints for 55 minutes at 10 pounds pressure and quarts for 1 hour and 30 minutes at 10 pounds pressure.

4.   The same as for DRY PACK (above).

KEEPING TIME: About one year.

TO FREEZE: Sweet potatoes and yams both freeze well, but they must be cooked and seasoned first. See recipes that follow.

TO PICKLE: Out of the question.

TO DRY: Also out of the question.

HOW TO WINTER OVER IN COLD STORAGE: Root cellars and metal drums buried outdoors are too cold and too humid for wintering sweet potatoes. You can, however, store sweet potatoes and yams safely throughout the fall, winter and early spring in a warmer, drier part of the cellar or in a spare room where temperatures will not drop below 50° F. and the humidity will not rise above 75%.

Unlike many vegetables that mature underground, sweet potatoes are easily damaged by killing frosts, so dig them *before* the first hard freeze. Sweet potatoes and yams are also easily bruised and nicked, so dig them carefully. Do not wash or clean them, but layer gently into slatted crates in the field, cover with a clean tarpaulin, then carry indoors and set in warm, moist spot to cure for 10 days (the temperature should be between 80° and 85° F. and the humidity about 85%).

After the 10-day curing period, transfer the crates of potatoes to a cooler, drier basement area or to a spare room where temperatures can be kept between 55° and 60° F. and the humidity between 70% and 75%.

KEEPING TIME: From fall through early spring.

FROZEN CANDIED SWEET POTATOES
Makes About 2 Pints

Before sweet potatoes are frozen they must first be cooked. If they are to be sliced and candied, you will find that they will have better texture and flavor if they are first baked rather than boiled or steamed.

6 large sweet potatoes or yams	*½ teaspoon ground cinnamon*
¼ cup lemon juice	*¼ teaspoon ground mace*
¼ cup orange juice	*¼ teaspoon ground cloves*
1 cup sugar or light brown sugar	

Scrub the potatoes well in cool water but do not peel. Bake uncovered in a hot oven (400° F.) for ¾ to 1 hour, just until tender. Remove potatoes from oven and cool until easy to handle.

Meanwhile, combine lemon and orange juices in a pie plate; also blend sugar and spices in a small bowl. Slip the skins off the potatoes and slice about ⅜" thick. Place slices in juice mixture, spooning juice on top so that they are well saturated; this is not only to keep the potatoes from darkening but also to give them flavor. Let potatoes stand in juice 4 to 5 minutes. Remove one at a time and roll in the spiced sugar until well coated. Pack the slices firmly in 1-pint freezer containers, pressing down lightly and filling to within ½" of the tops. Snap on lids, label and quick-freeze.

To serve: Thaw potatoes until easy to separate, layer into a small casserole, dotting liberally with chips of butter as you go and sprinkling, if you like, with a little extra sugar or brown sugar or drizzling lightly with maple syrup. Cover with

127

foil and bake 25 to 30 minutes in a moderate oven (350° F.) until bubbly-hot. From a 1-pint container, you will have enough for 2 to 4 servings.

FROZEN MASHED SWEET POTATOES
Makes About 2 Pints

If mashed sweet potatoes or yams are to be frozen, they should be soft rather than dry, so the best way to cook them is to boil them in their skins.

8 medium-size sweet potatoes or yams
2 tablespoons lemon juice or 1 tablespoon
each lemon and orange juice

Scrub the potatoes well in cool water but do not peel; boil in enough water to cover 35 to 40 minutes or just until tender. Remove the skins, mash the potatoes well and mix in the lemon juice.

Pack tightly in 1-pint freezer containers, filling to within ½″ of the tops. Snap on lids, label and quick-freeze.

To serve: Thaw the sweet potatoes until soft, then bring slowly to serving temperature in a heavy, covered saucepan. Season to taste with butter, salt and pepper, and if you like, sweeten with a little brown sugar or maple syrup. From a 1-pint freezer container you will have enough for 2 to 4 servings.

You can also make perfectly delicious sweet potato pie using the frozen mashed sweet potatoes.

SWEET POTATO PIE
Makes Two 9-Inch Single-Crust Pies

A spicy, custard-smooth pie that Southerners often serve in place of pumpkin pie.

1 pint Frozen Mashed Sweet Potatoes,
completely thawed (recipe precedes)
⅓ cup butter
1 cup sugar
½ cup firmly packed light brown sugar
1 cup milk
2 large eggs

1 teaspoon finely grated orange rind
¼ teaspoon ground cinnamon
¼ teaspoon ground nutmeg
⅛ teaspoon ground cloves
½ teaspoon vanilla
¼ teaspoon salt
2 (9-inch) unbaked pie shells

Place the thawed mashed sweet potatoes in a large heavy saucepan, add the butter and sugars, and heat and stir over low heat just until butter melts and sugar dissolves. Off heat, beat in the milk, then the eggs, one at a time, mixing only enough to blend. Stir in the orange rind, cinnamon, nutmeg, cloves, vanilla and salt. Pour the mixture into the two pie shells, dividing the total amount evenly.

Bake uncovered in a hot oven (400° F.) 30 to 35 minutes until the pastry is touched with brown and the filling seems set around the edges. Remove the pies from the oven and cool to room temperature before cutting.

SPINACH AND OTHER GREENS

Included in "other greens" are beet tops, chard, collards, kale, mustard and turnip greens. It is possible, of course, to can these leafy green vegetables, but the long pressure processing needed for their safekeeping makes them so olive-drab and soft and strong-flavored that we think canning a miserable way of putting them by for future enjoyment. Greens cannot be pickled or dried or stored in root cellars. But they do freeze quite acceptably.

TO FREEZE: If greens are to freeze well, they must be young and tender, insect- and blemish-free. *Amount of fresh leafy greens (untrimmed) needed to fill a 1-pint freezer container:* 1 to 1½ pounds.

1. Gather the greens shortly before you will freeze them and sort meticulously, discarding bruised, withered or yellowed leaves. Remove coarse stems and veins and discard. Wash the greens several times in a sinkful of cool water, letting them soak for a minute or two, then moving them very gently in the water so that the grit floats out and sinks to the bottom. Lift the greens into a colander, agitating the water as little as possible so that all grit and sand remain behind in the bottom of the sink. Rinse the greens well and drain.

2. For blanching, you will need 2 gallons of boiling water for each 1 pound of greens. Scald the greens 2 minutes, moving them gently in the blanch water so that they will scald evenly without matting or clumping. Drain the greens and plunge immediately into ice water. Chill 2 minutes and drain thoroughly.

3. Leave the leaves whole, or if you prefer, chop them coarsely (but do so as quickly as possible). Pack in 1-pint freezer containers, filling to within ¼" of the brim. Snap on lids, label cartons and quick-freeze.

KEEPING TIME: About one year at 0° F., although the greens will be of higher quality if eaten within 6 months.

SQUASH (SUMMER)

Unhappily, there are few ways you can conserve these delicate varieties—yellow squash, zucchini and pattypan or cymling. They are all so full of water that both pressure processing and freezing reduce them to mush. (Yes, you will find directions in other books for canning and freezing summer squash. But in my opinion

—with the exception of frozen puréed squash—the end products are so watery and tasteless that they do not merit inclusion here.) You cannot dry summer squash and you cannot hold them in cold storage either.

Fortunately, however, both zucchini and yellow squash make delicious pickles. Both may also be cooked and puréed and then frozen to use later in making soups and soufflés (recipes follow). Purées are also an excellent way to use up those enormous conversation-piece squashes. (You can probably expect one of these giants if you have put in more than a couple of rows of squash.)

Try the recipes that follow if you have on hand more fresh summer squash than you can enjoy or share with friends. They are the best ways I know of "stretching" the short summer squash season.

FROZEN PURÉED SUMMER SQUASH
Makes 5 to 6 Pints

6 pounds of summer squash (zucchini, yellow squash or pattypan)
2 large Spanish or Bermuda onions, peeled and coarsely chopped
⅓ cup butter

2 to 3 tablespoons water (only enough to keep squash from sticking as it cooks)
2 teaspoons salt
¼ teaspoon white pepper

Wash the squash well in cool water and trim but do not peel; cut in small cubes (¼" is a good size). Stir-fry the squash and onions in the butter in a very large heavy kettle over moderate heat about 15 minutes until golden and limp. If the kettle seems dry (a fair amount of liquid should have oozed out of the squash), add just enough water to moisten. Cover the kettle, lower heat and let the squash steam about 15 minutes until very tender. Purée the squash by pressing through a food mill or by buzzing, a little at a time, in an electric blender at high speed. Rinse and dry the kettle. Return the puréed squash to the kettle, add salt and pepper and let steam, uncovered, 2 to 3 minutes longer to drive off excess moisture. Cool the purée to room temperature.

Pack firmly into 1-pint freezer containers, filling to within ½" of the tops. Snap on lids, label containers and quick-freeze.

CREAM OF SQUASH SOUP
Makes 4 to 6 Servings

2 tablespoons butter
¼ teaspoon crumbled leaf rosemary or dill weed

3 tablespoons flour
2 cups chicken broth
1 cup milk

1 pint Frozen Puréed Summer Squash,
   thawed (recipe precedes)

1 cup light cream
Salt and white pepper to taste

Melt the butter in a large heavy saucepan over moderate heat, add the rosemary or dill and cook and stir about 1 minute to develop the herb flavor. Blend in the flour, then slowly stir in the chicken broth and milk and heat, stirring constantly, until thickened and smooth—3 to 4 minutes. Add the squash purée and heat, stirring, 3 to 4 minutes longer; add the light cream and heat and stir just until a good serving temperature. Taste for salt and pepper and add more of each, if needed. Ladle into soup bowls and serve.

SUMMER SQUASH SOUFFLÉ
Makes 4 Servings

Especially good with broiled chicken or lean white fish. Good, too, with poached salmon.

3 tablespoons butter
¼ teaspoon dill weed
Pinch of ground mace
5 tablespoons flour
¾ cup chicken broth
1 pint Frozen Puréed Summer Squash,

thawed completely (recipe precedes)
2 tablespoons grated parmesan cheese
4 egg yolks, lightly beaten (use large eggs)
5 egg whites (use large eggs)
Pinch of cream of tartar

Melt the butter in a medium-size heavy saucepan over moderate heat, add the dill and mace and heat and stir about 1 minute to develop their flavors. Blend in the flour until smooth, then add the chicken broth and squash purée and heat, stirring constantly, until thickened and smooth—3 to 4 minutes. Mix in the parmesan and heat, stirring, another 5 minutes. Briskly mix a little of the hot sauce into the beaten egg yolks, stir back into sauce and heat and stir for 1 minute—no longer or it may curdle (do not allow to boil either). Remove sauce from heat and continue stirring for about 1 minute. Cool for 15 minutes to 20 minutes or until lukewarm, stirring often to prevent a "skin" from forming on top of the sauce.

    Place the egg whites in a very large bowl and add the cream of tartar. Using a rotary egg beater, beat until the egg whites form peaks that curl over when the beater is withdrawn. Quickly mix about 1 cup of the beaten whites into the cooled sauce, then pour sauce over beaten egg whites and fold in gently using a rubber spatula and an over and over motion. Handle very carefully so as not to break down the volume of the egg whites.

    Pour into an ungreased 6-cup soufflé dish and bake in a moderate oven (350° F.) for about 30 minutes or until the soufflé is puffy and touched with brown. Serve immediately.

PICKLED ZUCCHINI
Makes 6 to 8 Pints

12 *medium-size tender young zucchini, trimmed, scrubbed but not peeled, then sliced ¼" thick (you will need 12 cups sliced zucchini in all)*
12 *cups thinly sliced, peeled white (silver-skin) onions (for this amount you will need about 3 dozen onions)*
6 *cups ice water mixed with ½ cup pick-ling salt (brine)*
2 *cups sugar*
1½ *teaspoons ground turmeric*
1 *teaspoon dill weed*
2 *teaspoons white mustard seeds*
1 *teaspoon celery seeds*
1 *quart white vinegar*

Layer zucchini and onion slices alternately into a very large bowl, pour in brine and let stand uncovered at room temperature for 3 hours. Drain, place in a colander and rinse well in cool water. Drain well again, pressing out as much liquid as possible.

Wash and rinse eight 1-pint preserving jars and their closures; keep jars and closures immersed in separate kettles of simmering water until you are ready to use them.

Blend sugar with turmeric, dill weed, mustard and celery seeds in a very large heavy enamel or stainless steel kettle; mix in vinegar. Set uncovered over high heat and bring to a boil, stirring until sugar dissolves. Add zucchini and onions and bring just to boiling, stirring gently. Using a wide-mouth canning funnel and a slotted spoon, pack pickles into hot preserving jars, filling to within ¼" of the tops. Pour in enough boiling pickling liquid to cover pickles at the same time leaving ¼" head space. Run a thin-blade spatula or table knife around inside edges of jars to release air bubbles; wipe jar rims and seal jars.

Process for 10 minutes in a boiling water bath (212° F.). Remove jars from water bath, complete seals if necessary, and cool thoroughly. Check seals, label jars and store on a cool, dark, dry shelf. Let the pickles season for at least a month before serving.

SWEET YELLOW SQUASH PICKLES
Makes 6 to 8 Pints

For best results, choose young, tender-skinned yellow squash for making these pickles. Either the straight-neck or crook-neck varieties may be used, however the straight-neck are preferable because they can be more evenly sliced.

12 *medium-size tender young yellow squash, trimmed, scrubbed but not peeled, then sliced ¼" thick (you will need 12 cups sliced squash in all)*

3 dozen small silverskin (white) onions, peeled and sliced very thin (you will need 12 cups sliced onions)
½ cup pickling salt
6 cups cracked ice cubes

3½ cups sugar
1 quart white vinegar
1¾ teaspoons ground turmeric
1¾ teaspoons celery seeds
1¾ teaspoons white mustard seeds

Layer sliced squash and onions alternately into a very large mixing bowl, sprinkling with pickling salt as you go. Pile cracked ice on top and let stand uncovered at room temperature for 3 hours. Drain, place in a colander and rinse well in cool water. Drain well again, pressing out as much liquid as possible.

Meanwhile, wash and rinse eight 1-pint preserving jars and their closures; keep hot in separate kettles of simmering water until you are ready to use them.

Bring sugar, vinegar, turmeric, celery and mustard seeds to a rolling boil over high heat in a large, heavy enamel or stainless steel kettle. Add squash and onions and stir gently. Bring just to the boiling point, then using a wide-mouth canning funnel, pack into hot preserving jars filling to within ¼" of the tops. Make sure squash and onions are covered with pickling liquid.

Wipe jar rims and seal jars. Process 10 minutes in a boiling water bath (212° F.). Remove jars from water bath, complete seals if necessary, and cool to room temperature. Check seals, label jars and store in a cool, dark, dry place.

TOMATOES

TO CAN: Many of today's tomatoes, as you can no doubt tell by tasting them, are significantly less tart (acid) than those of 25 or 50 years ago. They verge, in fact, on being low-acid, which means they *may* foster the growth of *Clostridium botulinum,* the villain in the deadly food poisoning known as botulism. For years, we have been taught that tomatoes are a high-acid food and that they may safely be processed in a boiling water bath. Well, some varieties of tomato are high-acid, but many others are not. If you intend to can tomatoes, it's important to know at the outset whether they are sufficiently acid to process in the boiling water bath or whether their acidity must be bolstered. Before you plant tomatoes, check with your county agricultural agent (he can be reached through county government offices) or with the home economics department of the state experiment station or state university in your area. Specialists here can recommend high-acid tomato varieties that will grow well in your area and they can advise you, too, as to local soil and climatic conditions that may alter the acidity of tomatoes. According to the U.S. Department of Agriculture, certain states now recommend that you routinely bolster the acidity of canned tomatoes and tomato juice to reduce spoilage and safeguard against botulism by adding citric acid as follows:

¼ teaspoon citric acid U.S.P. to each pint

½ teaspoon citric acid U.S.P. to each quart

You can buy or order citric acid at almost any pharmacy and it's a good idea to add it in the above proportions to any tomatoes or tomato juice of *unknown* acidity as well as to those of low acidity. Simply measure the tomato juice or tomatoes before you heat them, then mix in the required amount of citric acid. It will dissolve and spread uniformly throughout the tomatoes. It will not dissolve, however, if added to a jar of cold tomatoes, and for that reason low-acid tomatoes should be packed by the HOT PACK method only. *Amount of fresh tomatoes needed to fill a 1-quart preserving jar: 2½ to 3½ pounds.*

NOTE: Cherry tomatoes are known to be low-acid; moreover, they can poorly. So enjoy them fresh instead of trying to can them. When canning tomatoes, be especially meticulous and follow the steps outlined below to the letter. Do not add onions or green pepper or celery to the tomatoes to flavor them. These are all low-acid foods and as such will lower the acidity of the tomatoes, meaning that they cannot be safely processed in a boiling water bath. Instead, turn to the recipes for flavored tomato juices, paste, and sauces that follow.

Cold (Raw) Pack (for high-acid tomatoes only):

1. Pick plump, red, firm-ripe (not overripe) tomatoes as soon as possible before you will can them. Wash well in cool water, remove the stems and green crowns, then place, 5 to 6 tomatoes at a time, in a wire basket and scald 30 seconds in boiling water. Plunge tomatoes immediately into cold water, core, remove any green spots and slip off the skins. Leave tomatoes whole or quarter.

2. Pack tomatoes firmly in hot 1-pint or 1-quart preserving jars, pressing them down as you go and filling to within ½" of the jar tops. When jars are filled, press tomatoes down again until you force out enough juice to cover them. To each 1-pint jar add ½ teaspoon salt and to each 1-quart jar, 1 teaspoon salt. Run a thin-blade spatula around inside edge of each jar to release air bubbles.

3. Wipe jar rims and seal jars. Process pints and quarts in a boiling water bath (212° F.), allowing 35 minutes of processing for the pints and 45 minutes for the quarts. Be sure that water in the water bath stays at a gentle but steady boil throughout processing.

4. Remove jars from water bath, complete seals if necessary, then cool to room temperature. Check seals, label jars, and store on a cool, dark, dry shelf.

Hot Pack:

1. The same as for COLD PACK (above).

2. Measure the tomatoes and for every quart of them, add 1 teaspoon salt. Also add, if the tomatoes are of low or unknown acidity, ½ teaspoon citric acid to each quart. Boil the tomatoes uncovered for 5 minutes in a large heavy enamel or stainless steel kettle, then using a wide-mouth canning funnel, pour boiling hot into hot 1-pint or 1-quart preserving jars, filling to within ½" of the tops. Run a thin-blade spatula around the inside of each jar to free air bubbles.

3. Wipe jar rims and seal jars. Process pints and quarts in a boiling water bath (212° F.), allowing 10 minutes of processing for pints and 15 minutes for quarts.

4. The same as for COLD PACK (above).

KEEPING TIME: About one year.

TO FREEZE: Freezing destroys nearly everything we like about fresh tomatoes, most particularly the texture. Yes, I know there are people who say they've frozen whole or quartered tomatoes sucessfully. I have friends, in fact, who claim to have had good results. But I have personally never managed the trick and as far as I am concerned, trying to freeze raw tomatoes is a waste of time to say nothing of tomatoes. I far prefer to cook them into a pasta sauce that *does* freeze well (recipe follows).

TO DRY: Impossible.

TO PICKLE AND PRESERVE: Catsup ... chili sauce ... marmalade ... piccalilli ... pickles. You'll find recipes for each in the pages that follow.

TO HOLD IN COLD STORAGE: If tomatoes are ripening in your garden faster than you can eat them or get them into preserving jars, don't panic. You can hold them for about a month in a cool room, particularly if the tomatoes were planted late and are ripening in the fall (midsummer tomatoes are more perishable and do not hold so well).

Pick the tomatoes *before* "first frost," choosing for storage those from hardy vines; if the vines are spent, the tomatoes will be more susceptible to decay. Remove the stems (so that they will not puncture the tomatoes), wash the tomatoes in cool water, and let them air-dry thoroughly. Do not wipe them clean because any soil or sand clinging to them is abrasive enough to scar the skins.

Sort the tomatoes, separating the red from the green (they should be stored separately). Pack the tomatoes one or two layers deep in slatted-wood crates, then store on a well-ventilated dark shelf in a cool (55° F.), moderately moist area (the basement root cellar will be too cold and too damp). If you want to ripen green tomatoes, store in a warmer spot (65° to 70° F.). They will be ready to eat in about two weeks. Green tomatoes will also ripen at 55° F., but more slowly (in about a month). Keep a close eye on the humidity of the storage area: if it is too moist, the tomatoes will mold and decay, if it is too dry, they will shrivel. Ideal humidity for storing tomatoes is about 85%.

KEEPING TIME: 4 to 6 weeks.

HOME-CANNED TOMATO JUICE
Makes About 4 Quarts

For this recipe, use only juicy, vine-ripened tomatoes with plenty of "fresh tomato bouquet." Tomatoes that have been picked green and left to ripen indoors are pithy and flavorless by comparison. It is important, too, that the tomatoes be unblemished, for the smallest moldy spot can spoil an entire batch of juice.

20 *very large, vine-ripe, unblemished to-matoes, washed, cored and cut in thin wedges (no need to peel)*
1 *medium-size sweet green or red pepper, cored, seeded and minced*
2 *large yellow onions, peeled and minced*
1 *clove garlic, peeled and crushed (optional)*
2 *celery stalks, diced*
⅓ *cup sugar*
¼ *cup lemon juice*
1 *tablespoon salt*

Simmer all ingredients, covered, in a large heavy enamel or stainless steel kettle over moderate heat 35 to 40 minutes, stirring now and then, until tomatoes have cooked down to juice. Put mixture through a food mill or press through a fine sieve, forcing out as much juice and solids as possible.

Meanwhile, wash and rinse four 1-quart preserving jars together with their closures. Keep jars and closures immersed in separate kettles of simmering water until you are ready to use them.

Return strained tomato juice to kettle and bring to a full boil. Pour into hot preserving jars, filling each to within 1″ of the top. Wipe jar rims and seal, then process for 30 minutes at 10 pounds pressure in a steam pressure canner. Remove jars from canner, complete seals if necessary, and cool to room temperature. Check seals, then label jars and store in a cool, dark, dry place.

END-OF-THE-GARDEN VEGETABLE TONIC
Makes About 4 Quarts

A delicious way to use up tag ends of the garden. Serve well chilled as a midmorning or afternoon refresher.

12 large, vine-ripe tomatoes, cored and cut
*   in thin wedges (no need to peel)*
4 medium-size cucumbers, diced
4 medium-size zucchini or yellow squash,
*   coarsely grated*
4 medium-size carrots, peeled and coarsely
*   chopped*
2 medium-size sweet green or red peppers,
*   cored, seeded and minced*
4 celery stalks, diced
2 large yellow onions, peeled and minced
2 cups coarsely shredded cabbage

1 clove garlic, peeled and minced
2 cups water
¼ cup lemon juice
⅓ cup sugar
1 tablespoon salt
½ teaspoon freshly ground black pepper
2 bay leaves, crumbled
2 sprigs fresh thyme or ½ teaspoon crum-
*   bled leaf thyme, or, if you prefer, 2*
*   large fronds fresh dill or ½ teaspoon*
*   dill weed*

Simmer all ingredients slowly in a covered, large heavy enamel or stainless steel kettle over low heat 45 to 50 minutes, stirring now and then, until vegetables are mushy. Strain through a fine sieve, forcing out as much juice as possible.

Meanwhile, wash and rinse four 1-quart preserving jars together with their closures. Keep immersed in separate kettles of simmering water until you are ready to use them.

Return strained juice to kettle and bring to a vigorous boil. Pour into hot preserving jars, filling each to within 1" of the top. Wipe jar rims and seal. Process for 30 minutes at 10 pounds pressure. Remove jars from canner, complete seals if necessary and cool to room temperature. Check seals, label jars and store in a cool, dark, dry place.

BLOODY MARY MIX
Makes About 4 Quarts

If you have a bumper crop of tomatoes, put some of the surplus by as Bloody Mary Mix. Use it for making Bloody Marys or serve as a nippy nonalcoholic tomato cocktail.

20 large, vine-ripe tomatoes, cored and cut
    in thin wedges (no need to peel)
2 large yellow onions, peeled and minced
2 cloves garlic, peeled and crushed
3 celery stalks, diced
1 medium-size sweet green or red pepper,
    cored, seeded and minced
¼ cup finely grated fresh horseradish or

¼ cup prepared horseradish
1½ teaspoons crushed dried red chili peppers or 1½ teaspoons liquid hot red pepper seasoning
¼ cup sugar
⅓ cup lemon juice
1 tablespoon salt

Simmer all ingredients, covered, in a large heavy enamel or stainless steel kettle over moderate heat about 40 minutes, stirring now and then, until tomatoes have cooked down to juice. Put mixture through a food mill or press through a fine sieve, forcing out as much juice as possible.

Meanwhile, wash and rinse four 1-quart preserving jars together with their closures; keep jars and closures immersed in separate kettles of simmering water until you are ready to use them.

Return strained juice to kettle and bring to a boil. Pour into hot preserving jars, filling each to within 1" of the top. Wipe jar rims and seal. Process for 30 minutes in a steam pressure canner at 10 pounds pressure. Remove jars from canner, complete seals if necessary, and cool to room temperature. Check seals, label jars and store in a cool, dark, dry place.

To make Bloody Marys: One quart Bloody Mary Mix will make 6 to 8 Bloody Marys. Measure 1½ to 2 ounces vodka into each of six to eight (8-ounce) Old Fashioned glasses. Add 2 to 3 ice cubes to each, then pour in enough Bloody Mary Mix to fill glasses. Stir, taste, and, if you like, add a little additional liquid hot red pepper seasoning and/or prepared horseradish for extra bite.

HOME-GARDEN TOMATO PASTE
Makes About 6 Half-Pints

Until you taste homemade tomato paste, you will never know how superior it is to the commercial. Because most recipes call for such small quantities of tomato paste, it is advisable to put it up in small jars—the half-pint size is perfect because each holds exactly 1 cup. You can improvise a bit with the seasonings, if you like, adding garlic or not as you choose, also adding such compatible herbs as basil, bay leaves, oregano or marjoram. If you have fresh basil and oregano or marjoram growing in the garden, by all means use them in preparing the following recipe. If not, substitute dried herbs; they are perfectly acceptable, merely not so fragrant as the fresh. Tomato paste, like tomato juice, should only be made with plump, vine-ripened tomatoes without any moldy or soft spots. Otherwise, your efforts may go for naught because the tomato paste may spoil.

5 quarts peeled, cored and chopped vine-ripe, unblemished tomatoes (about 3 dozen large tomatoes)

1 cup minced sweet red pepper

1 clove garlic, peeled and crushed (optional)

1 tablespoon minced fresh basil or ½ teaspoon crushed dried basil (optional)

2 teaspoons minced fresh oregano or marjoram or ¼ teaspoon crushed dried oregano or marjoram (optional)

2 bay leaves (optional)

3 tablespoons lemon juice

2 tablespoons sugar

1 tablespoon salt

Place all ingredients in a large, very heavy enamel or stainless steel kettle and simmer uncovered over moderate heat 1 hour. Purée all in a food mill or press through a fine sieve, extracting as much juice and solids as possible. Return puréed mixture to kettle, set over low heat, and cook uncovered very slowly about 2 to 2½ hours or until reduced to a thick paste. You'll have to watch the kettle closely and stir occasionally to prevent the mixture from sticking to the kettle and scorching (particularly important toward the end of cooking).

Meanwhile, wash and rinse 6 half-pint preserving jars together with their closures. Keep closures and jars immersed in separate kettles of simmering water until you are ready to use them.

When tomato paste is the proper consistency (it should mound on a spoon), pour into hot preserving jars, filling each to within ¼" of the top. Wipe jar rims and seal jars. Process 45 minutes in a boiling water bath (212° F.). Remove jars from boiling water bath, complete seals if necessary, and cool thoroughly. Check seals, then label jars and store in a cool, dark, dry place.

NOTE: Once a jar of tomato paste has been opened, store, covered, in the refrigerator.

FROZEN PASTA SAUCE
Makes About 4 Quarts

Tomatoes are surprisingly prolific and if they are ripening in your garden faster than you can eat them, can them or preserve them, make up a batch of this pasta sauce which freezes beautifully. One quart of it is enough for 4 servings of spaghetti.

2 large Spanish onions, peeled and finely chopped

2 large cloves of garlic, peeled and minced

1/3 cup olive oil

2 dozen large, juicily ripe tomatoes, peeled, cored and coarsely chopped (reserve all juice)

1 medium-size sweet red pepper, cored, seeded and finely chopped

2 teaspoons crumbled leaf basil

1 teaspoon crumbled leaf oregano or marjoram

½ teaspoon crumbled leaf summer savory

2 bay leaves (do not crumble)

¼ teaspoon ground mace

2 tablespoons light brown sugar (or more if needed to mellow the tartness of the tomatoes)

1 tablespoon salt (about)

1 teaspoon freshly ground black pepper

3 cups dry red or white wine

Stir-fry the onions and garlic in the olive oil in a very large heavy, broad-bottomed kettle over moderate heat for 10 to 15 minutes until golden and touched with brown. Add the tomatoes (including their juice) and all remaining ingredients and cook, stirring, until mixture comes to a boil. Adjust heat so that mixture bubbles gently, cover and cook for 1 hour, stirring occasionally. Remove cover and continue cooking, stirring frequently, for about 1 hour longer or until mixture is smooth and thick and flavors are well blended. Taste and add more brown sugar and/or salt if needed. Remove the bay leaves.

Cool to room temperature, then pack into one-quart freezer containers, filling to within ½" of the tops. Snap on lids, label and quick-freeze.

SPICY CHILI SAUCE
Makes 5 to 6 Pints

This is an unpuréed and unsieved chili sauce so its texture is not as thick and compact as that of commercial chili sauces. Its flavor, however, will be uncommonly rich if you use vine-ripened tomatoes at their peak of maturity. Tomatoes ripened off the vine are both too flavorless and too pithy to make a worthwhile chili sauce.

4 quarts peeled, cored and coarsely chopped vine-ripened tomatoes (about 2 dozen medium-size tomatoes)	1 tablespoon white mustard seeds
	2 bay leaves, crumbled
	1 teaspoon whole cloves
1 pint finely chopped yellow onions	1 teaspoon ground ginger
1 pint finely diced sweet red peppers	1 teaspoon ground nutmeg
1 small hot red pepper, cored, seeded and minced or ½ teaspoon crushed dried red chili peppers	2 cinnamon sticks, each broken into several pieces
2 cloves garlic, peeled and minced fine	1½ cups firmly packed light brown sugar
2 tablespoons celery seeds	3 cups cider vinegar
	2 tablespoons salt

Mix tomatoes, onions, sweet and hot peppers in a very heavy, large enamel or stainless-steel kettle. Tie garlic, celery and mustard seeds, bay leaves, cloves, ginger, nutmeg and cinnamon loosely in several thicknesses of cheesecloth and drop into kettle. Set over high heat and bring to a boil, then lower heat and boil slowly, uncovered, until volume is reduced between one-half and two-thirds, about 2½ to 3 hours. Watch the kettle closely, especially toward the end of cooking, and stir often to prevent scorching.

Add the sugar, vinegar and salt, then boil, uncovered, as rapidly as you dare until again thick. This will take about 45 minutes and you'll have to stir the kettle frequently to keep the chili sauce from sticking to the kettle and burning.

Meanwhile, wash and rinse six 1-pint preserving jars and their closures; keep closures and jars immersed in separate kettles of simmering water until you are ready to use them.

When the chili sauce has cooked down to a consistency you like, pour boiling hot into hot jars, using a wide-mouth canning funnel to reduce the risk of spills and filling jars to within ¼″ of the tops. Wipe jar rims and seal.

Process jars for 10 minutes in a boiling water bath (212° F.). Remove jars from water bath, complete seals if necessary, then cool completely. Check seals, label jars and store on a cool, dark, dry shelf. Let the chili sauce "season" for about a month before serving.

TOMATO CATSUP
Makes About 3 Pints

Use only vine-ripened, unblemished tomatoes for making catsup, otherwise the color and flavor will not be as rich as they should be.

4 quarts peeled, cored and coarsely chopped ripe tomatoes (about 2 dozen medium-size tomatoes)
1 large yellow onion, peeled and chopped fine
1 medium-size sweet red pepper, cored, seeded and chopped fine
1 cinnamon stick, broken in several places

2 cloves garlic, peeled and minced fine
1½ teaspoons whole cloves
1½ cups cider vinegar
¾ cup sugar
2 teaspoons salt
2 teaspoons paprika
¼ teaspoon cayenne pepper

Place tomatoes, onion and sweet pepper in a large heavy enamel or stainless steel kettle and boil, uncovered, about ¾ hour until very soft. Press through a fine sieve, extracting as much liquid and pulp as possible. Return sieved mixture to rinsed-out kettle, set over low heat and simmer uncovered 2 to 2½ hours or until the volume is reduced by one-half to two-thirds. Watch kettle closely and stir as needed to prevent scorching.

Meanwhile, tie cinnamon, garlic and cloves in several thicknesses of cheese-cloth. Place vinegar in a small heavy saucepan, drop in spice bag and simmer slowly, uncovered, 30 to 40 minutes or until volume is reduced by half.

While tomatoes and vinegar cook, wash and rinse three 1-pint preserving jars and their closures; keep closures and jars immersed in separate kettles of simmering water until you are ready to use them.

When tomato mixture is very thick, add the spiced vinegar, the sugar, salt, paprika and cayenne pepper. Boil uncovered, stirring frequently, about 30 minutes until again thick (the consistency of catsup).

Using a wide-mouth canning funnel, pour boiling catsup into hot jars, filling to within ¼" of the tops. Wipe jar rims and seal jars. Process for 10 minutes in a boiling water bath (212° F.). Remove jars from water bath, complete seals if necessary, and cool thoroughly. Check seals, label jars and store on a cool, dark, dry shelf. Let catsup mellow for about a month before serving.

TOMATO MARMALADE
Makes About 5 Half-Pints

For a full-flavored marmalade, you must use tomatoes picked at their peak of maturity. If they are picked too green, the marmalade will be bitter.

*8 cups coarsely chopped, peeled and cored
    tomatoes (for this amount you will
    need about 5 pounds of tomatoes;
    make sure that you include all tomato
    juice that has oozed out during the
    chopping).*
1 navel orange
1 large lemon

⅓ cup cider vinegar
1 teaspoon ground cinnamon
½ teaspoon ground ginger
½ teaspoon ground cloves
¼ teaspoon ground allspice
¼ teaspoon ground cardamom
2½ cups sugar
½ cup firmly packed light brown sugar

Place the tomatoes in a very large, heavy, broad-bottomed kettle and set aside. Using a vegetable peeler, peel the thin, outer, colored rind from the orange and the lemon, then finely sliver the rind; add to kettle. Cut away and discard all the inner white rind from the orange and lemon, then section and seed each fruit. Chop the sections coarsely (and make sure that you catch and save all the juice). Add chopped fruit and the juice to the kettle. Stir in all remaining ingredients. Insert a candy thermometer.

Set the kettle over moderate heat and bring slowly to a boil, stirring constantly. Adjust heat so that mixture bubbles gently, then cook, uncovered, stirring frequently to prevent scorching, 2 to 2½ hours until glossy and thick—when the marmalade is the proper consistency, the candy thermometer will register between 218° and 220° F.

Toward the end of cooking, wash and sterilize 5 half-pint preserving jars and their closures; keep jars and closures immersed in separate kettles of simmering water until you are ready to use them.

Pour the boiling marmalade into hot jars, filling to within ¼" of the tops. Wipe jar rims and seal jars. Process for 10 minutes in a simmering water bath (185° F.). Remove jars from water bath, complete seals if necessary and cool thoroughly. Check seals, label jars and store on a cool, dark, dry shelf.

CRISPY-SWEET GREEN TOMATO PICKLES
Makes 6 to 8 Pints

Long soaking in lime water (made with slaked lime or calcium hydroxide, which is available at most drugstores) is what makes these pickles extra crisp. In the South, they rival watermelon pickles as the favorite. Serve them with roast meat or fowl or better still, with baked ham.

1 gallon firm, small green tomatoes, sliced ¼" thick (do not peel)	2 quarts white vinegar
	½ teaspoon whole cloves
2 gallons cool water mixed with 1½ cups slaked lime (calcium hydroxide)	½ teaspoon blade mace
	½ teaspoon whole allspice
5 pounds sugar	1 cinnamon stick, broken into small pieces

Soak the tomatoes in the mixture of cool water and slaked lime in a very large enamel or stainless steel kettle for 24 hours. Drain well, then soak for 4 hours in clear water, changing the water every hour. Drain the tomatoes well again. Place in a large heavy enamel or stainless-steel kettle with all remaining ingredients, bring to a slow boil, then remove from heat, cover and let stand 24 hours.

Next day, set kettle over moderately low heat and bring, uncovered, to a slow boil. Let bubble gently for 1 hour, stirring now and then.

Meanwhile, wash and rinse eight 1-pint preserving jars and their closures; keep jars and closures immersed in separate kettles of simmering water until you are ready to use them.

Ladle tomato slices and syrup (including some whole spices) into hot jars, filling to within ¼" of the tops. Wipe jar rims and seal jars. Process for 20 minutes in a boiling water bath (212° F.). Remove jars from water bath, complete seals if necessary, and cool to room temperature. Check seals, then label jars and store in a cool, dark, dry place.

PICCALILLI
Makes 3 to 4 Pints

If this green tomato relish is to have good color and crunch, the tomatoes must be truly green and hard. The cucumbers should be on the firm side, too, otherwise the piccalilli will reduce to mush during processing.

2 quarts coarsely chopped, cored but un-peeled hard green tomatoes (you will need about 1½ dozen smallish	tomatoes)
	1½ cups coarsely chopped sweet green peppers

1 cup coarsely chopped yellow onion
1½ cups coarsely chopped and seeded but
    unpeeled firm cucumber
½ cup pickling salt
1 cup sugar

3 cups white vinegar
1 tablespoon mustard seeds
2 tablespoons mixed pickling spices, tied in
    cheesecloth

Place tomatoes, sweet peppers, onion and cucumber in a large bowl, sprinkle with pickling salt and toss to mix. Cover and let stand overnight. Next day drain, then rinse vegetables in a large, fine sieve, pressing out as much liquid as possible. Place sugar, vinegar, mustard seeds and spice bag in a large heavy kettle and set uncovered over moderate heat. Bring to a boil, stirring until sugar dissolves, then boil uncovered for about 10 minutes.

Meanwhile, wash and rinse four 1-pint preserving jars and their closures; keep jars and closures immersed in separate kettles of simmering water until needed.

Stir drained vegetables into kettle and bring just to boiling. Ladle hot relish into hot jars, filling to within ⅛" of the tops. Run a thin-blade spatula or knife around inside edges of jars to free air bubbles; wipe jar rims and seal jars. Process for 10 minutes in a boiling water bath (212° F.). Remove jars from water bath, complete seals if necessary and cool completely. Check seals, label jars and store on a cool, dark, dry shelf.

TURNIPS AND RUTABAGAS

These root vegetables are too strong-flavored to can and too watery to freeze. They don't pickle and they won't dry. They will, however, winter over in a metal drum buried out-of-doors, provided it is sufficiently insulated to protect them from alternate freezing and thawing. Turnips and rutabagas are both too odoriferous to keep in a basement root cellar; their strong smell will permeate the house.

TO STORE IN A METAL DRUM BURIED OUTDOORS: Leave turnips and rutabagas in the ground until after the first few fall frosts, then dig them while the soil is still dry. Don't leave them in the field once they have been dug, but get them into cold storage as fast as possible so that they do not wind-dry. Cut the green tops off about ½" above the crowns, but do not remove the root ends.

Cushion the bottom of the metal drum well first with a moist (not wet) layer of sand or soil, then with a thick bed of dry, clean straw, hay or leaves. Layer turnips and/or rutabagas into the drum, cushioning them with additional straw or leaves and filling in spaces around them with more of the same. Top with a thick insulating layer of straw or leaves, then weight down with moist soil or sand. Roll the drum's door in place and pad it thickly with straw or leaves. If conditions are ideal inside the drum (a temperature fairly constant at 32° F. and a humidity between 90% and 95%), turnips and rutabagas will survive the winter well. It is difficult, of course, to control conditions precisely in a drum buried outside; however, if you make certain that both it and the vegetables inside it are thickly padded with straw, hay or leaves, you'll find that turnips and rutabagas will weather the cold in good shape.

KEEPING TIME: 2 to 4 months.

WINTER SQUASH AND PUMPKIN

The family of winter squash includes all the hard-skinned, golden-fleshed varieties—acorn, butternut, Hubbard, turban and so on. Pumpkins are, of course, fruits (and so, for that matter, are the squash), but because they are low-acid foods, they are prepared and processed like vegetables.

TO CAN: Choose, first of all, hard-skinned pumpkins or squash. If you have difficulty nicking the skins with your thumbnail, the pumpkins or squash are sufficiently dry-fleshed to can well. Soft or moist ones will absorb too much moisture during cooking and after puréeing, will be disagreeably soupy. Canned chunks of pumpkin or squash tend to be watery, too, and for that reason, we suggest canning them only as purées. These are uncommonly versatile—particularly if they have not had sugar, salt or spices added—and are ready to be stirred into your favorite pie, pudding, bread and cake recipes. Pumpkin and squash purées must both be packed hot, and they must also be pressure processed for long periods of time. *Amount of fresh pumpkin or winter squash (untrimmed) needed for 1 quart of canned purée:* 3 to 3½ pounds.

Hot Pack:

1. Quarter the pumpkin or squash, scoop out seeds and stringy portions, peel, then cut in 1″ to 2″ chunks. Place chunks on a large steamer rack, set in a large kettle over simmering water, cover and steam just until fork-tender—about 15 minutes.

2. Purée by pressing through a food mill or by buzzing, a few chunks at a time, in an electric blender at high speed. Place purée in a large kettle, add only enough water to keep it from sticking and bring slowly to a simmer.

3. Pack purée tightly into hot 1-pint or 1-quart preserving jars, filling to within ½″ of the tops. Press down to remove any trapped air bubbles.

4. Wipe jar rims, seal jars, then PRESSURE PROCESS at 10 pounds pressure, allowing 65 minutes for pints and 1 hour and 20 minutes for quarts.

5. Remove jars from pressure canner, complete seals, if necessary and cool completely. Check seals, label jars and store on a cool, dark, dry shelf. KEEPING TIME: About one year.

TO FREEZE: Resist the temptation to spice or sweeten the purée before you freeze it because the flavors may overdevelop to the point of bitterness during their stay in the freezer. Unseasoned purée, moreover, is more useful because it can be thawed, then seasoned as individual pudding, pie, bread or cake recipes direct. *Amount of fresh pumpkin or winter squash (untrimmed) needed to fill a 1-pint freezer container:* 1½ to 2 pounds.

1. Quarter the pumpkin or squash, remove seeds and stringy parts, then peel and cut in 1" to 2" chunks. Place chunks on a large steamer rack, set in a large kettle over simmering water, cover and steam until you can pierce the chunks easily with a sharp-pronged fork—about 15 minutes.

2. Purée the pumpkin or squash by pressing through a food mill or by buzzing, a few chunks at a time, in an electric blender at high speed.

3. Pack the purée firmly into 1-pint freezer containers, filling to within ½" of the tops. Cool to room temperature, snap on lids, label containers and quick-freeze.

KEEPING TIME: About one year at 0° F.

TO PICKLE OR PRESERVE: In the old days, women did make pumpkin preserves. But we frankly think the canned or frozen purée superior. Certainly it is easier to prepare to say nothing of being more useful.

TO DRY: Impossible.

TO WINTER OVER IN COLD STORAGE: Like sweet potatoes, pumpkins and winter squash cannot withstand the high humidity and low temperatures of basement root cellars or metal drums buried out-of-doors. But they will, with the exception of acorn squash, last the winter in warmer, drier areas. Acorn squash is too perishable to store for more than a month or so because it soon discolors, dries and becomes stringy.

Pumpkins and winter squash are both severely damaged by hard freezes, so you must gather them *before* (all due respect to James Whitcomb Riley) "the frost is on the punkin." Choose for cold storage only those pumpkins and squash that are mature and blemish-free. And when you cut them from the vine, leave about 2" of stem on. Do not wash or wipe clean.

Acorn squash should go directly into cold storage without any transitional curing or conditioning, which will merely hasten their decomposition. Line them up in rows in slatted crates and store uncovered in a dry area where you can maintain the humidity at about 70% and the temperature between 45 ° and 50 ° F.

KEEPING TIME: 6 weeks maximum.

Pumpkins and other varieties of winter squash require about 10 days of curing in a warm spot (80° to 85° F.) before they go into cold storage so that their rinds will harden and any nicks or cuts will heal.

After the 10-day curing period, simply line the pumpkins or squash up on wooden shelves in a dry (70% humidity), cool (55° F.) area. Handle them gently because they bruise easily.

KEEPING TIME: About 6 months.

Home-grown Fruits:
How to conserve them

Apples ... peaches ... pears ... berries ... cherries ... grapes. These are the fruits most commonly grown at home and the ones we will concentrate upon in the pages that follow. We will also include, for those lucky enough to own bearing fig bushes, avocado or citrus trees, directions for conserving these subtropical fruits.

If there are mature fruit trees or berry bushes in your garden, you should, before setting out to can or freeze or store the harvest, determine whether or not your particular varieties are suited to canning or freezing or storing. All of them aren't. (Your local agricultural or home economics extension agent can advise you; they are headquartered in your county seat and can be reached through the county government offices.) If, on the other hand, you have not yet planted trees or bushes, you should choose species of fruits that can be conserved well by one means or another. Remember, however, that the trees or bushes will not bear for several years.

Some fruits can commendably and some, no matter what variety, do not. Many freeze splendidly, but not, alas, all. A few can be held several months in cold storage, and a few can be dried in the oven. Fortunately, almost any fruit, whether or not it can be conserved by any other means, will make superlative preserves, jams, marmalades or jellies, both solo and in combination with other fruits.

Our purpose, then, will be to discuss the fruits individually and alphabetically, recommending what we consider to be the most favorable ways of conserving each. We will not mince words. Or waste space in describing a method we think ill-suited to any fruit. Why, for example, spend hours canning whole grapes when canned grape juice is preferable? To say nothing of grape jam or jelly? Our intent, at all times, is to be selective. To focus upon those methods that will preserve as much of the garden-freshness of your home-grown fruits as possible.

NOTE: All processing times and pounds of pressure given in the recipes and canning instructions that follow are for altitudes at or near sea level. If you live at an elevation of 1,000 feet or more, see the Appendix for tables of adjustments that must be made in water bath and steam pressure processing.

Altitude must also be considered when you are making jams, jellies, preserves, marmalades and butters. To make certain they are the proper consistency, use a candy thermometer and cook them until they are 9° F. above the boiling point of water in your particular area.

APPLES

TO CAN: The varieties of apples that will can best as slices or quarters are those that will not be reduced to mush during processing: Rome Beauty, for example, Stayman, Winesap or York Imperial. For applesauce, of course (see recipe), you will want apples that do soften and cook down. Rhode Island Greening and Newton Pippin are both good choices. Apples and applesauce should both be packed *hot*, and they should also be packed with an anti-browning agent to keep them from turning brown in the preserving jar. Be sure that you have on hand both powdered or crystalline ascorbic acid and citric acid before you begin the job of canning. *Amount of fresh apples needed to fill a 1-quart preserving jar:* 2½ to 3 pounds if canned as slices or quarters, 3 to 3½ pounds if canned as applesauce.

Hot Pack:

1.   Choose firm-ripe, plump apples full of flavor and pick them shortly before you will can them.

2.   Prepare either a *light* or *medium sugar syrup,* depending upon how sweet you want the canned apples. (See index for the table of Sugar Syrups for Canning Fruit for proportions.) As for quantity, you will need 1 to 1½ cups of syrup for packing each 1-quart jar.

3.   Wash the apples in cool water, then peel, core and quarter or slice. To prevent the apples from darkening before you get them into the preserving jars, let the slices or quarters drop, as you cut them, into 1 gallon of cold water mixed with 1 teaspoon ascorbic acid and 1 tablespoon citric acid. You may use instead 2 tablespoons of salt and 2 tablespoons of cider vinegar although the combination of ascorbic and citric acids is more effective.

4. In a large heavy enamel or stainless steel kettle, bring the necessary amount of sugar syrup to a boil. Drain the apples (but do not rinse), dump into the boiling syrup and boil uncovered for 5 minutes.

5. Using a slotted spoon and a wide-mouth canning funnel to make the jar-filling both faster and neater, ladle apples into hot 1-pint or 1-quart preserving jars, filling to within ½" of the tops. Pour enough boiling syrup into jars to cover apples, at the same time allowing ½" head space. To each 1-pint jar, add ⅛ teaspoon powdered or crystalline ascorbic acid and to each 1-quart jar, add ¼ teaspoon. Run a small spatula around inside edge of each jar to free air bubbles.

6. Wipe jar rims and seal jars. Process pints and quarts for 20 minutes in a boiling water bath (212° F.).

7. Remove jars from water bath, complete seals if necessary, then cool thoroughly. Check seals, label jars and store on a cool, dark, dry shelf. KEEPING TIME: About one year.

TO FREEZE: There are two ways of packing apples for the freezer—in syrup or in dry sugar, and which method you choose depends upon how you intend to use the frozen apples. If the apples are to be thawed and served as is or in a fruit cocktail, pack in syrup. If, on the other hand, they are to be baked into pies or cobblers, pack them in dry sugar. Varieties of apples that freeze best: Rome Beauty, Stayman, York Imperial, Winesap and Limbertwig. *Amount of fresh apples needed to fill a 1-pint freezer container:* About 1½ pounds.

Syrup Pack:

1. Prepare and chill enough *medium (40%) sugar syrup* to pack the quantity of apples you will be freezing. For each 1 pint of packed fruit you will need ½ to ⅔ cup of syrup; you will find proportions and directions for the *medium syrup* elsewhere in this book; see index for page number. Measure the syrup and to each 1 quart of it, add ½ teaspoon powdered or crystalline ascorbic acid to keep the apples from browning in the freezer.

2. For best results, select firm, fully ripe apples without bruises or blemishes. Wash in cool water, peel, then core and slice, letting the apple slices drop into 1 gallon of cold water mixed with 1 teaspoon ascorbic acid and 1 tablespoon citric acid.

3. To pack the apples, pour ½ cup of the syrup into a 1-pint freezer container, then using a slotted spoon, lift the apple slices from the acidulated water and pack into the container, filling to within ½" of the top. Press the apple slices down, then pour in enough additional syrup to cover them, but leave ½" head space. Snap on the lids, label containers and quick-freeze.

Sugar Pack:

1.   Choose firm-ripe apples showing no signs of mealyness. Wash in cool water, then peel, core and slice, letting slices fall into 1 gallon of cold water mixed with 1 teaspoon ascorbic acid and 1 tablespoon citric acid. Drain apples but do not rinse.

2.   To retard browning further, spread apple slices out in a single layer on a steamer rack, cover and steam 1½ minutes *over* (not *in*) boiling water. Quick-chill in ice water and drain.

3.   Measure out apple slices, 1 quart at a time, and sprinkle evenly with ½ cup sugar that has been well mixed with ⅛ teaspoon powdered ascorbic acid. Stir to mix.

4.   Pack into 1-quart freezer containers, pressing fruit down gently but firmly and leaving 1" of head space so that the apples will have room to expand as they freeze. Snap on lids, label and quick-freeze.

KEEPING TIME: About one year at 0° F. although the apples will be better if eaten within 6 months.

TO DRY: Dried apples are what the Pennsylvania Dutch call *schnitz*. They have a flavor and texture altogether different from fresh, canned or frozen apples and are delicious made into pie and *Schnitz und Kneppe* (recipes follow). You can dry the apples in the oven, but because they are not so moisture-free as commercially dried apples, we suggest for safekeeping that you bundle them into freezer bags and store in the freezer. Apple varieties particularly suited to drying: McIntosh, Newtown Pippin, Rome Beauty, Red Delicious and Rhode Island Greening. *Amount of fresh apples needed to equal 1 cup of dried apple slices:* About 1 pound.

1.   Wash apples well in cool water and dry. Pare, core and slice about ⅛" thick. Spread the slices out one layer deep on a large baking sheet or metal tray lined with several thicknesses of paper toweling or with a clean white dish towel. Set uncovered in a very slow oven (175° F.) and let dry until slices are leathery and pale tan. This will take 16 to 20 hours.

2.   Cool the slices, then bundle into 1-pint freezer bags, press out all air pockets, twist tops into tight goosenecks and secure with twist bands. Store in the freezer.

KEEPING TIME: About one year.

TO PICKLE AND PRESERVE: Apples make splendid butters, chutneys and jellies (see recipes for each).

TO STORE IN A ROOT CELLAR: The apples that will keep best in the home root cellar are such late-maturing varieties as Yellow Newtown, Winesap, Arkansas

(Mammoth Black Twig) and York Imperial. Earlier varieties (Grimes Golden, Jonathan, Golden or Red Delicious and Stayman), unfortunately, will quickly overripen. If apples are to weather cold storage well, conditions must be ideal: temperatures of around 31° to 32° F. and a humidity between 80% and 90%. You cannot count on maintaining these conditions in a metal drum buried outdoors, so store the apples in the fruit section of the basement root cellar—well away from potatoes because apples quickly absorb the potatoes' musty-earthy aroma.

Pick the apples in cold weather when they are ripe but still good and hard (red apples should be uniformly bright red). And select for storage only those apples that are in perfect condition—no bruises, blemishes, nicks or insect damage. For best results, wrap each apple individually in tissue, then layer into perforated cardboard cartons lined with perforated polyethylene sheets (each sheet should have about 10 to 12 evenly spaced perforations measuring about ¼″ in diameter). Cover the apples loosely with another perforated polyethylene sheet. Check the apples from time to time to see that they are storing well, not decaying or shriveling. And discard any apples that are faring poorly.

KEEPING TIME: 4 to 6 months.

AUTUMN APPLESAUCE
Makes About 4 Pints

A basic home-canned applesauce made with crisp, tart "cooking apples" plus two variations: Honeyed Applesauce and Spicy Applesauce.

4 pounds Greenings, Jonathan or McIntosh apples	¼ cup lemon juice
1¾ cups water	1⅓ cups sugar
	¼ teaspoon salt

Peel, core and slice the apples. Bring water, lemon juice, sugar and salt to a boil in a large heavy enamel or stainless steel kettle, stirring until sugar dissolves. Add apples, cover and cook about 10 minutes until apples are almost tender. Turn heat off and let apples stand, covered, for 10 minutes to plump and finish cooking. Sieve the applesauce or not, as you choose.

Wash and rinse four 1-pint preserving jars and their closures. Pack the hot applesauce into the hot jars, filling to within ½″ of the tops. Run a thin-blade spatula or table knife around inside edges of jars to remove air bubbles. Wipe jar rims and seal jars. Process for 10 minutes in a boiling water bath (212° F.). Remove jars from water bath, complete seals if necessary and cool completely. Check seals, label jars and store on a cool, dark, dry shelf.

VARIATIONS:

Honeyed Applesauce. Prepare as directed for Autumn Applesauce, but use ⅓ cup golden honey and 1 cup sugar instead of 1⅓ cups sugar. Pack and process as above.

Spicy Applesauce. Prepare as directed for Autumn Applesauce, but add ¼ teaspoon each ground cinnamon, cloves and nutmeg to kettle along with apples. Pack and process as above.

SCHNITZ UND KNEPPE
Makes 6 Servings

Schnitz und Kneppe (Dried Apples and Dumplings), like so many Pennsylvania Dutch recipes, is both frugal and filling. Depending upon the meatiness of the ham hock used to prepare it, it can be served either as a main dish or as an accompaniment to the main dish (served in place of potatoes). You can, if you like, substitute leftover cubed ham for the hock (you should have 2 to 2½ cups of it), or if you prefer, use about ⅓ pound very lean smoky bacon, cut in small cubes (about ⅜").

1 large, meaty, smoked ham hock
8 cups chicken stock or broth
2 cups dried apples
4 teaspoons light brown sugar
Salt to taste

Kneppe (Dumplings):
2 cups sifted all-purpose flour
2½ teaspoons baking powder
¾ teaspoon salt
1 cup milk (at room temperature)
2 large eggs, lightly beaten (at room temperature)
5 tablespoons melted unsalted butter

Cut the rind from the ham hock and discard; also trim away excess fat and discard. Cut the ham into bite-size chunks and place in a large, broad-bottomed kettle; drop in the ham bone, add chicken stock, dried apples and brown sugar. Cover, set over moderately low heat and simmer 35 to 40 minutes until the apples are tender. Taste for salt and add as needed.

For the Kneppe, sift the flour with the baking powder and salt into a large mixing bowl. Combine the milk, eggs and butter. Make a well in the center of the dry ingredients, pour the combined liquid ingredients in all at once and stir briskly just enough to mix—don't overbeat or the dumplings will be tough.

Remove ham bone from kettle, bring liquid to a rolling boil, then drop in the Kneppe from mounded tablespoons, spacing them as evenly as possible over the surface of the liquid. Cover tight and boil 12 minutes without sneaking a look into the kettle. Spoon the Kneppe into large soup bowls, then smother with apples, ham and broth.

SPICY SCHNITZ PIE
Makes 8 Servings

Dried apples make a delicious pie. The filling has an almost applesauce consistency and a caramel-like flavor.

4 cups dried apple slices
3¹2 cups cold water
Finely grated rind of 1 lemon
1 tablespoon lemon juice
¾ cup firmly packed light brown sugar
4 teaspoons cornstarch
½ teaspoon ground cinnamon

¼ teaspoon ground cloves
⅛ teaspoon ground nutmeg or mace
¼ teaspoon salt
2 tablespoons butter
Pastry for a 9-inch, double-crust pie (use your favorite recipe)

Cook the apples in the water in a covered heavy saucepan over moderate heat about 20 minutes until firm-tender, not mushy. Remove from heat, mix in lemon rind and juice and cool slightly. Mix the brown sugar with the cornstarch, spices and salt, rubbing between your fingers to press out all lumps. Quickly stir the sugar mixture into the apples, return to a moderate heat and cook and stir until thickened and clear—3 to 4 minutes. Remove from heat, mix in butter and cool to room temperature.

Meanwhile, roll out half of the pastry and fit into a 9-inch pie pan. Fill with cooled apples; roll top crust and fit in place; trim pastry overhang so that it is about 1″ larger all around than the pie pan. Roll the overhang (of both crusts) up onto pie pan rim and crimp, making a high fluted edge. Cut decorative steam vents in the top crust.

Bake in a moderately hot oven (375° F.) for 30 to 40 minutes or until the pastry is pale tan and the apple filling bubbly. Remove pie from oven, set on a wire rack and cool to room temperature before cutting. Excellent as is, but better still topped with vanilla ice cream or softly whipped heavy cream.

GINGERED APPLE CHUTNEY
Makes 8 Pints

A dark, sweet-sour chutney with plenty of nip. Be prepared to spend the better part of the day preparing this recipe–the chutney must cook down, down, down until very glossy and thick (about 5 hours). Your efforts will be rewarded, however, because this is a good all-purpose condiment, delicious with roast fowl, game birds, venison, lamb, pork and ham as well as with curries.

6 medium-size yellow onions, peeled and
    quartered
2 cloves garlic, peeled
1 pound golden seedless raisins
8 pounds tart, firm apples, peeled, cored
    and cut in 1" chunks
1 pound dried currants
1 pound crystallized ginger, coarsely
    chopped

Grated rind of 1 orange
Grated rind of 1 lemon
2 quarts cider vinegar
2 pounds light brown sugar
2 pounds granulated sugar
1 tablespoon powdered mustard
1 tablespoon salt
¼ teaspoon cayenne pepper

Put onions, garlic and raisins through a food chopper fitted with a coarse blade. Combine with all remaining ingredients in a large, very heavy enamel or stainless steel kettle (preferably one that measures at least 12" across the top). Set uncovered over moderately high heat and bring to a rolling boil. Reduce heat slightly so that mixture boils gently, then cook uncovered 4½ to 5 hours until very thick, glossy and dark. Watch the kettle closely toward the end and stir frequently lest the mixture stick and burn.

About ½ hour before chutney is done, wash and rinse eight 1-pint preserving jars and their closures. Immerse jars in a kettle of simmering water until needed; set closures in a pan of simmering water, turn heat off and let stand in the hot water until needed.

Ladle hot chutney into hot jars, filling to within ¼" of the tops. Wipe jar rims and seal. Process for 10 minutes in a boiling water bath (212° F.). Remove jars from water bath, complete seals if necessary and cool to room temperature; check seals, then label and store on a cool, dark, dry shelf.

SHENANDOAH APPLE BUTTER
Makes About 4 Pints

For apple butter, you need apples that will cook down to mush–Greenings, for example, or McIntosh or Jonathan. You will also need a very heavy, large, broad-bottomed kettle so that you can cook the apples slowly down to butter without danger of their sticking and scorching.

8 pounds tart cooking apples, washed, cored and sliced thin but not peeled	*sweetness of the apples)*
	1 teaspoon ground cinnamon
1 quart apple cider	*½ teaspoon ground ginger*
2 cups water	*½ teaspoon ground cloves*
Sugar (you will need ½ to ¾ cup for each 1 cup of apple pulp, depending upon	*¼ teaspoon ground nutmeg*
	¼ teaspoon ground allspice

Place apples, apple cider and water in a very large (about 3- to 4-gallon) heavy kettle and boil gently, uncovered, 25 to 30 minutes until apples are very soft. Press apples and liquid through a large fine sieve into a large mixing bowl, forcing out as much pulp as possible with a wooden spatula or spoon. Measure the apple pulp carefully and make a note of the total amount. Return apple pulp to rinsed-out kettle, and then for every 1 cup of apple pulp, add ½ to ¾ cup sugar, depending on how tart or sweet the apples are. Mix in all spices.

Set kettle over low heat and cook slowly, uncovered, 1½ to 2 hours, stirring often, until very thick and smooth (a little of the hot mixture, spooned onto a cold saucer, should as it cools firm up without any liquid oozing out). The butter will be the right consistency when it has reached 218° to 220° F. (test with a candy thermometer, but warm it first by immersing in water and bringing to a boil).

Toward the end of cooking, wash and sterilize four 1-pint preserving jars and their closures; keep jars and closures immersed in separate kettles of simmering water until you are ready to use them.

When the apple butter is of the right consistency, ladle boiling hot into hot jars, filling to within ¼" of the tops. Wipe jar rims and seal jars. Process in a simmering water bath (185° F.) for 10 minutes. Remove jars from water bath, complete seals if necessary, and cool completely. Check seals, label jars and store on a cool, dark, dry shelf.

VARIATION: *Orange Apple Butter.* Prepare as directed for Shendandoah Apple Butter but use 1 cup strained fresh orange juice and 1 cup water instead of the 2 cups of water called for. Also add 1 teaspoon finely grated orange rind along with the spices.

APPLE AND TOMATO BUTTER
Makes 4 to 5 Half-Pints

New York's Finger Lakes region is apple country, and the unusual recipe that follows is an old Upstate farm favorite. It is delicious served with roast pork or chicken or baked ham.

10 cups (2½ quarts) coarsely chopped unpeeled and unseeded *apples (use Greenings for best results)*	Coarsely grated rind of 2 oranges
	3 cups sugar
5 cups coarsely chopped peeled and cored plump-ripe tomatoes	2 cinnamon sticks
	2 tablespoons cider vinegar
	⅔ cup orange juice

Place apples, tomatoes and orange rind in a large, heavy, broad-bottomed, enamel or stainless steel kettle, set over moderate heat and bring to a boil. Lower heat slightly, cover and cook 25 to 30 minutes until apples and tomatoes are very soft. Press mixture through a large, fine sieve, extracting as much juice and pulp as possible. Return sieved mixture to kettle, add sugar, cinnamon and vinegar; insert a candy thermometer. Bring slowly to a boil, stirring until sugar dissolves, then boil as rapidly as you dare, uncovered, until glossy and thick—about 20 to 25 minutes. Keep a close eye on the kettle and stir as needed to prevent butter from sticking.

Meanwhile, wash and sterilize 5 half-pint preserving jars and their closures; keep jars and closures immersed in separate kettles of simmering water until you are ready to use them.

When butter is good and thick, remove cinnamon sticks and stir in orange juice; continue boiling uncovered until again thick—the candy thermometer should register about 218° to 220° F. Ladle boiling hot into hot jars, filling to within ¼" of the tops. Wipe jar rims and seal jars. Process in a simmering water bath (185° F.) for 10 minutes. Remove jars from water bath, complete seals if necessary, and cool thoroughly. Check seals, label jars and store on a cool, dark, dry shelf.

NATURAL GREENING JELLY
Makes Enough to Fill 4 (8-ounce) Jelly Glasses

Rhode Island Greenings make a particularly good apple jelly because they contain pectin enough for the juice to jell naturally without added commercial pectin. They have refreshingly tart flavor and they give the jelly a delicate yellow-green hue. You can use the extracted apple juice for a variety of herbal jellies, if you like—rosemary, lemon verbena, rose geranium, sage, mint, tarragon or thyme. See the jelly variations that follow.

4 pounds firm-ripe (not overripe) Rhode Island Greenings, stemmed and washed but not peeled or cored
1 quart water
½ cup lemon juice
Sugar (you will need ¾ cup of sugar for each 1 cup of extracted apple juice)

Slice the apples directly into a large enamel or stainless steel kettle (include skins, seeds and cores because these all contain pectin). Add the water and lemon juice, cover and boil 15 to 20 minutes until the apples are very mushy. Line 2 very large colanders with 4 thicknesses of clean, damp cheesecloth and set each over a very large heatproof bowl.

Or, if you have 2 jelly bags, dampen them in cold water, wring dry, suspend from the jelly bag stands and set each over a very large heatproof bowl. Pour half of the hot apple mixture into each colander or jelly bag and let drip through *undisturbed.* Do not squeeze or massage the bags to force the juice through because the jelly will then be cloudy. It must drip through of its own accord, which will take an hour, perhaps two.

Meanwhile, wash and sterilize 4 (8-ounce) jelly glasses and keep submerged in simmering water until you are ready to fill them. Also melt paraffin for sealing the jelly glasses.

When all of the apple juice has dripped through, combine the two lots, measure precisely and make a note of the total amount. Place the apple juice in a very large, heavy, broad-bottomed enamel or stainless steel kettle and then add, for each 1 cup of juice, ¾ cup of sugar; stir to mix. Insert candy thermometer.

Set the uncovered kettle over moderate heat and bring slowly to the boil without stirring; boil rapidly without stirring 20 to 25 minutes or until thermometer registers 218° F. Take up a small amount of the hot mixture on a metal spoon, cool and tilt; if the drops slide together in a single jelly-like mass, the jelly is done. If not, continue cooking to 220° F. and test again for sheeting. If mixture still does not sheet, cook to 222° F.

As soon as mixture sheets, remove from the heat and skim off froth. Pour boiling hot jelly into hot jelly glasses, filling to within ¼" of the tops. Seal with ⅛" of melted paraffin, pricking any bubbles in the paraffin with a sterilized needle. Cool the jelly completely, then cover the glasses with their metal caps, label and store on a cool, dark, dry shelf.

VARIATIONS:

Spicy Apple Jelly. Prepare as directed, but when you begin to cook the apples, add to the kettle 1 cinnamon stick, broken into several pieces, 1 teaspoon whole cloves and 2 blades of mace tied loosely in several thicknesses of cheesecloth. Remove spice bag before pouring apples into colanders or jelly bags.

Rose Geranium Jelly. Pick 10 to 12 tender young rose geranium leaves, crush slightly with your hands, then tie loosely in several thicknesses of cheesecloth. Drop into the kettle and cook along with the apples. Remove before pouring apples into colanders or jelly bags. Otherwise, proceed as directed for Natural Greening Jelly.

Lemon Verbena Jelly. Tie ⅔ cup slightly bruised, young, tender lemon verbena leaves loosely in a double thickness of cheesecloth, drop into kettle and cook along with the apples. Remove before pouring apples into colanders or jelly bags. Otherwise, proceed as directed for Natural Greening Jelly.

Apple-Mint Jelly. Tie 1 cup coarsely chopped young, tender mint leaves loosely in a double thickness of cheesecloth, drop into kettle and cook along with the apples. Remove before pouring apples into colanders or jelly bags. Otherwise, proceed as directed for Natural Greening Jelly. NOTE: The mint jelly will have a yellow-tan color; commercial jellies are bright green because artificial coloring has been added.

Apple-Tarragon Jelly. Tie 1 cup slightly bruised, fragrant young tarragon leaves in a double thickness of cheesecloth, drop into kettle and cook along with the apples. Remove before pouring apples into colanders or jelly bags. Otherwise, proceed as directed for Natural Greening Jelly.

Rosemary, Sage or Thyme Jelly. Tie ½ cup slightly bruised, young and tender rosemary, sage or thyme leaves loosely in a double thickness of cheesecloth, drop into the kettle and cook along with the apples. Remove the bag of herbs before you pour the apples into colanders or jelly bags. Otherwise, proceed as directed for Natural Greening Jelly.

APRICOTS

TO CAN: Apricots, like apples and peaches, will darken as soon as they are exposed to the air, so they must be dipped in acidulated water (water mixed with ascorbic and citric acids) the minute they are peeled and cut open. And, if they are to retain their sunny color after canning, a minute quantity of ascorbic acid must be added to each preserving jar. *Amount of fresh apricots needed to fill a 1-quart preserving jar:* 2 to 2½ pounds.

Cold (Raw) Pack:

1. For best results, choose tree-ripened but still firm apricots and pick them just before you are ready to can them.

2. Prepare either a *light* or a *medium sugar syrup,* using the proportions given in the table of Sugar Syrups for Canning Fruit; see index for page number.

You will need 1 to 1½ cups of syrup for each 1-quart jar of fruit, so make up enough at the start to pack all the apricots you have picked.

3. Wash apricots in cool water, blanch 30 seconds in boiling water, then quick-chill in cold water. Slip off the skins, halve and pit the apricots, letting the halves fall into 1 gallon of cold water mixed with 1 teaspoon ascorbic acid and 1 tablespoon citric acid.

4. With a slotted spoon, lift the apricot halves from the acidulated water and pack snugly, placing the halves hollow sides down and slightly overlapping, in hot 1-pint or 1-quart preserving jars. Pack each jar to within ½″ of the top. Pour enough boiling syrup into each jar to cover the apricots, at the same time leaving ½″ head space. To each 1-pint jar add ⅛ teaspoon powdered or crystalline ascorbic acid, and to each 1-quart jar add ¼ teaspoon. Run a small spatula around inside edge of each jar to free trapped air bubbles.

5. Wipe jar rims and seal jars. Process pints for 25 minutes and quarts for 30 minutes in a boiling water bath (212° F.).

6. Remove jars from water bath, complete seals if necessary, and cool completely. Check seals, label jars and store on a cool, dark, dry shelf.

Hot Pack:

1., 2., & 3. The same as for COLD PACK (above).

4. In a large heavy enamel or stainless steel kettle, bring the sugar syrup to a boil. Working with about a half-dozen apricots at a time, drain, then cook in boiling syrup just long enough to heat through—2 to 3 minutes. Pack the apricot halves firmly, hollows down and slightly overlapping, in hot 1-pint or 1-quart preserving jars, leaving ½″ head space. Pour enough boiling syrup into jars to cover fruit, but leave ½″ of room at the top. To each 1-pint jar add ⅛ teaspoon ascorbic acid and to each 1-quart jar add ¼ teaspoon. Run a thin-blade, small spatula around inside edges of jars to release air bubbles.

5. Wipe jar rims and seal jars. Process in a boiling water bath (212° F.), allowing 20 minutes for pints and 25 minutes for quarts.

6. The same as for COLD PACK (above).

KEEPING TIME: About one year.

TO FREEZE: Apricots may be frozen as halves or slices, and they may also be packed either in syrup (recommended when the apricots are to be served uncooked) or in dry sugar (when they are to be baked into puddings or pies). *Amount of fresh apricots needed to fill a 1-pint freezer container:* About ¾ to 1 pound.

Syrup Pack:

1. Prepare and chill enough *medium (40%) sugar syrup* to pack the amount of apricots you intend to freeze (for each 1 pint of packed apricots you will need between ½ and ⅔ cup of syrup; directions and proportions for the syrup can be found under Sugar Syrups for Freezing Fruit: see index for page number). If the apricots are to keep their bright orange color in the freezer, you must add ascorbic acid to the syrup. The proper amount is ¾ teaspoon powdered or crystalline ascorbic acid per 1 quart of syrup.

2. For freezing, pick firm, perfect, uniformly golden apricots. Wash in cool water, then scald 30 seconds in boiling water, quick-chill in cold water and slip off the skins. Halve the apricots and pit. Leave halves intact or, if you prefer, slice about ¼" thick. As soon as you peel and cut the apricots, drop them into 1 gallon of cold water mixed with 1 teaspoon ascorbic acid and 1 tablespoon citric acid to keep them bright. Drain but do not rinse.

3. Pack the apricots into 1-pint freezer containers, leaving ½" space at the top. Pour in enough chilled syrup to cover apricots but leave ½" head space. Snap on container lids, label and quick-freeze.

Sugar Pack:

1. Wash firm-ripe apricots in cool water, blanch 30 seconds in boiling water to loosen skins, then quick-chill in cold water. Slip off the skins, halve and pit apricots, then leave as halves or slice. Work with only a few apricots at a time lest they darken, and when you have 1 quart of them halved or sliced, sprinkle over them ¼ cup cold water in which you have dissolved ¼ teaspoon powdered or crystalline ascorbic acid. Next add ½ cup sugar and stir gently until sugar dissolves.

2. Pack apricots into 1-quart freezer containers, pressing down until the sweetened juices cover the fruit. Leave ½" head space. Place lids on containers, label and quick-freeze.

KEEPING TIME: About one year at 0° F.

TO DRY: You cannot dry apricots effectively at home without special drying equipment.

TO PICKLE AND PRESERVE: Excellent ways to put today's harvest by for enjoyment later (see recipe below).

TO STORE IN A ROOT CELLAR: You can't. Apricots are much too perishable.

PICKLED APRICOTS OR PEACHES
Makes 6 to 8 Pints

If the apricots or peaches are to be plump and full of flavor, you must let them stand in the pickling syrup overnight at room temperature.

6 pounds small firm-ripe apricots or peaches

1 gallon cold water mixed with 1 teaspoon ascorbic acid and 1 tablespoon citric acid (acidulated water)

2 cups white vinegar

1 cup cider vinegar

3 cups water

4½ cups sugar

3 cinnamon sticks, each broken in several pieces

3 blades of mace

1 thin strip of orange or lemon rind (the colored part of the rind only)

Whole cloves (you will need 2 cloves for each apricot or peach)

Blanch the apricots or peaches, about 2 pounds at a time, in boiling water for 30 seconds. Plunge in ice water to quick-chill, then slip off the skins, letting the peeled whole fruit fall directly into the cold acidulated water (this is to keep them from turning brown).

Place white and cider vinegars, water and sugar in a very large enamel or stainless steel kettle. Tie the cinnamon, mace and orange or lemon rind loosely in several thicknesses of cheesecloth and drop into kettle. Set kettle, uncovered, over moderate heat and bring slowly to the boil. Working with 4 to 6 apricots or peaches at a time, lift from acidulated water, stud each with 2 cloves, then simmer uncovered for 5 minutes in the boiling syrup. Lift apricots or peaches to a large mixing bowl with a slotted spoon. Continue studding the apricots or peaches, simmering them, and transferring them to the bowl. When all have been cooked, bring the syrup to a full boil, return the peaches or apricots to the kettle and remove from the heat at once. Cover and let stand overnight at room temperature.

In the morning, wash and rinse eight 1-pint preserving jars and their closures; keep jars and closures immersed in separate kettles of simmering water until you are ready to use them.

Using a slotted spoon, lift apricots or peaches from syrup and place in a large mixing bowl. Set kettle of syrup over moderate heat and bring slowly to the boil; remove spice bag.

Pack the apricots or peaches as snugly and attractively as possible into hot preserving jars, filling to within ¼" of the tops. Pour enough boiling pickling syrup into each jar to cover fruit, at the same time leaving ¼" head space. Run a thin-blade spatula or table knife around inside edges of jars to release air bubbles. Wipe jar rims and seal jars.

163

Process jars for 15 minutes in a boiling water bath (212° F.). Remove from water bath and complete seals if necessary. Cool completely, check seals, then label and store on a cool, dark, dry shelf. Let the apricots or peaches "season" for about one month before serving.

AVOCADOS

The only way you can conserve these fragile, butter-smooth fruits is to purée them and freeze the purée. Avocados blacken under the merest breath of air, so they must be mixed with ascorbic acid if their color is to remain relatively true. The avocado purée may be packed unseasoned (best for use in soups and other savory dishes) or it may be sweetened and packed. *Sweetened?* Yes, mixed with sugar. Sweetened avocado purée makes a delicate and silky ice cream (see recipe). *Amount of fresh avocados needed for 1-pint of purée:* 2 to 3 large avocados.
    TO FREEZE:

Unseasoned Purée:

1. Choose large just-ripe avocados that are neither hard nor mushy. The rinds should be bright green and blemish-free. Halve the avocados, pit, and scoop out the flesh. Mash well with a potato masher and mix ⅛ teaspoon powdered or crystalline ascorbic acid into each 1 quart of purée.
2. Pack as fast as possible into 1-pint freezer containers, filling to within ¼" of the tops. Snap on lids, label and quick-freeze.

Sweetened Purée:

1. Prepare and mash avocados as directed in Step 1 for Unseasoned Purée. Measure purée and to each quart, add 1 cup of sugar and ⅛ teaspoon powdered or crystalline ascorbic acid. Blend well.
2. Pack into 1-pint freezer containers, losing no time and filling each to within ¼" of the top. Place lids on containers, label and quick-freeze.
    KEEPING TIME: About 6 months at 0° F.

CURRIED AVOCADO SOUP
Makes 4 Servings

A fragrant, smooth soup that puts frozen unsweetened avocado purée to good use.

3 tablespoons unsalted butter
2 tablespoons finely grated yellow onion
2 to 3 teaspoons curry powder (depending
upon how strong a curry flavor you like)
3 tablespoons all-purpose flour

2 cups chicken broth
2 cups light cream or milk
1 pint unsweetened frozen avocado purée,
    thawed completely (recipe precedes)

⅛ teaspoon ground nutmeg
¾ teaspoon salt
⅛ teaspoon white pepper

Melt the butter in a large heavy saucepan over moderate heat, add the grated onion and stir-fry 3 to 4 minutes until limp; blend in the curry powder and continue stir-frying about 3 to 4 minutes longer to mellow the raw taste of the curry. Blend in the flour and heat and stir 2 to 3 minutes longer. Add the chicken broth and light cream and heat, stirring constantly, until thickened and smooth—about 3 minutes. Mix in the thawed avocado purée, nutmeg, salt and pepper and heat, stirring occasionally, 5 to 10 minutes until flavors are well balanced. Taste for salt and pepper and add more if needed. Ladle into soup bowls and serve. For an elegant garnish, float a few cubes of fresh avocado in each bowl, or if you prefer, slim avocado crescents.

AVOCADO ICE CREAM
Makes 1½ Quarts

Avocado ice cream? It's unusually smooth and refreshing and the best of all ways to use sweetened, frozen avocado purée.

1¼ cups sugar
2 teaspoons cornstarch
1 quart milk
3 eggs, separated
1 pint sweetened frozen avocado purée,
    completely thawed (recipe precedes)

2 tablespoons lemon juice
1 teaspoon very finely grated orange rind
½ teaspoon almond extract
1 cup heavy cream, softly whipped

Blend the sugar and the cornstarch well in the top of a double boiler. Stir in the milk gradually, blending well. Beat the egg yolks lightly and mix in, too. Set the double boiler top over simmering (not boiling) water and cook and stir until thickened and smooth, about 15 minutes. Quick-chill in an ice bath, stirring frequently to prevent a skin from forming. When cool, mix in the avocado purée, lemon juice, orange rind and almond extract. Beat the egg whites to soft peaks and fold in gently but thoroughly until no streaks of white or green remain. Pour into 2 refrigerator trays and freeze until mushy.

Place the partially frozen ice cream in a large mixing bowl and beat hard with an electric mixer set at high speed until fluffy. Quickly fold in the whipped cream, spoon into 3 refrigerator trays and freeze until firm.

BLACKBERRIES, BOYSENBERRIES, DEWBERRIES, LOGANBERRIES, RASPBERRIES AND YOUNGBERRIES

TO CAN: These, frankly, all can best as juice. They are, in fact, so soft that if canned whole they pretty much cook down to juice anyway. *Amount of fresh berries needed to equal 1 quart of juice:* About 4 pounds.

Berry Juice:

1. Choose plump-ripe berries full of fragrance, wash well in cool water, and hull. Place berries in a large enamel or stainless steel kettle and crush well with a potato masher. Heat just to the simmering point (185° to 190° F.) or just until juices run freely out of berries.

2. Strain the juice through a cloth bag or through several thicknesses of cheesecloth. Measure the amount of juice and to each quart add ¼ cup of sugar or more, if needed, to suit your taste.

3. Return juice to kettle and bring again to simmering. Pour into hot 1-pint or 1-quart preserving jars, filling to within ½" of the tops.

4. Wipe jar rims and seal jars. Process pints and quarts in a boiling water bath (212 ° F.) for 15 minutes. Remove jars from water bath, adjust seals if necessary, then cool completely. Check seals, label jars and store on a cool, dark, dry shelf.

KEEPING TIME: One year.

TO FREEZE: If you simply want to thaw the berries and serve, pack them whole in syrup. If you want to bake them into pies or cobblers or boil them into jam, pack them whole in dry sugar. Soft (but unblemished) berries will fare better if they are crushed or puréed, sweetened and frozen (use these for making dessert sauces or ice creams; see recipes). *Amount of berries needed to fill a 1-pint freezer container:* About 1⅓ to 1½ pints if packed whole, 2½ to 3 pints if crushed or puréed.

Whole Berries (Syrup Pack):

1. Prepare and chill enough *medium (40%) sugar syrup* to pack the quantity of berries you intend to freeze. For each pint of berries, you will need ½ to ⅔ cup syrup; you will find proportions and directions for making the syrup under Sugar Syrups for Freezing Fruit; see index for page number.

2. Pick firm, plump, full-flavored berries shortly before you will freeze them. Wash gently in cold water so as not to bruise the berries, drain, then hull or stem.

3. Pack the berries in 1-pint freezer containers, shaking them down lightly and leaving ½″ head space. Pour in enough well-chilled syrup to cover the berries, at the same time leaving ½″ head room. Snap on container lids, label and quick-freeze.

Whole Berries (Sugar Pack):

1. Again, pick the plumpest, firm-ripe berries and wash tenderly in cold water. Drain, hull or stem. Measure berries and to each 1 quart add ¾ cup sugar. Toss berries gently until almost all of the sugar has dissolved.

2. Pack berries in 1-pint freezer containers, lightly shaking them down and filling to within ½″ of the tops. Place lids on containers, label and quick-freeze.

Crushed or Puréed Berries:

1. Choose soft-ripe berries full of flavor but make certain they show no signs of mold or decay. Hull, wash in cold water, drain well, then crush with a potato masher or purée by pressing through a fine sieve or buzzing in an electric blender (blender puréed berries should then be sieved to remove seeds). Measure purée and to each 1 quart, add 1 cup sugar. Stir until sugar is dissolved.

2. Pack the purée tightly into 1-pint freezer containers, filling to within ½″ of the tops. Place lids on containers, label and quick-freeze.

KEEPING TIME: About one year at 0° F.

TO DRY: It can't be done.

TO PRESERVE: These berries all make first-rate jams and preserves (see recipe that follows, also Grandma's Cooked Berry Jam under Strawberries).

TO STORE IN A ROOT CELLAR: Impossible. Berries are far too fragile and perishable.

BERRY ICE CREAM
Makes About 1½ Quarts

With frozen puréed or crushed berries on hand, you have the makings of berry ice cream. This particular recipe is smooth and velvety although it is frozen in the refrigerator rather than in a hand-crank freezer.

¾ cup sugar
2 tablespoons cornstarch
1 quart milk
4 eggs, separated
Finely grated rind of 1 lemon

2 teaspoons lemon juice
1 pint frozen puréed or crushed berries,
  thawed
1 cup heavy cream, whipped to soft peaks

Blend the sugar and cornstarch in the top of a double boiler until no lumps remain, then mix in milk gradually. Beat the egg yolks until frothy, then mix in. Set over simmering water and cook, stirring constantly, until smooth and custard-like—this will take about 15 minutes. Set double-boiler top in an ice bath and quick-chill, stirring constantly to prevent a skin from forming or the sauce from lumping. Combine the lemon rind and juice with the berries, then add slowly to the cooled sauce, beating hard to prevent curdling (the acid in the berries sometimes causes milk or eggs to curdle, but if you add them slowly enough, you should have no difficulty). Beat the egg whites to soft peaks, then fold into the berry mixture until no streaks of white remain. Pour into 2 refrigerator trays and freeze until mushy-firm.

   Spoon the partially frozen ice cream into largest mixer bowl and beat hard at high speed until fluffy (don't overbeat or mixture will melt). Fold in the whipped cream, spoon into 3 refrigerator trays and freeze until firm.

BERRY SAUCE
Makes About 2 Cups

You can make this glistening sauce from almost any frozen puréed berries, but the best to use are blackberries or raspberries. Serve over ice cream or custard or plain cake.

1 pint frozen puréed berries, thawed
½ cup red currant jelly
1 tablespoon lemon juice

5 teaspoons cornstarch or arrowroot
  blended with 3 tablespoons cold water

Combine all ingredients in a heavy saucepan, set over moderate heat and cook and stir until thickened and clear—about 3 minutes. Cool to room temperature, stirring often to prevent a skin from forming on the surface of the sauce, then serve.

BLUE RIDGE BLACKBERRY JELLY
Makes Enough to Fill Four (8-ounce) Jelly Jars

Making blackberry jelly the old-fashioned way is somewhat tricky because the quantity of pectin in the berries varies according to ripeness. As a precaution against runny jelly, add 1 Greening apple per quart of berries. NOTE: Do not double this recipe.

2½ *Rhode Island Greening apples,*
    washed and sliced thin but not peeled
    or cored
1 *cup water*

2½ *quarts firm-ripe blackberries, washed*
    and drained
3 *cups sugar (about)*

Place apples (stems, seeds, cores, too, because these are what contain the pectin that makes the jelly "set up") and water in a very large, heavy enamel or stainless steel kettle, cover and boil 15 minutes. Add blackberries, crush well with a potato masher, cover and boil 5 minutes longer. Meanwhile, suspend 2 damp jelly bags over large heatproof bowls or line 2 large colanders with 4 thicknesses of cheesecloth, letting ends lop over; set in bowls. Pour half the fruit mixture into each bag or colander and let juice drip through undisturbed. This will take considerable time—an hour or more, perhaps—so have patience.

Meanwhile, wash and sterilize 4 (8-ounce) jelly jars, stand upside down on a baking sheet and keep hot in a very slow oven (250°) until needed. When the juice has been extracted, measure carefully. You should have about 4 cups. Pour extracted juice into a large, clean, heavy enamel or stainless steel kettle and for each 1 cup of extracted juice, add ¾ cup sugar. Insert a candy thermometer in kettle and boil mixture uncovered, without stirring, about 15 minutes until thermometer reaches 218° to 220° F. Begin testing for sheeting, however, after 5 minutes. Take up a little juice in a large metal spoon, cool slightly, then tilt; if drops run together in a jelly-like sheet, jelly is done. Remove from heat and skim off froth. Fill jars to within ½" of tops and seal with ⅛" melted paraffin. Cool, cover jars with their caps, label and store in a cool, dark, dry place.

How to Test Fruit Juices for Pectin Content

If you intend to make fruit jellies without using commercial pectin preparations (they are available in liquid and powder form), you must know whether or not the particular fruit contains sufficient natural pectin to jell. Many fruits are rich in protein—apples, crabapples and quinces, to name three—but the pectin content of each varies. All jellies are a delicate balance of acid, pectin and sugar and the pectin content determines precisely how much sugar must be added in order for the jelly to jell. There are two methods of determining the pectin content of extracted fruit juices:

To Determine Pectin Content with a Jelmeter: This is the surer way. Jelmeters, nothing more than calibrated glass tubes, are sold in many hardware stores and housewares departments of large stores. They are accompanied by full instructions and the best plan is to follow them. Briefly, here's how they work: Fill the Jelmeter with extracted fruit juice, then time how long it takes for the juice to drain through. The speed with which the juice flows through the tube indicates the pectin content, which, in turn indicates how much sugar is needed for a good jell. That's all there is to it.

To Determine Pectin Content with Alcohol: An old-fashioned yet fairly reliable method. You will need pure grain (ethyl) alcohol, not rubbing alcohol and you can buy it at any drugstore. To test for pectin, place 1 tablespoon of alcohol in a small cup, then add 1 tablespoon of extracted fruit juice; let stand for 1 minute, then pour the mixture into a second cup. If a hard solid curd forms, the fruit juice is rich in pectin and should be mixed cup for cup with sugar. If the curd is crumbly, you should use ¾ cup sugar to each 1 cup of extracted juice. And if it is very soft, use ½ cup sugar to each 1 cup of fruit juice.

BLUEBERRIES, ELDERBERRIES AND HUCKLEBERRIES

TO CAN: You'll be happier if you freeze the berries.

TO FREEZE: Berries that will later be baked into muffins, pies and cobblers will hold their shape better during baking if they are packed whole in freezer containers without any syrup or sugar. If, on the other hand, you simply want frozen berries that you can thaw and serve straightaway as dessert, pack them in syrup. The syrup will plump and soften them. *Amount of fresh berries needed to fill a 1-pint freezer container:* About 1⅓ to 1½ pints.

Whole Berries (Syrup Pack):

1. Prepare and chill enough *medium (40%) sugar syrup* to pack the amount of berries you will be freezing (for each pint of berries you will need ½ to ⅔ cup syrup; proportions and directions for making sugar syrup are included under Sugar Syrups for Freezing Fruit; see index for page number).

2. Pick berries of as nearly the same size as possible, selecting those that are tender-skinned, firm-ripe and full-flavored. Sort the berries according to size, wash in cold water, drain and stem.

3. Place berries in a large fine-mesh basket and steam 1 minute over boiling water (this helps intensify the flavor of the berries). Quick-chill in ice water; drain.

4. Pack the berries in 1-pint freezer containers, shaking them down gently as you go and leaving ½" head space. Pour in enough chilled syrup to cover berries, filling each container to within ½" of the top. Snap lids on containers, label and quick-freeze.

Whole Berries (Packed Plain):

1. Pick plump, tender-skinned, well-flavored berries and sort according to size. Wash in cold water, drain and stem.

2. Pack berries into 1-pint freezer containers, filling to within ½" of the tops and shaking the berries down lightly so that they will be more compact. Snap lids on containers, label and quick-freeze.

KEEPING TIME: About one year at 0° F.

TO DRY: Don't bother.

TO PICKLE OR PRESERVE: The best way to preserve these berries is as jam (see Grandma's Cooked Berry Jam; it is a basic recipe that can be used for most varieties of berries).

TO STORE IN A ROOT CELLAR: No point in trying. The berries will mold and decay.

CHERRIES

TO CAN: Whether sweet or sour, cherries will be plumper and finer flavored if they are packed in syrup instead of in water. A *medium sugar syrup* will suffice for both the sweet and the sour, although if the cherries are mouth-puckeringly tart, you should pack them in a *heavy sugar syrup*. Should cherries be pitted before canning? That depends upon how you will use them. If they are to be served as is (in a dessert, say, or in a fruit cocktail), they need not be pitted. But if they are to be used for making pies or cobblers or crisps, they should be pitted. Pitting is, at best, a tedious business, even if you have a proper cherry pitter (and do, by all means, buy one if you have many quarts of cherries to can). Better still, buy *several* cherry pitters, then draft what volunteers you can to help get the job done fast. You must work quickly with cherries, especially with sweet cherries, because they will discolor on standing. All cherries, by the way, will fade in canning. There is no way to maintain their tree-ripe brilliance short of adding red food coloring, and that we do not recommend. *Amount of cherries, unpitted, needed to fill a 1-quart preserving jar:* About 2 to 2½ pounds.

Cold (Raw) Pack:

1.   Pick the cherries as soon as possible before you will can them, selecting those that are plump but firm and of good, uniform color. Sort according to size, stem, wash in cool water and drain. Leave the pits in the cherries if they will not later be used in cooking, but do prick the skin of each cherry with a sterilized needle to keep the cherries from bursting during processing.

2.   Prepare enough *medium or heavy sugar syrup* (depending upon whether cherries are sweet or sour) to pack the quantity of cherries you intend to can. Directions for making the syrup are included under Sugar Syrups for Canning Fruit; see index for page number. You will need 1 to 1½ cups syrup for each 1-quart jar.

3.   Pour ½ cup boiling medium or heavy syrup into a hot 1-pint or 1-quart preserving jar, pack with raw cherries, shaking them down as you go and filling to within ½" of the jar top. Pour in enough additional boiling syrup to cover the cherries, at the same time leaving ½" head space. Repeat until all jars are filled.

4.   Wipe jar rims and seal jars. Process in a boiling water bath (212° F.), allowing 20 minutes for pints and 25 minutes for quarts.

5.   Remove jars from water bath and adjust seals if necessary. Cool thoroughly, check seals, label jars and store on a cool, dark, dry shelf.

Hot Pack:

1.   The same as for COLD PACK (above).

2. Measure the cherries and for each 1 quart of them, add ½ to ¾ cup sugar, depending upon whether the cherries are sweet or sour. Place cherries in a large heavy enamel or stainless steel kettle and heat slowly, just until the sugar dissolves and the cherries are heated through. Using a slotted spoon, fill hot 1-pint or 1-quart preserving jars with cherries, shaking the jars as you go so that the cherries will pack compactly without crushing. Fill jars to within ½" of the tops, then pour in enough hot cherry juice from the kettle to cover the cherries, but leave the necessary ½" head space. If there is insufficient cherry juice to cover the cherries, pour in boiling water or *light sugar syrup* (see index to find the proportions under Sugar Syrups for Canning Fruit).

3. Wipe jar rims and seal jars. Process in a boiling water bath (212° F.), allowing 10 minutes for pint jars and 15 minutes for quarts.

4. Remove jars from water bath, adjust seals if necessary, and cool completely. Check seals, then label jars and store on a cool, dark, dry shelf.

KEEPING TIME: About one year.

TO FREEZE: Both sweet and sour cherries freeze successfully, but the techniques for each are slightly different because sour cherries, obviously, will require more sweetening and sweet cherries, unless treated with an anti-browning agent, will discolor. Sour whole cherries may be packed either in syrup (preferable when they are simply to be thawed and served in fruit cocktail or as dessert) or in sugar (when they are to be used in baking). Sweet cherries, on the other hand, are best packed in syrup, no matter how they will be used ultimately. Both varieties of cherries can, of course, be frozen as purée or juice, however you will find that you will have more use for frozen whole cherries. These, moreover, can always be reduced to purée or juice after they have been thawed. So we recommend that you save preparation time at the outset and freeze the cherries whole. *To pit or not to pit?* It's a good idea to remove pits from cherries before they are frozen because the pits, for some reason, give them a strong almond flavor. *Amount of raw cherries needed to fill a 1-pint freezer container:* About 1¼ to 1½ pounds.

Whole Sour Cherries (Syrup Pack):

1. Prepare and chill enough *very heavy (60%) sugar syrup* to pack the amount of cherries you intend to freeze. You will need between ½ and ⅔ cup syrup for each pint container. Proportions and directions for making the syrup are included under Sugar Syrups for Freezing Fruit; see index for page number.

2. Pick bright red, tree-ripe cherries shortly before you will freeze them. Sort according to size, stem and wash in cool water. Drain and remove pits.

3. Pack cherries into 1-pint freezer containers, agitating the containers gently so that you can pack the cherries compactly without bruising them. Fill each container to within ½" of the top, then pour in enough chilled syrup to cover the cherries, at the same time leaving ½" head space. Snap lids on containers, label and quick-freeze.

Whole Sour Cherries (Sugar Pack):

1. Pick and prepare cherries for freezing as directed in Step 2 under SYRUP PACK (above). Measure the cherries, and for each 1 quart of them, add ¾ cup sugar. Toss gently until sugar is dissolved.

2. Pack cherries into 1-pint freezer containers, shaking them down gently as you go and filling to within ½" of the tops. Snap lids on containers, label and quick-freeze.

Whole Sweet Cherries (Syrup Pack); sweet red cherries freeze more successfully than the pale-skinned varieties:

1. Prepare enough *medium (40%) sugar syrup* to pack the quantity of cherries you intend to freeze. You will need from ½ to ⅔ cup for each 1-pint container. Directions for making the sugar syrup are included under Sugar Syrups for Freezing Fruit; see index for page number. Measure the total quantity of syrup, and for every 1 quart of it, add ½ teaspoon powdered or crystalline ascorbic acid. It is needed to keep the cherries from browning in the freezer. Chill the syrup well.

2. Pick the cherries shortly before you will freeze them, choosing those that are plump, bright red and sweet. Sort the cherries according to size, stem, then wash well in cool water. Drain the cherries and pit.

3. Pack cherries into 1-pint freezer containers, shaking them down lightly and filling to within ½" of the tops. Pour in enough chilled syrup to cover the cherries, at the same time allowing the necessary ½" head space. Snap on container lids, label and quick-freeze.

KEEPING TIME: About one year at 0° F.

TO DRY: Impossible.

TO PICKLE AND PRESERVE: Cherries pickle and preserve exceptionally well (see recipes below).

TO STORE IN A ROOT CELLAR: Cherries do not take to cold storage.

PICKLED SWEET BLACK CHERRIES
Makes 8 to 10 Pints

Not the usual condiment but an excellent one that partners well with roast meat, fowl and game.

10 pounds firm-ripe sweet black cherries	*1 tablespoon whole cloves, bruised*
2 cups white vinegar	*1 tablespoon whole allspice, bruised*
2 cups cider vinegar	*3 cinnamon sticks, each broken in several*
2 cups water	*places*
3 cups sugar	*2 blades of mace*

Wash the cherries well in cool water and stem but do not pit. Drain well. To prevent cherries from bursting during processing, prick each with a sterilized needle.

Wash and rinse ten 1-pint preserving jars and their closures; keep jars and closures immersed in separate kettles of simmering water until you are ready to use them.

Place white and cider vinegars, water and sugar in a large heavy enamel or stainless steel kettle. Tie all the spices loosely in several thicknesses of cheesecloth and drop into the kettle. Set uncovered over moderate heat and bring to a boil. Add the drained cherries to the boiling syrup, and the instant syrup returns to a boil, boil the cherries for 2 minutes exactly. Using a slotted spoon, pack the hot cherries into the hot jars, shaking them down for a more compact fit and filling to within ½" of the jar tops. Pour enough boiling pickling syrup into each jar to cover cherries, at the same time leaving ½" head space. Run a thin-blade spatula or table knife around inside edges of jars to remove trapped air bubbles. Wipe jar rims and seal jars.

Process for 10 minutes in a boiling water bath (212° F.). Remove jars from water bath, complete seals if necessary and cool completely. Check seals, then label and store on a cool, dark, dry shelf. Let the cherries season for about a month before serving.

CHERRY PRESERVES
Makes About 6 Half-Pints

Begin this recipe one afternoon, let the cherries plump overnight in their juices, then finish the preserves the following morning.

2 quarts firm-ripe tart red cherries
Sugar (you will need ¾ cup for each 1 cup
    of prepared fruit)
2 tablespoons lemon or orange juice

Stem the cherries and wash well in cool water; pit the cherries. Measure the total quantity of cherries and for each 1 cup of them, measure out ¾ cup sugar. Place cherries and sugar in a very large, heavy, broad-bottomed enamel or stainless steel kettle and let stand 15 minutes at room temperature or until the sugar has drawn some of the juices from the fruit. Set the kettle uncovered over moderate heat and bring cherries slowly to the boil; boil uncovered for 5 minutes, stirring occasionally.

Remove kettle from heat, cover and let cherries plump overnight in their syrup so that they will hold their shape fairly well.

Next day, wash and sterilize 6 half-pint preserving jars and their closures; keep jars and closures immersed in separate kettles of simmering water until you are ready to use them.

Set the kettle of cherries over moderate heat, stir in lemon or orange juice, insert a candy thermometer, and bring slowly to a boil; boil uncovered as rapidly as you dare, stirring often to prevent scorching, until mixture is glossy and thick (when the preserves are at the proper consistency, the candy thermometer will register between 218° and 220° F.).

Pour the boiling preserves into the hot jars, filling to within ¼″ of the tops. Wipe jar rims and seal jars. Process for 10 minutes in a simmering water bath (185° F.). Remove jars from water bath, complete seals if necessary, then cool completely. Check seals, label jars and store on a cool, dark, dry shelf.

CRANBERRIES AND CURRANTS

We don't think much of canned cranberries or currants, or, for that matter, of those frozen in syrup or sugar. As far as we're concerned, the best way to conserve these tart red berries is simply to pop them into freezer containers—as is—and freeze them. What could be easier? Best of all, the frozen whole berries can be used exactly like the freshly picked ones for making sauces or conserves.

176

TO FREEZE: Amount of fresh cranberries or currants needed to fill a 1-pint freezer container: ½ to ¾ pound.

1. Pick plump, fully ripe scarlet berries. Sort according to size and remove stems. Wash the berries in cool water and drain.

2. Pack into 1-pint or 1-quart freezer containers, shaking the berries down so that they will fit more snugly. Leave ½" head space at the top of each container. Snap the lids on, label and quick-freeze. That's all there is to it.

KEEPING TIME: About one year at 0° F.

CRANBERRY AND ALMOND CONSERVE
Makes About 8 Half-Pints

In autumn when cranberries are plentiful, put up this tart and crunchy conserve to enjoy until the next cranberry season. It is especially good with roast turkey and chicken, duck and goose, venison, pork, ham and lamb.

2 medium-size oranges, halved, seeded and chopped fine (rind, pulp and all)
Grated rind of 1 lemon
1 quart water
3 cups granulated sugar

3 cups firmly packed light brown sugar
2 quarts cranberries, stemmed
½ cup seedless raisins
½ cup dried currants
1¼ cups chopped blanched almonds

Place oranges, lemon rind and water in a large, heavy enamel or stainless steel kettle, set over moderately high heat and boil uncovered for 25 minutes or until rind is tender.

Meanwhile, wash and sterilize 8 half-pint preserving jars and their closures; keep closures and jars immersed in separate kettles of simmering water until you are ready to use them.

When rind is tender, add granulated and brown sugars to kettle and as soon as they are dissolved, stir in cranberries, raisins and currants. Let mixture come slowly to the boil, then boil hard, uncovered, stirring frequently to prevent scorching, 5 minutes. Mix in almonds. Continue boiling rapidly and stirring 5 to 10 minutes longer until mixture is thick and jelly-like (about 220° F. on a candy thermometer).

Ladle boiling hot into hot jars, filling to within ⅛" of the tops. Wipe jar rims and seal jars. Process for 10 minutes in a simmering water bath (185° F.). Remove jars from water bath, complete seals if necessary, and cool to room temperature. Check seals, then label and store on a cool, dark, dry shelf.

177

FIGS

Because we are concerned here only with the best ways of conserving your home garden fruits, we don't advise canning figs (they are too mushy) or drying them (too risky) or putting them in cold storage—pointless because the figs will not keep.

Figs do, to be sure, make splendid preserves (see recipes). And they freeze beautifully if packed whole in syrup with just enough ascorbic acid added to keep them from darkening.

TO FREEZE: Two varieties of fig that freeze particularly well are Brown Turkey and Celeste. *Amount of fresh figs needed to fill 1-pint freezer container:* ¾ to 1 pound.

1. Prepare enough *medium (40%) sugar syrup* to pack the quantity of figs you intend to freeze. You will need from ½ to ⅔ cup for each 1-pint container (directions for making the sugar syrup are included under Sugar Syrups for Freezing Fruit; see index for page number). Measure the total quantity of syrup, and for every 1 quart of it, mix in ½ teaspoon powdered or crystalline ascorbic acid. It will prevent the figs from discoloring in the freezer. Chill the syrup well.

2. Gather the figs in the cool of the morning shortly before you will freeze them and be especially choosy about the ones you select. They should be fully ripe, soft but not mushy or shriveled. Figs are both fragile and perishable, so handle them quickly but gently.

3. Wash the figs in cool water, drain and remove stems. Pack whole unpeeled figs in 1-pint freezer containers, fitting them in as snugly as possible without mashing them and filling to within ½" of the tops. Pour in enough chilled syrup to cover the figs, but again leave ½" head space. Snap the lids on the containers, label and quick-freeze.

KEEPING TIME: About one year at 0° F. although the figs will have superior flavor and texture if eaten within 6 months.

PICKLED FIGS
Makes 8 to 10 Pints

10 pounds firm-ripe figs
1 gallon boiling water
1 quart cider vinegar
1 quart cold water
6 cups sugar
2 tablespoons whole cloves, bruised

1 tablespoon whole allspice, bruised
2 cinnamon sticks, each broken in several
    places
2 long thin strips of lemon rind (the yellow
    part only)

Wash the figs well in cool water and drain; do not stem or peel. To prevent the figs from bursting during processing, prick each once or twice with a sterilized needle. Place the figs in a large heavy kettle, pour in the boiling water and let stand until the water cools to room temperature. Drain the figs.

Place the vinegar, cold water and sugar in a large heavy enamel or stainless steel kettle. Tie the cloves, allspice, cinnamon and lemon rind loosely in several thicknesses of cheesecloth and drop into kettle. Set kettle uncovered over moderate heat and bring to a boil. Add all the figs, reduce heat slightly so that syrup boils gently, then boil uncovered for ¾ to 1 hour or until figs are translucent and tender. Remove spice bag.

Meanwhile, wash and rinse ten 1-pint preserving jars and their closures; keep jars and closures immersed in separate kettles of simmering water until you are ready to use them.

Using a slotted spoon, pack the hot figs in the hot jars, arranging as snugly and attractively as possible and filling the jars to within ¼″ of the tops. Pour enough boiling pickling syrup into each jar to cover the figs, at the same time leaving ¼″ head space. Run a thin-blade spatula or table knife around inside edges of jars to free air bubbles. Wipe jar rims and seal jars.

Process the pickled figs for 15 minutes in a boiling water bath (212° F.). Remove the jars from the water bath, complete seals if necessary, and cool completely. Check seals, then label jars and store on a cool, dark, dry shelf. Let the figs develop flavor for about a month before serving.

PRESERVED FIGS
Makes 4 Half-Pints

½ cup water

3 cups sugar

Juice of 1 lemon

1 quart peeled, firm-ripe figs

Bring water, sugar and lemon juice to a boil in a large, heavy enamel or stainless steel kettle, stirring until sugar dissolves. Add figs and cook uncovered 10 to 15 minutes until figs are clear. Remove from heat, cover and let stand overnight at room temperature to "plump" the figs.

Next day, wash and sterilize 4 half-pint preserving jars and their closures; keep jars and closures immersed in separate kettles of simmering water until you are ready to use them.

Bring figs and syrup slowly to a boil, skim off any froth and with a slotted spoon, pack figs into hot jars, filling to within ¼″ of the tops. Pour in enough boiling syrup to cover figs, at the same time leaving ¼″ head space. Wipe jar rims and seal jars. Process for 30 minutes in a simmering water bath (185° F.). Remove jars from water bath, complete seals if necessary, and cool thoroughly. Check seals, then label jars and store on a cool, dark. dry shelf. Let stand for several weeks before serving.

GOOSEBERRIES

Make them into jam, make them into jelly, or freeze them. There is not much else you can do to conserve these tart green berries because no other method truly does them justice.

TO FREEZE: We frankly think that gooseberries freeze best when packed whole without any sugar or syrup. Certainly, this is the way they should be frozen if you ultimately intend to make them into pies, puddings or preserves. *Amount of fresh gooseberries needed to fill a 1-pint freezer container:* About 1⅓ to 1½ pints.

1. Pick plump, fully ripe berries (unless you will use the frozen berries later for making jelly, in which case they should be a shade underripe). Sort the berries according to size, stem them, then wash well in cool water and drain.

2. Pack the whole berries into 1-pint freezer containers, shaking down loosely for a more compact fit and filling to within ½″ of the container tops. Snap on the lids. label the containers and quick-freeze.

KEEPING TIME: About one year at 0° F.

GOOSEBERRY JAM
Makes About 4 Half-Pints

Because gooseberries have fairly tough skins, you will find that your jam will be more tender if you cook the berries *before* you add the sugar and boil them into jam.

2 quarts firm-ripe gooseberries   *Sugar (you will need ¾ cup of sugar for*
½ cup water   *each 1 cup of cooked gooseberries)*

Stem the gooseberries and remove the blossom ends but do not peel; wash well in cool water and drain. Put the gooseberries through a food chopper fitted with a coarse blade, letting the ground berries fall directly into a large, heavy, broad-bottomed enamel or stainless steel kettle. When all berries are ground, mix in the water, cover and boil over moderate heat for about 10 minutes until the berries are very soft. Measure the total amount of cooked berries and for each 1 cup of them, add ¾ cup sugar.

Wash and sterilize 4 half-pint preserving jars and their closures; keep jars and closures immersed in separate kettles of simmering water until you are ready to use them.

Return the sweetened berries to the rinsed-out kettle and insert a candy thermometer. Set uncovered over moderate heat and bring to a boil; boil rapidly, uncovered, stirring as needed to prevent scorching, until mixture is glossy and thick (the candy thermometer will register about 218° F.).

Pour the hot jam into the hot jars, filling to within ¼″ of the tops. Wipe jar rims and seal jars. Process for 10 minutes in a simmering water bath (185° F.). Remove jars from water bath, complete seals if necessary, then cool completely. Label jars and store on a cool, dark, dry shelf.

GOOSEBERRY JELLY
Makes Enough to Fill 3 to 4 (8-ounce) Jelly Glasses

2 quarts gooseberries (about ¼ of them should be a shade underripe, the rest firm-ripe)

½ cup water
Sugar (you will need ¾ cup of sugar for each 1 cup of extracted juice)

Stem the gooseberries but do not peel; wash well in cool water; drain. Place berries in a large heavy enamel or stainless steel kettle and crush well with a potato masher; add the water, cover and simmer over moderate heat 10 to 15 minutes until very soft.

Meanwhile, line 2 very large colanders with 4 thicknesses of damp cheesecloth, letting the ends overhang the colanders about 4″ all around; stand each colander in a very large mixing bowl. Or, if you have 2 jelly bags, dampen them with cold water, wring out and suspend from the jelly bag stands; set each over a large bowl.

Pour half of the gooseberries into each colander or jelly bag and let the juice trickle out at its own speed; this will take an hour, perhaps two, but do not rush the process by squeezing the bags or pressing the juices through the colander. Your jelly will be cloudy if you do.

Meanwhile, wash and sterilize 4 (8-ounce) jelly glasses; keep glasses immersed in simmering water until you are ready to use them. Also melt paraffin for sealing the glasses.

When all the gooseberry juice has been extracted, measure precisely, then add ¾ cup of sugar to each 1 cup of juice. If you are anxious about whether or not your jelly will jell, test for pectin using one of the methods described under How To Test Fruit Juices for Pectin Content; see index for page number.

Place the sweetened gooseberry juice in a very large, heavy, broad-bottomed enamel or stainless steel kettle, insert a candy thermometer and set uncovered over moderately high heat. Bring to the boil, then boil uncovered without stirring 20 to 25 minutes or until the mixture will sheet—that is, a little of the hot mixture taken up on a metal spoon will, when cooled and tilted, slide together in a single jelly-like sheet; sheeting usually occurs when the candy thermometer registers between 218° and 220° F.

When jelly sheets, remove from heat and skim off the froth. Pour hot jelly into hot glasses, filling to within ¼″ of the tops. Seal with ⅛″ melted paraffin, pricking any bubbles in the paraffin with a sterilized needle. Cool jelly thoroughly, cover jelly glasses with their metal caps, label and store on a cool, dark, dry shelf.

GRAPEFRUITS AND ORANGES

TO CAN: Freezing is preferable. It's easier, quicker, and unlike canning, neither alters nor intensifies the fruits' tang.

TO FREEZE: Grapefruit and orange sections both freeze well; so, too, do their juices. To preserve as much of their fresh natural flavor as possible, pack in glass freezer jars (citrus fruits, being sharply acid, sometimes develop "off" flavors if packed in plastic containers). *Amount of fresh grapefruit needed to fill a 1-pint freezer jar:* About 1 medium-size grapefruit if packed as sections and 1½ to 2 grapefruits if packed as juice. *Amount of fresh oranges needed to fill a 1-pint freezer jar:* 2 to 3 medium-to-large oranges if packed as sections, 4 if packed as juice.

Grapefruit or Orange Sections:

1.   Prepare enough *medium 40% sugar syrup* to pack the quantity of fruit you intend to freeze. You will need from ½ to ⅔ cup syrup for each 1-pint freezer jar. Directions for making the sugar syrup are included under Sugar Syrups for Freezing Fruit; see index for page number. Measure the total quantity of syrup, and for every 1 quart of it, add ½ teaspoon powdered or crystalline ascorbic acid. Its purpose is not, as with other fruits, to prevent darkening; it is to give the frozen fruits better flavor and texture. Chill the syrup well.

2.   Pick firm-ripe, fragrant grapefruits or oranges that seem heavy for their size. Peel, making sure you remove all the bitter white parts of the rind, then section, removing all membranes, pith and seeds.

3.   Pack sections into 1-pint freezer jars, shaking them down lightly for a more compact fit and filling to within ½″ of the jar tops. Pour in enough chilled syrup to cover fruit, at the same time leaving ½″ head space. Screw lids on jars, label and quick-freeze.

Grapefruit or Orange Juice:

1.   Pick tree-ripened fruit that is juicy and full of flavor. Halve the fruits and squeeze, using a juicer that does not mash the rinds or press out their bitter

oils. Strain the juice, if you like. Measure the total quantity of juice and to each 1 quart, mix in 2 tablespoons sugar and a scant ¼ teaspoon powdered or crystalline ascorbic acid.

2.   Pour juice into 1-pint freezer jars, filling to within ½" of the tops. Screw on lids, label and quick-freeze.

KEEPING TIME: About one year at 0° F. for juice and sections although each will have finer flavor if served within 6 months.

TO DRY: Impossible.

TO PICKLE OR PRESERVE: Grapefruits and oranges make delicious marmalades (recipes follow), and they are, of course, used in preparing many other preserves and chutneys. The ultimate in conservation? Save the rinds and candy them (see recipe).

TO STORE IN A ROOT CELLAR: Grapefruits and oranges will hold well for as long as 6 weeks, provided you can maintain in your basement root cellar a temperature of 32° F., a humidity between 80% and 90% and *slight* ventilation. The hitch, of course, is that in areas where oranges and grapefruits grow, these conditions are difficult to achieve without mechanical refrigeration.

The fruits should be picked when firm-ripe, preferably on a cool morning, then layered into perforated cartons and stored uncovered in the fruit section of your basement root cellar. Check often and discard any fruits that are softening or molding.

KEEPING TIME: 4 to 6 weeks.

GRAPEFRUIT MARMALADE
Makes About 6 Half-Pints

You begin this marmalade one day and finish it the next because the rind must be left to tenderize overnight.

3 large grapefruits
1 large orange
3 quarts + 3 cups water
Sugar (you will need 1 cup sugar for each 1

cup of grapefruit mixture)
⅓ cup finely slivered crystallized ginger
(optional but a nice, nippy addition)

Peel the grapefruits and orange with a vegetable peeler so that you have long thin strips of the colored part of the rind; cut rind in fine slivers and reserve. Peel all bitter inner white rind from grapefruits and orange, then section the fruits, discarding seeds, white membranes and pith. Coarsely chop the sections, saving every bit of juice.

Place the grapefruit and orange rind in a small heavy saucepan, add 1 quart of the water and bring, uncovered, to a boil; drain the rind, then once again cover with 1 quart of water and bring to a boil. Drain and repeat once more.

Place the drained rind, the chopped fruit and juice and the 3 cups water in a large, heavy, broad-bottomed enamel or stainless steel kettle, leave uncovered and bring slowly to boiling over moderate heat. Lower heat slightly and simmer uncovered for 15 minutes. Remove from heat, cover and let stand overnight in a cool place.

Next day, wash and sterilize 6 half-pint preserving jars and their closures; keep jars and closures immersed in separate kettles of simmering water until you are ready to use them.

Measure the grapefruit mixture and for every 1 cup of it, add 1 cup of sugar. Place grapefruit mixture, sugar and, if you like, the slivered ginger in the large kettle and insert a candy thermometer. Set over moderately low heat and let come slowly to the boil; boil uncovered about 35 to 40 minutes until clear and jelly-like and the candy thermometer registers 218° to 220° F. Take up a little of the hot mixture on a metal spoon, cool and tilt; if the marmalade slides together in a single jelly-like sheet, it is done. If not done, continue cooking until it will "sheet."

Remove marmalade from heat and stir gently for 1 minute; skim off any froth, then pour hot marmalade into hot jars, filling to within ¼" of the tops. Wipe jar rims and seal jars. Process for 10 minutes in a simmering water bath (185° F.). Remove jars from water bath, complete seals if necessary and cool completely. Check seals, label jars and store on a cool, dark, dry shelf.

ORANGE MARMALADE
Makes About 6 Half-Pints

When making marmalade (or, for that matter, any jams, jellies and preserves), you should use a heavy, broad-bottomed kettle of about three times the volume of the ingredients put into it so that there is plenty of room for the marmalade to boil up without boiling over. The best kettle to use is an enameled cast-iron one because it will conduct the heat evenly and because its porcelain lining is inert, meaning that it will not react with the acid in fruits to produce "off" or metallic flavors. The marmalade below is a fairly mellow one. If you prefer a bittersweet marmalade, simply substitute two tangerines for one of the large oranges, using both their rind and their pulp.

3 large oranges
1 large lemon
3 cups water

Sugar (you will need 1 cup of sugar for each 1 cup of orange mixture)

Using a vegetable peeler, peel the outer colored rind from the oranges and the lemon; trim off and discard any bitter white parts of inner rind that cling to the colored rind. Sliver the colored rind very fine and reserve. Using a paring knife, peel all white inner rind from the oranges and lemon, section them, remove seeds and pith, then coarsely chop the sections, being careful to save all juice. Place the slivered rind, chopped oranges and lemon and their juices in a large heavy enamel or stainless steel kettle. Stir in water, set over moderate heat and bring just to the boiling point. Reduce heat slightly and simmer uncovered for 15 minutes. Remove from heat, cover and let stand overnight in a cool spot.

Next day, wash and sterilize 6 half-pint preserving jars and their closures; keep jars and closures immersed in separate kettles of simmering water until you are ready to use them.

Measure the orange mixture precisely and make a note of the total amount. Return to the kettle, then add 1 cup of sugar for each 1 cup of orange mixture. Insert a candy thermometer. Set over moderately low heat and bring slowly to the boil, stirring until sugar dissolves. Continue boiling, uncovered, 35 to 40 minutes until clear and jelly-like (about 218° to 220° F. on the candy thermometer). Take up a bit of the hot mixture on a metal spoon, cool, then tilt; if the drops slide together in a jelly-like mass, the marmalade is done. Remove from heat, stir marmalade for 1 minute, then skim off froth.

Pour hot marmalade into hot jars, filling to within ¼″ of the tops. Wipe jar rims and seal jars. Process for 10 minutes in a simmering water bath (185° F.). Remove jars from water bath, complete seals if necessary and cool thoroughly. Check seals, label jars and store on a cool, dark, dry shelf.

CANDIED GRAPEFRUIT OR ORANGE RIND
Makes About 2 Pounds

You cannot candy orange or grapefruit rind successfully unless the rind is good and thick, so use thick-skinned varieties. Lemon or lime rind may also be candied using the recipe below; you'll need the rind of about 10 large lemons or limes. Do not attempt this recipe on a damp day; it won't work.

Rind of 4 grapefruits or 7 navel oranges (remove in large sections)
Cold water
5¾ cups sugar

1 cup hot water
2 teaspoons unflavored gelatin softened in 2 tablespoons cold water

Place the rind in medium-size heavy enamel or stainless steel kettle and pour in 6 cups cold water. Bring to a boil, uncovered, then drain. Once again cover rind with 6 cups cold water, bring to a boil and drain. Repeat the boiling and draining three more times—this is to extract as much bitterness from the rind as possible and to soften it. Cut the rind in strips 2" to 3" long and about ⅛" wide and spread out on paper toweling.

In the same large kettle, mix 4 cups of the sugar and the hot water and bring slowly to the boil over low heat, stirring until sugar dissolves. Add the rind and boil slowly, uncovered, 25 to 30 minutes until rind is clear and sparkling. You'll have to stir fairly constantly to keep the mixture from scorching. Mix in the softened gelatin and simmer 5 minutes longer. Remove kettle from heat and cool 3 to 5 minutes. Meanwhile, spread remaining 1¾ cups of sugar out on a baking sheet. Using a slotted spoon, lift a few pieces of rind out of the syrup, letting all excess syrup drain back into kettle. Roll rind in sugar to coat well, then spread sugared rind out to air-dry on wire racks set over a counter lined with wax paper. When all pieces of rind have been rolled in sugar and air-dried, store in airtight cannisters. The rind should keep well for several months.

GRAPES

If you are going to can grapes, you should can them as juice. Whole grapes must be seeded and stemmed and to be honest, the quality of the end product does not justify the tedious means. The same might be said for freezing. In my view, it is not a very worthwhile way of conserving grapes. Drying, on a small, home scale is out of the question. But jams and jellies! They are something else again. Grapes make more fragrant and tender jelly than almost any other fruit. And they cook down into superbly thick, full-flavored jam. You may be interested to know, too, that grapes can be held over for some weeks in cold storage. You will find below recipes for making and canning grape juice, also for old-fashioned grape jelly and jam. As for putting grapes in cold storage, here's how you should go about it.

TO STORE GRAPES IN A ROOT CELLAR: First of all, you will only be able to hold grapes successfully in cold storage if you live in the North where grapes mature in autumn after temperatures have dropped down around 32° F. The varieties most suited to cold storage are, in order: Catawba, Tokay and Concord.

The basement root cellar is where you should store grapes because you can control, fairly precisely, its temperature (32° F. is the ideal) and its humidity (anything between 80% and 90% is optimum). You must, however, store the grapes in the fruit section of the root cellar, well away from other fruits and vegetables because grapes so readily absorb and hold alien odors.

Gather the grapes when they are firm-ripe, and remove from each bunch any grapes that are bruised, withering or decaying. Layer the bunches in sturdy cartons lined with a 1½″ bed of clean dry straw, and cushion successive layers with more straw. Do not pack the grapes more than three layers deep lest the weight of the grapes on top crush those underneath. Cover the grapes loosely with clean dry straw.

KEEPING TIME: 1 to 2 months, but inspect the grapes now and again for signs of spoilage and remove at once any that are going bad.

HOME-CANNED GRAPE JUICE
Makes About 3 to 4 Quarts

The best grapes to use in making grape juice are Concord, or better yet, the wild Scuppernong or Muscadine because they have dark skins (which will give the juice good color) and a robust "grape" flavor. Pick the grapes when they are plump and juicy and full of bouquet.

10 pounds stemmed, plump-ripe grapes
Water (you will need ¼ cup for each 1 quart of crushed grapes)

Sugar (you will need ¼ to ½ cup for each quart of juice, depending upon the natural sweetness of the grapes)

Wash the grapes well in cool water, then working with about a fourth of them at a time, place in a large mixing bowl and crush thoroughly with a potato masher. Measure the crushed grapes and for every 1 quart of them, add ¼ cup water. Place water and crushed grapes in a large heavy enamel or stainless steel kettle. Continue crushing the grapes, measuring and adding the required amount of water until all grapes have been crushed and added to the kettle. Bring slowly to the boil, then boil gently, uncovered, for 15 minutes to force the juice out of the grapes and develop its flavor.

Line a very large colander with several thicknesses of cheesecloth (cut the pieces of cheesecloth large enough so that they will overhang the colander 3" to 4" all around). Set the colander over a very large enamel or stainless steel kettle and again, working with about a fourth of the grapes at a time, pour into the colander and let the juices drain through. Using a wooden spoon, press and force out as much juice as possible. When all of the grapes have been drained and only skins and seeds remain in the cheesecloth, bundle into a bag and twist, extracting every last bit of juice. Cover the kettle of juice and chill overnight in the refrigerator. Next day, strain the juice once again through several thicknesses of cheesecloth. Measure the total quantity of juice and for each 1 quart of it, add ¼ to ½ cup of sugar–the amount needed will depend upon the tartness of the juice.

Wash and rinse four 1-quart preserving jars and their closures; keep jars and closures immersed in separate kettles of simmering water until you are ready to use them.

Place sweetened grape juice in a large heavy enamel or stainless steel kettle (you can use the same one, rinsed out and dried), set over moderate heat and bring slowly to a simmer (190° F.). Pour simmering juice into hot jars, filling to within ¼" of the tops. Wipe jar rims and seal jars. Process for 10 minutes in a boiling water bath (212° F.). Remove jars from water bath, complete seals if necessary, and cool thoroughly. Check seals, label jars and store on a cool, dark, dry shelf.

COUNTRY KITCHEN GRAPE JAM
Makes About 6 Half-Pints

4 pounds stemmed Concord, Scuppernong or Muscadine grapes	*6 cups sugar*
⅔ cup water	*1 tablespoon lemon juice*

Wash the grapes well in cool water and drain. Peel the grapes; place the skins in a large heavy saucepan and the peeled grapes in a large, heavy, broad-bottomed enamel or stainless steel kettle. Add the water to the skins, cover, set over moderate heat and boil 20 minutes until skins are tender. Meanwhile, cover kettle of grapes and simmer about 20 minutes until grapes are mushy. Put grapes through a food mill or press through a fine sieve, forcing out as much pulp and liquid as possible. Return grape pulp to the kettle, add the grape skins and their liquid, the sugar and the lemon juice. Insert a candy thermometer. Set over moderate heat and bring slowly to a boil, uncovered. Stir frequently until sugar dissolves, then cook rapidly, uncovered and stirring occasionally, until mixture reaches the jelling point (the candy thermometer will register between 218° and 220° F.).

Meanwhile, wash and sterilize 6 half-pint preserving jars and their closures; keep jars and closures immersed in separate kettles of simmering water until you are ready to use them.

Pour boiling hot jam into hot jars, filling to within ¼" of the tops. Wipe jar rims and seal jars. Process for 10 minutes in a simmering water bath (185° F.). Remove jars from water bath, complete seals if necessary, and cool thoroughly. Check seals, label jars and store on a cool, dark, dry shelf.

GRAPE AND PECAN CONSERVE
Makes 6 to 7 Half-Pints

4 pounds stemmed Concord, Scuppernong or Muscadine grapes	1 teaspoon finely grated orange rind
	1 teaspoon finely grated lemon rind
⅔ cup water	1 cup moderately coarsely chopped pecans
6 cups sugar	

Wash grapes in cool water and drain; peel the grapes, then place the skins in a large heavy saucepan and the grapes in a large, heavy broad-bottomed enamel or stainless steel kettle. Add water to the grape skins, cover and boil 20 minutes until tender; reserve. At the same time, cover the kettle of grapes and boil gently about 20 minutes until grapes are mushy. Sieve the grapes, pressing out as much pulp and juice as possible. Return sieved grapes to kettle, mix in grape skins and their liquid, the sugar, orange and lemon rinds. Insert a candy thermometer. Stir well to mix, set over moderate heat and bring slowly to a boil, stirring until sugar dissolves. Raise heat slightly and boil rapidly, uncovered, stirring as needed to prevent scorching, for 10 minutes. Add the pecans and boil and stir about 5 minutes longer or until candy thermometer registers 220° F.

While the conserve cooks, wash and sterilize 7 half-pint preserving jars and their closures; keep jars and closures immersed in separate kettles of simmering water until you are ready to use them.

Pour boiling hot conserve into hot jars, filling to within ¼" of the tops. Wipe jar rims and seal jars. Process for 15 minutes in a simmering water bath (185° F.). Remove jars from water bath, complete seals if necessary, and cool completely. Check seals, label jars and store on a cool, dark, dry shelf.

OLD-FASHIONED GRAPE JELLY
Makes Enough to Fill 6 (8-ounce) Jelly Glasses

Grapes, and particularly wild grapes such as Scuppernongs, contain tartaric acid which, unless filtered out of the extracted grape juice, will crystallize and make grape jelly unpleasantly gritty. The trick, then, of sparkling, tender grape jelly is to let the extracted juice stand overnight in the refrigerator. Much of the tartaric acid will crystallize and sink to the bottom of the container, so that all you need do is pour off the juice, leaving the sediment behind. One other important point: If your grape jelly is to be the perfect consistency—quivery but firm enough to stand on its own when unmolded—you must use grapes that are *firm-tender*, not soft or mushy. If grapes are picked too green, the jelly will be stiff; if they are picked too ripe, it will be runny.

4½ pounds firm-ripe *Concord or Scup-*
  pernong grapes
1⅛ cups cold water (or to simplify the

measuring, 1 cup + 2 tablespoons)
Sugar (you will need ¾ cup for each 1 cup
  of extracted grape juice)

Stem the grapes and wash well in cool water; do not peel or seed (grape skins and seeds both contain pectin, which is what makes jelly jell; the skins, moreover, are what give the jelly is deep purple hue). Place the grapes and water in a large, heavy enamel or stainless steel kettle and crush well, using a potato masher. Cover the kettle and bring to a boil over high heat; reduce heat to moderate and let the grapes boil, covered, for 15 minutes.

Meanwhile, line 2 very large colanders with 4 thicknesses of damp cheesecloth, letting the ends overhang the colanders about 4″ all around; stand each colander in a very large mixing bowl. Or, if you have 2 jelly bags, dampen them with cold water, wring out and suspend from jelly bag stands, each set over a large mixing bowl.

Pour half of the grapes and juice into each colander or jelly bag and let drip through *undisturbed*. This will take an hour, perhaps two, but do not rush the process by squeezing the jelly bags or pressing the grapes through the colander. If you do, your jelly will be cloudy and granular. Simply go about your business and let the grape juice drip through at its own slow speed. When all juices have drained through, remove colanders or bags (again refrain from squeezing them). Combine the two lots of grape juice in a single bowl, cover and refrigerate overnight.

Next day, wash and sterilize 6 (8-ounce) jelly glasses and keep immersed in simmering water until you are ready to use them. Also melt paraffin for sealing the glasses.

Line a fine-mesh, large sieve with 4 thicknesses of damp cheesecloth and set over a large mixing bowl. Very slowly pour the grape juice through so as not to stir up the sediment at the bottom of the bowl. The sediment, it goes without saying, should be left behind in the bowl and not be poured into the strainer.

Measure the strained grape juice precisely and for each 1 cup of it, add ¾ cup sugar. Pour the sweetened juice into a very heavy, large enamel or stainless steel kettle and insert a candy thermometer. Set over high heat and bring quickly to the boil. Lower heat slightly, then boil the grape juice, uncovered and *without stirring,* until the candy thermometer reaches 218° F. Begin testing at once for sheeting, that is, take up a small amount of the hot mixture on a metal spoon, let cool, then tilt. If the drops slide together in a single jelly-like sheet, the jelly is done. If not, continue boiling until the jelly will sheet.

Remove kettle from heat, skim froth from jelly, then pour boiling hot into hot jelly glasses, filling each to within ¼″ of the top. Pour in a ⅛″ layer of melted paraffin, making sure that it touches the edges of the jelly glasses all around. If there are any bubbles in the paraffin, prick with a sterilized needle while the paraffin is still liquid. Cool jelly to room temperature, place metal caps on glasses, label and store on a cool, dark, dry shelf.

MELONS

Firm-ripe cantaloupes can be pickled, as can watermelon rind; see recipes. And all of the popular melon varieties (cantaloupe, crenshaw, honeydew, Persian and watermelon) can be cut into cubes or balls and frozen in sugar syrup. So much for the ways of conserving melons.

TO FREEZE: Amount of fresh melon needed to fill a 1-pint freezer container: Difficult to ascertain because melons vary so in size. You should, however, be able to cut enough melon cubes or balls from one large honeydew to fill two 1-pint containers.

1.   Prepare and chill enough *light (30%) sugar syrup* to pack the amount of melon you will be freezing. You'll need between ½ and ⅔ cup of syrup for each 1-pint container (directions for making the syrup are included under Sugar Syrups and Freezing Fruit; see index for page number).

2.   Pick melons shortly before you will freeze them, choosing those that are firm-fleshed, well-colored and full of flavor. Halve the melons, scoop out seeds, then cut the flesh into balls or cubes of about 1″.

3.   Pack the melon cubes or balls into 1-pint freezer containers, fitting as snugly as possible without crushing and filling to within ½″ of the tops. Pour in

enough chilled syrup to cover melon, at the same time leaving ½" head space. Snap on container lids, label and quick-freeze.

KEEPING TIME: About 6 months at 0° F.

PICKLED CANTALOUPE
Makes About 5 to 6 Pints

Pick cantaloupes a shade underripe for pickling. The flesh must be good and firm so that it will not soften. These pickles are somewhat like watermelon rind pickles, a bit sweeter and not quite so crisp. Making these pickles is a two-day job, so do not attempt it until you have time.

2 fairly large underripe cantaloupes (they should weigh about 3½ to 4 pounds each)
1 gallon cold water mixed with 1 cup pickling salt (brine)
6 pounds sugar
1 gallon cold water
3 cinnamon sticks, each broken in several places

2 tablespoons whole cloves, bruised
4 teaspoons whole allspice, bruised
3 (2") cubes of ginger root, peeled and scored with a knife in a crisscross fashion
3 blades of mace
1 quart cider vinegar

Halve the melons, scoop out seeds, then cut off skin and all green rind. Cut the pink flesh into ½" cubes or, if you prefer, into ½" balls using a melon baller (if you make melon balls, you will have about 1 pint less of pickles). Place the melon cubes or balls in a large heavy enamel or stainless steel kettle and pour in brine. Let stand uncovered for 3 hours at room temperature. Drain cantaloupe well in a large colander, rinse under a stream of cool water and drain well again. Rinse out kettle.

Place 4 pounds of the sugar in the kettle and mix in the water; set uncovered over moderate heat and bring slowly to the boil, stirring until sugar dissolves; boil rapidly for 5 minutes. Add cantaloupe, stir to mix, and boil uncovered for 5 minutes. Turn heat off, set lid on kettle, slightly askew, and let cantaloupe plump in the syrup overnight at room temperature.

In the morning, tie all the spices loosely in several thicknesses of cheesecloth and drop into kettle. Mix in the remaining 2 pounds of sugar and cider vinegar. Set uncovered over moderately low heat and bring slowly to a boil; continue to boil the cantaloupe, uncovered, stirring now and then, 15 to 20 minutes or until sparkling and clear.

Meanwhile, wash and rinse six 1-pint preserving jars and their closures; keep jars and closures immersed in separate kettles of simmering water until you are ready to use them.

Using a slotted spoon and a wide-mouth canning funnel to facilitate filling, pack the cantaloupe into the jars, shaking down firmly and filling to within ¼" of the tops. Pour in boiling pickling syrup to cover the pickles, at the same time leaving ¼" head space. Run a thin-blade spatula or table knife around inside edges of jars to release air bubbles. Wipe jar rims and seal jars.

Process jars for 10 minutes in a boiling water bath (212° F.). Remove jars from water bath, complete seals if necessary, and cool completely. Check seals, then label and store jars on a cool, dark, dry shelf.

MOTHER'S WATERMELON RIND PICKLES
Makes About 8 Pints

For watermelon rind pickles you need a rind at least ¾-inch thick and better yet, 1-inch thick. This old-fashioned, two-day recipe calls for individual whole spices tied in cheesecloth, but you can substitute, if you like, two (1¼-ounce) boxes mixed pickling spices. These pickles are both sweet and spicy.

8 pounds trimmed, thick watermelon rind (trimmed means trimmed both of green skin and any remnants of pink flesh)
1 cup pickling salt dissolved in 1 gallon cold water (brine)
1 gallon water (for cooking watermelon rind)
6 pounds sugar
4½ cups cider vinegar
1 quart water (for pickling syrup)
4 chili pequins (tiny dried whole hot red chili peppers)

2 cinnamon sticks, each broken in several places
2 blades of mace
2 tablespoons whole allspice
4 teaspoons whole cloves
1 tablespoon white mustard seeds
2 cardamom pods, lightly crushed
2 bay leaves, crumbled
2 pieces dried or fresh peeled ginger root, each about 1" long, cracked or crushed
1 lemon, sliced and seeded

Cut the watermelon rind in 1" cubes. Place in a very large enamel or stainless steel kettle, add brine, cover and let stand 12 hours or overnight.

Next day, drain and rinse the rind. Also rinse the kettle. Add drained rind to kettle along with 1 gallon clear water and cook, uncovered, over moderate heat until crisp-tender, about 10 to 15 minutes; drain rind well in a large colander. Place sugar, vinegar and 1 quart water in kettle and stir to mix. Tie chili pequins, all spices and lemon slices loosely in a double thickness of cheesecloth and drop into kettle.

Set uncovered over moderately high heat and boil uncovered for 10 minutes, stirring until sugar dissolves. Add the well-drained rind and when mixture returns to the boil, cook uncovered until watermelon rind is sparkling and clear—approximately 15 to 20 minutes.

Meanwhile, wash and rinse eight 1-pint preserving jars and their closures; keep jars and closures immersed in separate kettles of simmering water until you are ready to use them.

When the pickles are done, remove spice bag. Using a wide-mouth canning funnel and a slotted spoon, pack hot pickles into hot jars, filling to within ¼″ of the tops. Pour enough boiling pickling syrup into each jar to cover pickles, at the same time leaving ¼″ head space. Run a thin-blade spatula or table knife around inside edges of jars to release air bubbles. Wipe jar rims and seal jars.

Process jars for 5 minutes in a boiling water bath (212° F.). Remove jars from water bath, complete seals if necessary and cool completely. Check seals, label jars and store on a cool, dark, dry shelf. Let the pickles mellow for about a month before serving.

PEACHES AND NECTARINES

Nectarines are a variety of peach—smooth-skinned, smaller than the average peach, sweeter and juicier. Like peaches, they may be successfully canned or frozen and the techniques, with few exceptions, are the same.

TO CAN: Clingstone peaches hold their shape better in canning than the freestone varieties, however they are more difficult to pit ("clingstone," not surprisingly, means that the stones or pits cling to the flesh. Pink-red fibers hold them fast and these, for cosmetic reasons, should be removed along with the pits. If left in the peach hollows, they will turn a dreary brown during processing). Peaches and nectarines will both darken in canning unless they are dipped in acidulated water as soon as they are peeled and cut. Peaches may be canned either as halves or slices but nectarines, being smaller and softer, can more satisfactorily as halves. Either may be packed RAW or HOT (raw peaches and nectarines will be slightly firmer, those packed hot will fill the jar more uniformly and attractively). *Amount of fresh peaches or nectarines needed to fill a 1-quart preserving jar:* 2 to 2½ pounds.

Cold (Raw) Pack:

1. Pick peaches or nectarines that are firm-ripe, full of bouquet, unbruised and unblemished and do so as soon as possible before you will can them. Sort the fruits according to size, then wash only enough for a single canner load (these fruits are unusually perishable, so it's best to work with small quan-

tities). Drain fruit, then place in a mesh basket, scald 30 seconds in boiling water to loosen the skins and plunge immediately in cold water to chill. Working with one piece of fruit at a time, slip off the skin, halve and pit. Leave nectarine halves intact, but, if you wish, slice the peaches about ¼" thick. As soon as each fruit is peeled and cut, immerse in 1 gallon of cold water mixed with 2 tablespoons each of salt and cider vinegar (this helps preserve the golden color).

2. Prepare enough *medium sugar syrup* to pack the quantity of fruit you intend to can. Directions for making the syrup are included under Sugar Syrups for Canning Fruit; see index for page number. You will need 1 to 1½ cups syrup for each 1-quart jar of fruit.

3. Fill hot 1-pint or 1-quart preserving jars, one at a time, packing the raw fruit fairly firmly and arranging the halves, hollow sides down and slightly overlapping. Fill jars to within ½" of the tops. Pour enough boiling syrup into jars to cover fruit, at the same time leaving ½" head space. Run a thin-blade spatula or table knife around inside edges of jars to free trapped air bubbles.

4. Wipe jar rims and seal jars. Process in a boiling water bath (212° F.), allowing 25 minutes for pints and 30 minutes for quarts.

5. Remove jars from water bath, complete seals if necessary, and cool thoroughly. Check seals, then label jars and store on a cool, dark, dry shelf.

Hot Pack:

1. & 2. The same as for 1. & 2. under COLD PACK (above).

3. Bring the sugar syrup to a gentle boil in a large enamel or stainless steel kettle, then cook a few peaches or nectarines (about what it will take to fill one jar) in the syrup just long enough to heat them through–2 to 3 minutes. Using a slotted spoon, lift fruit to a hot 1-pint or 1-quart preserving jar, arranging halves hollow sides down and slightly overlapping. Fill jar to within ½" of the top. Pour in enough boiling syrup to cover fruit, at the same time leaving ½" head space. Run a thin-blade spatula or table knife around inside edge of jar to release air bubbles. Wipe jar rim and seal jar. Repeat until you have filled and sealed enough jars for one canner load.

4. Process jars in a boiling water bath (212° F.), allowing 20 minutes for pints and 25 minutes for quarts.

5. The same as for COLD PACK (above).
KEEPING TIME: About one year.

TO FREEZE: Nectarines fare best if sliced and packed in sugar syrup. As for peaches, slices will freeze more successfully than halves. They may be packed *either* in syrup or in dry sugar. *Amount of fresh peaches or nectarines needed to fill a 1-pint freezer container:* About 1 to 1½ pounds.

Sliced Peaches or Nectarines (Syrup Pack):

1.   Prepare enough *medium (40%) sugar syrup* to pack the quantity of fruit you will be freezing. You will need between ½ and ⅔ cup of syrup for each 1-pint freezer container. Directions for making the syrup are included under Sugar Syrups for Freezing Fruits; see index for page number. Measure the total quantity of syrup, and for every 1 quart of it, add ½ teaspoon powdered or crystalline ascorbic acid. Chill the syrup well.

2.   Pick tree-ripe, firm, richly colored and well-flavored peaches or nectarines. Wash well in cool water and drain. Working with one piece of fruit at a time, peel, pit and slice directly into a 1-pint freezer carton containing ½ cup of chilled syrup. Fill the carton as fast as you can, shaking the fruit down lightly and filling to within ½" of the top. Press fruit down gently, then pour in enough additional cold syrup to cover it, at the same time leaving ½" head space. Snap lid on container, label and quick-freeze. Repeat until you have frozen all the fruit you have picked.

Sliced Peaches (Sugar Pack)

1.   Pick plump, ripe fruits in the peak of condition minutes before you will freeze them. Wash in cool water and drain. Peel, pit and slice, working with only 5 to 6 peaches at a time and wasting no time lest they darken. Measure sliced peaches, then to each 1 quart, add ⅔ cup sugar and ¼ cup water mixed with ¼ teaspoon powdered or crystalline ascorbic acid. Toss gently to mix.

2.   Pack in 1-pint freezer containers, shaking the fruit down lightly for a more compact fit and filling each container to within ½" of the top. Snap on lids, label and quick-freeze.

KEEPING TIME: About one year at 0° F. For higher quality, serve within 6 months.

TO DRY: You can't do it safely at home without special low-temperature drying equipment.

TO PICKLE AND PRESERVE: See the recipe collection below.

TO STORE IN A ROOT CELLAR: There's no point in trying. Neither peaches nor nectarines can be held at home in cold storage.

196

BRANDIED OR BOURBONED PEACHES OR APRICOTS
Makes 6 to 8 Pints

A favorite Southern way to pack peaches or apricots is in smooth, well-aged bourbon instead of in brandy. Try it.

6 pounds small firm-ripe peaches or apricots
1 gallon cold water mixed with 1 teaspoon ascorbic acid and 1 tablespoon citric acid (acidulated water)
6 cups water

6 cups sugar
Brandy or bourbon (you will need 1 cup of brandy or bourbon for each 1 cup of syrup used to pack the peaches or apricots, about 3 cups in all)

Wash and rinse eight 1-pint preserving jars and their closures; keep jars and closures immersed in separate kettles of simmering water until you are ready to use them.

Blanch the peaches or apricots, about 2 pounds at a time, in boiling water for 30 seconds; plunge in ice water to quick-chill. Slip the skins off the fruit and let the peeled whole fruit fall directly into the cold acidulated water (this is to prevent discoloring).

Place water and sugar in a large heavy enamel or stainless steel kettle, set uncovered over moderate heat and bring to a boil; reduce heat slightly so that liquid simmers gently, then add peaches or apricots, 6 to 8 at a time and boil 5 minutes. With a slotted spoon, lift fruit from the syrup and pack as firmly and attractively as possible in hot jars, filling to within ¼" of the tops. Repeat until all peaches have been cooked and packed.

Insert a candy thermometer in the kettle of syrup and boil rapidly, uncovered, until syrup reaches 220° F. Turn heat off and let syrup cool for 5 minutes. Measure out 3 cups of the syrup and mix in 3 cups of brandy or bourbon. Place in a medium-size saucepan and heat just to the simmering point; do not boil. Pour enough hot syrup into each jar to cover fruit, at the same time leaving ¼" head space. Run a thin-blade spatula or table knife around inside edges of jars to release air bubbles. Wipe jar rims and seal jars.

Process jars for 10 minutes in a boiling water bath (212° F.). Remove jars from water bath, complete seals if necessary and cool thoroughly. Check seals, label jars and store on a cool, dark, dry shelf. Let the peaches or apricots "age" for about 6 weeks before serving.

PEACH JAM
Makes About 8 Half-Pints

Make the jam spicy or make it plain. It is delicious either way. Because the peaches must all be pitted, you will find that the preparation goes about twice as fast if you use the freestone varieties instead of the clingstone. This recipe works equally well with nectarines.

18 to 20 medium-size, juicy, ripe peaches	*1½ teaspoons whole cloves (optional)*
½ cup water	*2 blades of mace (optional)*
Sugar (you will need ¾ cup sugar for each	*1 cinnamon stick, broken into several pieces*
1 cup of peach mixture)	*(optional)*
2 tablespoons lemon juice	

Wash peaches well in cool water and drain; blanch peaches in boiling water for 30 seconds, quick-chill in ice water, then slip off the skins. Pit the peaches and slice thin directly into a large, heavy enamel or stainless steel kettle. Mash the peaches with a potato masher, add the water and simmer uncovered about 10 minutes until peaches are soft. Measure the peach mixture and for every 1 cup of it, add ¾ cup sugar; return to kettle, add lemon juice and, if you like, the spices tied in cheesecloth. Insert a candy thermometer, bring to a boil over moderate heat, then boil, uncovered, stirring often, until mixture is glossy and thick (218° to 220° F. on the candy thermometer). The jam should be done in 15 to 20 minutes, but to test, take a little of the hot mixture up on a metal spoon, cool, then tilt; if drops slide together in a single sheet, the jam is done. Remove spice bag.

While jam cooks, wash and sterilize 8 half-pint preserving jars and their closures; keep jars and closures immersed in separate kettles of simmering water until you are ready to use them.

Pour the boiling hot jam into hot preserving jars, filling to within ¼" of the tops. Wipe jar rims and seal jars. Process for 10 minutes in a simmering water bath (185° F.). Remove jars from water bath, complete seals if necessary and cool thoroughly. Check seals, label jars and store on a cool, dark, dry shelf.

GEORGIA PEACH BUTTER
Makes 3 to 4 Pints

A smooth amber spread that is delicious on fresh-baked biscuits or toasted English muffins. Try spreading it on buttered waffles, too, instead of drizzling them with syrup. For best results, use fully ripe peaches that are at their peak of flavor. Leave the butter plain, or spice it, if you like (the spices are listed as optional ingredients in the recipe below).

18 medium-size juicily ripe peaches
1 cup water
Sugar (you will need ½ cup of sugar for
    each 1 cup of peach purée)
1 teaspoon finely grated orange rind
    (optional)

1 teaspoon ground ginger (optional)
½ teaspoon ground mace (optional)
¼ teaspoon ground cinnamon (optional)

Blanch the peaches in enough boiling water to cover for 30 seconds, then plunge in a large pan of ice water to quick-chill. Peel and pit the peaches, then chop fairly coarsely. Place the peaches and the water in a very large heavy kettle, cover, set over moderately low heat and bring to a boil. Continue cooking the peaches until they are soft enough to purée–about 15 to 20 minutes. Watch them closely and stir or add a little additional water as needed to keep them from scorching. Press the peaches through a fine sieve or put through a food mill. Measure the peach pulp carefully, then for each 1 cup of it, add ½ cup of sugar.

Place the sweetened peach pulp in a very heavy, broad-bottomed, large kettle. Add the optional orange rind and spices if you like. Set uncovered over moderate heat and bring slowly to the boil, stirring until sugar dissolves. Continue cooking uncovered (the mixture should bubble gently) for 30 to 40 minutes until very thick–about the consistency of jam–and translucent. You'll have to watch the kettle carefully and stir almost constantly to keep the peach butter from burning.

While the peach butter cooks, wash and sterilize four 1-pint preserving jars and their closures; keep jars and closures immersed in separate kettles of simmering water until you are ready to use them.

Pour the boiling hot peach butter into hot jars, filling to within ¼" of the tops. Wipe jar rims and seal jars. Process for 10 minutes in a simmering water bath (185° F.). Remove jars from water bath, complete seals if necessary, then cool thoroughly. Check seals, label jars and store on a cool, dark, dry shelf.

PEARS

Pears can better than they freeze, and they preserve even better still (see recipe collection that follows). Pears cannot be dried satisfactorily at home without especially built dryers. But they can be held several months in a basement root cellar if the temperature is sufficiently low and the humidity sufficiently high.

TO CAN: Bartletts are the preferred "canning pears" because they hold their shape so well under processing. Kieffer pears may also be canned, but don't expect them to be as attractive or fine-textured as the Bartletts. Both varieties should be picked while they are still pale green and quite hard, then brought indoors and ripened in a cool spot (60° to 65° F.) before they are canned. Bartletts should ripen in a week to 10 days, Kieffers in 2 to 3 weeks. Like apples, pears will darken unless they are treated with an anti-browning agent, and because they must be partially cooked before they are canned, they are packed *HOT* only. *Amount of fresh pears needed to fill a 1-quart preserving jar:* 2 to 3 pounds, when packed as halves (the most handsome way to pack them).

Hot Pack:

1. Prepare enough *light sugar syrup* to pack all of the pears you intend to can. You will need from 1 to 1½ cups of syrup for each 1-quart jar. Directions for preparing the syrup are included under Sugar Syrups for Canning Fruit; see index for page number. TIP: For spicy canned pears, add 2 cinnamon sticks to the syrup; for orange or lemon-flavored ones, add 2 long thin strips of orange or lemon peel (remove peel from the orange or lemon with a vegetable peeler so that you get the colored part only, not the bitter white under-rind). Remove cinnamon or rind from syrup before packing pears in jars.

2. Remove from cool storage only those pears that are uniformly firm-soft, blemish-free and full of bouquet. Stem the pears, sort according to size, wash in cool water and drain. Peel the pears, halve and core, making sure that you cut away all grittiness around the cores. Leave the pears as halves, or halve each half lengthwise. As soon as the pears are peeled and cut, immerse in 1 gallon of cold water mixed with 1 teaspoon ascorbic acid and 1 tablespoon citric acid (or if you prefer, 1 gallon cold water mixed with 2 tablespoons each salt and cider vinegar). The acidulated water bath helps keep the pears creamy-white.

3. Place the sugar syrup in a large heavy enamel or stainless steel kettle (include cinnamon sticks, orange or lemon peel, if you like) and bring slowly to a boil. Add pears and simmer uncovered for 5 minutes.

4. Pack the hot pears into hot 1-pint or 1-quart preserving jars, arranging them as compactly and attractively as possible and filling the jars to within ½" of the tops. Pour in enough boiling syrup to cover the pears, at the same time allowing ½" head space. Run a thin-blade spatula or table knife around inside edges of jars to free air bubbles.

5. Wipe jar rims and seal jars. Process in a boiling water bath (212° F.), allowing 20 minutes for pints and 25 minutes for quarts.

6. Remove jars from water bath, complete seals if necessary and cool completely. Check seals, then label and store on a cool, dark, dry shelf.
KEEPING TIME: About one year.

TO STORE PEARS IN A ROOT CELLAR: Anjou, Bosc and Comice pears will all hold well for several months in a basement root cellar if you can maintain the temperatures at 32° F., the humidity between 85% and 90% and keep the circulation of air at a minimum. Bartletts and Kieffers can also be stored in the basement root cellar, although for a shorter period of time (about 2 months).

Pick the pears while they are pale (not dark) green and hard, then bring them indoors without delay. To condition the pears for cold storage, let them stand in a cool (60° to 65° F.) spot for one week. Sort the pears carefully, rejecting for cold storage any that show blemishes or signs of softening. Wrap the perfect pears individually in tissue, then layer into perforated cardboard cartons lined with perforated polyethylene sheets (each sheet should have about 10 to 12 evenly spaced perforations measuring about ¼″ in diameter). Cover the pears loosely with another perforated plastic sheet. Store in the fruit section of the basement root cellar and check the pears from time to time, discarding at once any that show signs of decay.

KEEPING TIME: 2 to 6 months.

JEAN ANDERSON'S GREEN THUMB PRESERVING GUIDE

PICKLED PEARS
Makes 6 to 8 Pints

You will find that Seckel pears are particularly suited to pickling—they are small enough to pack prettily in jars and firm enough to hold their shape. The pears will develop more uniform flavor and texture if they are plumped overnight in the pickling syrup, so begin this recipe one afternoon and finish it the following morning.

6 pounds firm-ripe Seckel pears
1 gallon cold water mixed with 1 teaspoon ascorbic acid and 1 tablespoon citric acid (acidulated water)
2 cups white vinegar
1 cup cider vinegar
3 cups water
6 cups sugar
2 cinnamon sticks, each broken in several pieces

3 blades of mace
1 tablespoon whole allspice, bruised
2 (2") cubes fresh ginger root, peeled and bruised (optional)
2 long thin strips of lemon rind (the yellow part only)
Whole cloves (you will need 2 cloves for each pear)

Wash the pears well in cool water, then pare, leaving the stems on. As you peel each pear, drop into the acidulated water so that it will not darken. Place the white and cider vinegars, the water and sugar in a large, heavy, enamel or stainless steel kettle. Tie the cinnamon, mace, allspice, ginger if you like, and the lemon rind loosely in several thicknesses of cheesecloth and drop into kettle. Set uncovered over moderate heat and bring to a boil. Working with about 6 pears at a time, lift them from the acidulated water and stud each with 2 cloves. Drop into boiling syrup and boil uncovered for 15 minutes, just until the pears are firm-tender. Using a slotted spoon, lift cooked pears to a large bowl. Continue studding the pears with cloves and cooking them, no more than 6 at a time, until all of them are cooked. Remove kettle of boiling syrup from the stove, add all pears, cover and let plump overnight at room temperature.

Next day, wash and rinse eight 1-pint preserving jars and their closures; keep jars and closures immersed in separate kettles of simmering water until you are ready to use them.

Lift the cold pears from the pickling syrup and pack as snugly and attractively as possible in hot preserving jars, filling each to within ¼" of the tops. Bring syrup rapidly to a boil, remove spice bag, then pour enough syrup into each jar to cover pears, at the same time leaving ¼" head space. Run a thin-blade spatula or table knife around inside edges of jars to free air bubbles. Wipe jar rims and seal jars.

Process for 15 minutes in a boiling water bath (212° F.). Remove jars from water bath, complete seals if necessary and cool thoroughly. Check seals, label jars and store on a cool, dark, dry shelf. Wait 4 to 6 weeks before serving the pears so that they will have a chance to develop flavor.

SPICY PEAR AND PEPPER RELISH
Makes About 8 Pints

A sweet and spicy pickle relish that partners well with roast pork or chicken or baked ham. For best results, use a firm pear–a Bartlett, for example–that will not soften too much during cooking and processing.

1 gallon peeled, cored and diced firm-ripe pears	*½ cup pickling salt*
8 medium-size sweet red peppers, cored, seeded and coarsely chopped	*4 cups sugar*
	2 teaspoons celery seeds
6 medium-size sweet green peppers, cored, seeded and coarsely chopped	*2 teaspoons ground cinnamon*
	2 teaspoons powdered mustard
6 medium-size yellow onions, peeled and coarsely chopped	*1 teaspoon white pepper*
	½ teaspoon ground mace
	1 quart white vinegar

Place pears, red and green peppers and onions in a very large bowl, sprinkle with salt, toss lightly, then let stand uncovered at room temperature for 3 hours. Drain well, rinse thoroughly and drain again, pressing out as much liquid as possible.

Wash and rinse eight 1-pint preserving jars and their closures; keep jars and closures immersed in separate kettles of simmering water until needed.

In a very large heavy enamel or stainless steel kettle mix sugar with celery seeds, cinnamon, mustard, pepper and mace; stir in vinegar. Set uncovered over moderate heat and bring just to boiling, stirring until sugar dissolves. Add pear mixture and as soon as it comes to a boil, cook and stir for 4 minutes—no longer or pears will overcook.

Ladle hot relish into hot jars, filling to within ⅛" of the tops and making sure that the pickling liquid covers the relish. Run a thin-blade spatula or knife around inside edges of jars to remove air bubbles; wipe jar rims and seal jars.

Process for 10 minutes in a boiling water bath (212° F.). Remove jars from water bath, complete seals if necessary and cool completely. Check seals, label jars and store on a cool, dark, dry shelf. Let the relish mellow for 4 to 6 weeks before serving.

203

NATCHEZ TRACE PEAR HONEY
Makes About 4 Half-Pints

For this recipe you will need a variety of pear that will soften to mush in cooking–Anjou, for example, or Bosc. For best results, the pears should be juicily ripe and full of bouquet. They will turn brown as you grind them, in fact they will all but disintegrate. But no matter. The finished pear honey will be smooth and the color of amber. Serve with fresh-baked biscuits or rolls. Or spread on toast.

1 quart peeled, cored and moderately coarsely ground ripe pears (you will need 10 to 12 medium-size to large pears)
3 lemons, quartered, seeded and finely ground (rind, pulp and all)
4 cups sugar
½ teaspoon ground ginger
¼ teaspoon ground nutmeg or mace

Place all ingredients in a large, heavy, broad-bottomed kettle and stir well to mix. Insert a candy thermometer. Set uncovered over low heat and bring slowly to a boil. Raise heat slightly and boil, uncovered, stirring often, for about 1 hour or until the color and consistency of a thick, amber honey (the candy thermometer will register between 218° and 220° F. when the mixture is the right consistency).

Meanwhile, wash and sterilize 4 half-pint preserving jars and their closures. Keep jars and closures immersed in separate kettles of simmering water until you are ready to use them.

Using a wide-mouth canning funnel, ladle pear honey into jars, filling to within ¼″ of the tops. Wipe jar rims and seal jars. Process for 10 minutes in a simmering water bath (185° F.). Remove jars from water bath, complete seals if necessary, and cool completely. Check seals, label jars and store on a cool, dark, dry shelf.

PLUMS

TO CAN: If you are to can plums successfully, you must choose a firm-fleshed variety such as the Green Gage. The soft and succulent Japanese plums are far too fragile to withstand the heat of processing. For best results, can plums whole–unpeeled and unpitted. Warm them gently in sugar syrup, then allow them to plump in the syrup, off heat, before you pack them so that they will hold their shape. *Amount of fresh plums needed to fill a 1-quart preserving jar:* 1½ to 2½ pounds.

Hot Pack (the preferred method of canning plums):

1. Pick firm-ripe plums free of blemishes and full of flavor shortly before you

204

will can them. Wash the plums well in cool water and drain. Do not pit or peel. Prick the plums with a sterilized needle to help keep them from bursting as they process. The skins will probably split, but if you prick the plums, they should hold their shape reasonably well.

2. Prepare enough *medium or heavy sugar syrup* (depending upon natural sweetness of the plums) to pack all of the plums you have picked. You will need from 1 to 1½ cups of syrup for each 1-quart jar. Directions for preparing the syrup are included under Sugar Syrups for Canning Fruit; see index for page number.

3. Place the syrup in a large heavy enamel or stainless steel kettle and bring slowly to the boil. Add the plums (but no more than enough for two layers in the kettle) and simmer 2 minutes. Remove kettle from the heat, cover, and let the plums stand in the syrup for 30 minutes.

4. Pack the plums into hot 1-pint or 1-quart preserving jars, fitting in as snugly and attractively as possible and filling jars to within ½" of the tops. Bring the sugar syrup to a boil, then pour enough into each jar to cover plums, at the same time leaving ½" head space. Run a thin-blade spatula or table knife around inside edge of each jar to release air bubbles.

5. Wipe jar rims and seal jars. Process in a boiling water bath (212° F.), allowing 20 minutes for pints and 25 minutes for quarts.

6. Remove jars from water bath, complete seals if necessary, and cool thoroughly. Check seals, label jars and store on a cool, dark, dry shelf.
KEEPING TIME: About one year.

TO FREEZE: How you intend to use frozen plums determines how you should pack them for the freezer. If you plan to use them for making jams, freeze them whole without either syrup or sugar. But if you will later make them into puddings or pies, halve, quarter or purée them, sweeten with syrup or sugar, then freeze. Plums, like peaches and apricots, will darken when peeled and cut open unless treated with an anti-browning agent. *Amount of fresh plums needed to fill a 1-pint freezer container:* About ¾ pound if packed whole, 1 to 1½ pounds if halved, quartered or puréed.

Whole Plums (Unsweetened):

1. Pick tree-ripe, firm-soft, blemish-free plums shortly before you will freeze them. Wash well in cool water and drain.

2. Pack whole (without syrup or sugar) into 1-pint or 1-quart freezer containers, filling to within ½" of the tops. Snap lids on containers, label and quick-freeze. *NOTE:* These plums are most suited to making jam; however, you can thaw them and serve whole as dessert. For best results, dip the solidly frozen fruit in cold water for 5 to 10 seconds. Peel, then let thaw in enough chilled *medium (40%) sugar syrup* to cover. Directions for making the syrup are included under Sugar Syrups for Freezing Fruit; see index for page number.

Halved or Quartered Plums (Syrup Pack):

1.   Prepare enough *heavy (50%) sugar syrup* to pack the quantity of plums you will be freezing. You will need ½ to ⅔ cup of syrup for each 1-pint freezer container. (Directions for making the syrup are included under Sugar Syrups for Freezing Fruit; see index for page number.) Measure the total quantity of syrup, and for every 1 quart of it, add ½ teaspoon powdered or crystalline ascorbic acid. Chill the syrup well.

2.   Gather the plums just before you are ready to freeze them, selecting those that are firm-ripe, richly colored and full of flavor. Reject any showing signs of insect damage or bruises. Wash the plums in cool water and drain. Do not peel. Halve the plums and remove pits; leave as halves or cut into quarters.

3.   Pack plums into 1-pint freezer containers, shaking them down lightly and filling to within ½" of the tops. Pour in enough cold syrup to cover plums, at the same time leaving ½" head space. Snap on lids, label containers and quick-freeze.

Plum Purée:

1.   Pick perfect, tree-ripe plums of deep color. Wash in cool water and drain. If the plums are soft enough, you can peel them, pit them and press through a fine sieve without heating. But if they are firm, you will need to cook them briefly before you purée them. Measure the peeled, halved and pitted plums and for every 1 gallon of them, add 1 cup of cold water. Place in a large heavy enamel or stainless steel kettle, bring slowly to a boil, then cook uncovered for 2 minutes. Cool plums and press through a fine sieve.

2.   Measure the plum purée (whether raw or cooked) and to each 1 quart of it add ¼ teaspoon powdered or crystalline ascorbic acid and, depending upon the natural sweetness of the fruit, from ½ to 1 cup sugar.

3.   Pack the purée tightly into 1-pint freezer containers, filling to within ½" of the tops. Place lids on containers, label and quick-freeze.
    KEEPING TIME: About one year at 0° F.
TO DRY: It's true that plums are dried commercially into prunes, but you cannot dry them successfully at home without special low-heat dryers.

TO PICKLE AND PRESERVE: Plums (and particularly Damsons) make splendid jams, sauces and preserves (see recipes below).

TO STORE IN A ROOT CELLAR: It can't be done.

ORIENTAL PLUM SAUCE
Makes 4 to 6 Half-Pints

Chinese-style plum sauce that is both tart and sweet. Serve with roast pork, duckling, goose or chicken.

4 cups finely chopped, peeled and pitted fresh sweet purple plums (include all juice)

2 cups finely chopped, peeled and pitted fresh apricots (include all juice)

2 cups finely chopped, peeled and pitted fresh loquats, nectarines or peaches (include all juice)

2 cups finely chopped, peeled and cored Greening apples (include all juice)

1 large sweet red pepper, cored, seeded and minced as fine as possible (include all juice)

3 cups granulated sugar

1 cup firmly packed light brown sugar

2½ cups cider vinegar

1 cinnamon stick, broken in several places

1 tablespoon whole cloves, bruised

2 long thin strips of orange rind (the orange part only)

Place all the chopped fruits, the sweet pepper, the granulated sugar, brown sugar and vinegar in a large, heavy, broad-bottomed enamel or stainless steel kettle. Tie the cinnamon, cloves and orange rind loosely in several thicknesses of cheesecloth and drop into kettle. Cover, set over moderate heat and bring slowly to the boil; boil, covered, for 15 to 20 minutes until fruits are very soft. Lift spice bag from kettle and reserve. Purée the kettle mixture in a food mill or press through a fine sieve, extracting as much pulp and liquid as possible. Return purée and spice bag to kettle and boil gently, uncovered and stirring often, for about 1 hour or until very glossy and thick—slightly thinner than catsup.

Meanwhile, wash and sterilize 6 half-pint preserving jars and their closures. Keep jars and closures immersed in separate kettles of simmering water until you are ready to use them.

Pour boiling sauce into hot preserving jars, filling to within ¼" of the tops and shaking it down for a more compact fit. Wipe jar rims and seal jars. Process for 10 minutes in a simmering water bath (185° F.). Remove jars from water bath, complete seals if necessary and cool thoroughly. Check seals, label jars and store on a cool, dark, dry shelf.

PLUM PRESERVES
Makes 4 to 5 Half-Pints

The principal difference between preserves and jams is the size of the fruit. For jams they are coarsely chopped, for preserves they are left whole or halved. Always use tart plums for making jams and preserves because only they will have sufficient pectin to give the jams and preserves body. The small black Damsons are far and away the best choice.

2½ to 3 pounds firm-ripe Damson plums, washed, halved and pitted but not peeled (you will need 5 cups of halved plums)
1 cup water

4 cups sugar
1 teaspoon finely grated orange or lemon rind
⅛ teaspoon ground mace or nutmeg

Wash and sterilize 5 half-pint preserving jars and their closures; keep jars and closures immersed in separate kettles of simmering water until you are ready to use them.

Place all ingredients in a large, heavy, broad-bottomed enamel or stainless steel kettle and set uncovered over moderate heat. Insert a candy thermometer. Bring slowly to the boil, then boil uncovered for 15 to 20 minutes until preserves are thick and glossy (218° to 220° F. on the candy thermometer). Stir often and watch the kettle closely lest the preserves scorch.

Ladle boiling hot preserves into hot jars, filling to within ¼" of the tops. Wipe jar rims and seal jars. Process for 15 minutes in a simmering water bath (185° F.). Remove jars from water bath, complete seals if necessary and cool completely. Check seals, label jars and store on a cool, dark, dry shelf.

PLUM JAM
Makes About 8 Half-Pints

For a delicately spicy jam, tuck a cinnamon stick into the plums as they cook, then remove before pouring jam into jars.

4½ to 5 pounds Damson plums, washed, pitted and coarsely chopped but not peeled (you will need 2 quarts chopped plums in all)
6 cups sugar

1½ cups water
2 tablespoons lemon juice
2 tablespoons orange juice
1 cinnamon stick (optional)

Wash and sterilize 8 half-pint preserving jars and their closures; keep jars and closures immersed in separate kettles of simmering water until you are ready to use them.

Place all ingredients in a large, heavy, broad-bottomed enamel or stainless steel kettle and set uncovered over moderate heat. Insert a candy thermometer. Bring slowly to the boil, then boil uncovered for 20 to 25 minutes, stirring frequently to prevent sticking, until thermometer registers 218° to 220° F. and jam is thick and glossy. To test for doneness, take a little of the hot jam up on a metal spoon, cool, then tilt; if drops slide together in a single sheet, the jam is done. Remove cinnamon stick, if used.

Pour boiling hot jam into hot jars, filling to within ¼″ of the tops. Wipe jar rims and seal jars. Process for 10 minutes in a simmering water bath (185° F.). Remove jars from water bath, complete seals if necessary, and cool to room temperature. Check seals, label jars and store on a cool, dry, dark shelf.

BAKED PLUM PUDDING
Makes 8 Servings

If you have frozen plum purée on hand, try this spicy plum pudding. It is not the English steamed plum pudding of Christmas (which, in truth, rarely contains plums), but a moist baked pudding that should be served warm–not hot–with gobs of softly whipped cream.

1 pint frozen plum purée, thawed completely
1 cup sugar
¼ cup firmly packed light brown sugar
3 eggs, lightly beaten
1¾ cups milk
2 cups sifted all-purpose flour
1 teaspoon baking soda
¾ teaspoon salt
¾ teaspoon ground ginger
½ teaspoon ground cinnamon
½ teaspoon ground mace
⅓ cup melted butter
2 teaspoons finely grated orange rind
1 teaspoon finely grated lemon rind

Place the thawed plum purée in a large mixing bowl, add the sugar and brown sugar and beat hard until no lumps of brown sugar remain. Stir in eggs and milk and set aside. Sift the flour with the soda, salt, ginger, cinnamon and mace into a second large mixing bowl.

Combine the melted butter with the grated orange and lemon rinds and let steep 2 to 3 minutes.

Make a well in the center of the sifted dry ingredients, then add the plum mixture, about a third of it at a time, beating after each addition only enough to combine the ingredients (overbeating will toughen the pudding). Stir in the melted butter. orange and lemon rinds and mix until blended.

Pour into a well-buttered, shallow 3-quart baking dish and bake uncovered in a slow oven (300° F.) for about 1 hour and 15 minutes or until a table knife inserted in the center of the pudding comes out clean. Remove pudding from oven and cool about 20 minutes before serving. Top each portion with softly whipped cream.

QUINCES

These ancient Oriental fruits are so hard and astringent that they cannot be eaten raw. They do, however, make supremely fragrant jellies and preserves as the following recipes prove.

GINGERED QUINCE PRESERVES
Makes About 4 Half-Pints

3 cups sugar
2 quarts water
3 to 3½ pounds firm-ripe quinces, peeled,
  quartered and cored (you will need 7

cups of cut-up quinces in all)
⅓ cup finely slivered crystallized ginger
1 teaspoon finely grated lemon rind

Place sugar and water in a very large, heavy, broad-bottomed enamel or stainless steel kettle and insert a candy thermometer. Set uncovered over moderate heat and boil 5 minutes to make a syrup. Add the quinces, the ginger and lemon rind and boil gently uncovered, stirring often, until thick and clear. This will take about 1 hour, perhaps longer, but when the preserves are the right consistency, the candy thermometer will register 218° F.

Toward the end of cooking wash and sterilize 4 half-pint preserving jars and their closures; keep jars and closures immersed in separate kettles of simmering water until you are ready to use them.

When preserves are the right consistency, ladle boiling hot into hot jars, filling to within ¼" of the tops. Wipe jar rims and seal jars. Process for 15 minutes in a simmering water bath (185° F.). Remove jars from water bath, complete seals if necessary, and cool completely. Check seals, label jars, and store on a cool, dark, dry shelf.

COLONIAL QUINCE JELLY
Makes Enough To Fill 3 to 4 (8-ounce) Jelly Glasses

Quinces cook into a lovely, tender jelly. Their natural pectin content is high, so you will not need to add any of the commercial pectin preparations. To be on the safe side—that is, to make certain your quince jelly will jell—you should test the extracted juices for pectin content so that you will know precisely the right amount of sugar to add. Too much sugar will make for a runny jelly, too little sugar a waxy one. (Two methods for determining pectin content are explained under How to Test Fruit Juices for Pectin Content; see index for page number.)

1 pound slightly underripe quinces, washed and stemmed
3 pounds firm-ripe quinces, washed and stemmed
Water (you will need 2 cups of water for each 4 cups of sliced quinces)

Sugar (the amount you will need will depend upon the amount of natural pectin contained in the extracted quince juice; usually ¾ cup of sugar per 1 cup of extracted juice will make a jelly of just the right consistency)

Slice the quinces (skins, cores and all), then measure. For each 4 cups (1 quart) of sliced quinces, add 2 cups (1 pint) of water. Place quinces and water in a large heavy enamel or stainless steel kettle, cover and boil about 30 minutes until the quinces are very mushy.

Line 2 large colanders with several thicknesses of damp cheesecloth and set over large heatproof bowls. Or, if you have 2 jelly bags, dampen them in cold water, wring dry, suspend from their stands and set each over a large heatproof bowl. Pour half of the quince mixture into each colander or jelly bag and let stand undisturbed for 1 to 2 hours until all the juices have drained through. Do not squeeze the bags to force the juices out because if you do, the jelly will be cloudy.

Meanwhile, wash and sterilize 4 (8-ounce) jelly glasses; keep glasses immersed in simmering water until you are ready to use them. Also melt paraffin for sealing the jelly glasses.

When all of the quince juice has been extracted, measure the total amount carefully. Take up a small amount of it and test for pectin using one of the methods described under How to Test Fruit Juices for Pectin Content; see index for page number. Add to the extracted juice the quantity of sugar indicated in the pectin test, or, if you have no means of measuring the pectin, add ¾ cup of sugar to each 1 cup of extracted juice (this proportion should produce good results).

Place the sweetened juice in a very large, heavy, broad-bottomed, enamel or stainless steel kettle, insert a candy thermometer and set uncovered over moderately high heat. Bring to the boil, then boil uncovered without stirring about 20 to 25 minutes until the mixture will sheet–that is, a little of the hot mixture taken up on a metal spoon will, when cooled and tilted, slide together in a single jelly-like sheet; sheeting usually occurs when the candy thermometer registers between 218° and 220° F.

When jelly sheets, remove kettle from heat and skim off the froth. Pour hot jelly into hot glasses, filling to within ¼" of the tops. Seal with ⅛" melted paraffin, pricking any bubbles in the paraffin with a sterilized needle. Cool jelly thoroughly, cover jelly glasses with their metal caps, label and store on a cool, dark, dry shelf.

RHUBARB

Botanically, rhubarb is not a fruit. But because it is prepared and preserved like fruit, we include it here instead of with vegetables. The crimson stalks are the only edible parts of rhubarb (both leaves and roots are toxic). Rhubarb stalks do not can especially well (other canning guides to the contrary), because they brown and oversoften under the heat of processing. They cannot be dried or held in cold storage, but they do make superlative preserves and chutneys (see recipes). And they freeze exceptionally well.

TO FREEZE: The first spring cuttings of rhubarb will freeze better than maturer stalks, which tend to be fibrous. If you want to put aside rhubarb to use later for making preserves, simply cut into chunks and freeze without sugar or syrup. But if you plan to use the rhubarb in baking (for pies or puddings), pack the chunks in syrup or, if you prefer, cook the rhubarb until tender, purée, sweeten and then freeze. *Amount of fresh rhubarb needed to fill a 1-pint freezer container:* About ¾ pound if frozen as chunks, about 1 pound if frozen as purée.

Rhubarb Chunks (Unsweetened):

1. Gather succulent, tender, evenly scarlet stalks. Trim off leaves and root ends, wash stalks well in cool water, then cut into 1" or 2" chunks.

2. To set the color and flavor of the rhubarb, blanch chunks 1 minute in boiling water. Quick-chill 1 minute in ice water and drain.

3. Pack into 1-pint freezer containers, shaking the rhubarb chunks down for a more compact fit and filling to within ½" of the container tops. Snap on lids, label and quick-freeze.

Rhubarb Chunks (Syrup Pack):

1. Prepare and chill enough *medium (40%) sugar syrup* to pack the amount of rhubarb you plan to freeze. You will need from ½ to ⅔ cup of syrup for each

1-pint container. (Directions for making the syrup are included under Sugar Syrups for Freezing Fruit; see index for page number).

2. Pick, prepare, blanch and quick-chill the rhubarb as directed in steps 1. & 2. for unsweetened rhubarb chunks (above).

3. Pack rhubarb into 1-pint freezer containers, shaking the chunks down lightly and filling to within ½″ of the tops. Pour in enough cold syrup to cover the rhubarb, at the same time leaving ½″ head space. Snap on lids, label containers and quick-freeze.

Rhubarb Purée:

1. Gather tender, crimson stalks, remove leaves and root ends, then wash stalks thoroughly in cool water; drain. Cut in 1″ chunks.

2. Measure the total amount of rhubarb chunks and for every 1½ quarts (6 cups) of them, add 1 cup water. Bring to a boil in a large heavy enamel or stainless steel kettle and boil uncovered for 2 minutes. Cool to room temperature and press through a fine sieve.

3. Measure the amount of purée and for each 1 quart of it, add ⅔ cup sugar. Mix well.

4. Pack purée tightly into 1-pint freezer containers, filling to within ½″ of the tops. Place lids on containers, label and quick-freeze.

KEEPING TIME: About one year at 0° F.

RHUBARB CHUTNEY
Makes 4 Pints

This is a splendid condiment to serve with roast pork or lamb, baked ham or roast saddle of venison. It is delicious, too, with curry.

4 pounds rhubarb, washed, trimmed of leaves and coarse stalk ends, then cut in ½" chunks (you will need 2 quarts cut-up rhubarb)
2 medium-size yellow onions, peeled and chopped fine
2 pounds light brown sugar

2 cloves garlic, peeled and minced
1½ teaspoons ground ginger
1 teaspoon powdered mustard
4 teaspoons salt
⅛ teaspoon cayenne pepper
1 cup cider vinegar
1 pound seedless raisins

Wash and rinse four 1-pint preserving jars and their closures; keep jars and closures immersed in separate kettles of simmering water until you are ready to use them.

Place all ingredients except raisins in a 2-gallon heavy enamel or stainless steel kettle, cover and bring to a boil over high heat. Reduce heat to moderate, mix well, re-cover and simmer 5 minutes until rhubarb is very soft. Stir in raisins and simmer uncovered 15 to 20 minutes until mixture is quite thick, about like marmalade. Ladle into hot jars, filling to within ¼" of the tops. Wipe jar rims and seal jars. Process 10 minutes in a boiling water bath (212° F.). Remove jars from water bath, complete seals if necessary, and cool thoroughly. Check seals, label jars and store in a cool, dark, dry place. Allow chutney to "season" at least 2 weeks before serving.

RHUBARB AND FIG PRESERVES
Makes 6 Half-Pints

Fresh rhubarb and dried figs simmered into a dark and glistening spread. Delicious with home-baked bread and rolls.

3 pounds rhubarb, washed, trimmed of leaves and coarse stalk ends, then cut in ½" chunks (you will need 1½ quarts cut-up rhubarb)
6 cups sugar

1 lemon
⅓ cup cold water
1 pound dried figs, stemmed and moderately finely chopped

Mix rhubarb and sugar in a heavy 2-gallon enamel or stainless steel kettle, cover and let stand overnight at room temperature. Using a vegetable peeler, cut yellow part of rind from lemon, then mince very fine; cut white pith from lemon and discard, then cut lemon into small cubes and discard seeds. Mix rind, lemon and water in a small bowl, cover and let stand overnight at room temperature also.

Next day, add figs and lemon mixture to rhubarb. Set kettle over moderately low heat and bring to a boil, uncovered, stirring constantly. Insert a candy thermometer. Raise heat to moderate and boil, uncovered, stirring occasionally, about 30 minutes or until quite thick and thermometer registers 218° to 220° F.

While the preserves cook, wash and sterilize 6 half-pint preserving jars and their closures. Keep jars and closures immersed in separate kettles of simmering water until you are ready to use them.

To test the preserves for doneness, take a little of the hot mixture up on a metal spoon, cool slightly, then tilt. If drops slide together in a single jelly-like sheet, the preserves are done.

Remove from heat at once, let stand 1 to 2 minutes, then skim foam from surface. Stir preserves, then pour into hot jars, filling to within ¼" of the tops. Wipe jar rims and seal jars. Process 15 minutes in a simmering water bath (185° F.). Remove jars from water bath, complete seals if necessary, then cool thoroughly. Check seals, label jars and store on a cool, dark, dry shelf.

RHUBARB JAM
Makes 4 Half-Pints

2 pounds rhubarb, washed, trimmed of
    leaves and coarse stalk ends, then cut
    in ½" chunks (you will need 1 quart
    cut-up rhubarb)

3 cups sugar
1 tablespoon lemon or lime juice
¼ cup cold water

Mix rhubarb and sugar in a large, heavy enamel or stainless steel kettle, cover, and let stand overnight at room temperature. Next day, mix lemon juice and water into rhubarb, insert a candy thermometer, set kettle over moderately low heat and bring to a boil, stirring constantly until sugar dissolves. Boil uncovered, stirring occasionally, 30 to 40 minutes until thick and thermometer registers 218° to 220° F.

While the jam cooks, wash and sterilize 4 half-pint preserving jars and their closures. Keep jars and closures immersed in separate kettles of simmering water until you are ready to use them.

To test the jam for doneness, take a little of the hot mixture up on a metal spoon, cool slightly, then tilt; if drops slide together in a jelly-like sheet, the jam is done. Remove from heat, let stand 1 to 2 minutes, then skim off froth. Stir jam 1 minute, then pour into hot jars, filling to within ¼" of the tops. Wipe jar rims and seal jars. Process for 10 minutes in a simmering water bath (185° F.). Remove jars

215

from water bath, complete seals if necessary, and cool completely. Check seals, label jars, and store on a cool, dark, dry shelf.

VARIATION: *Rhubarb-Strawberry Jam.* Makes 8 half-pints. Mix the 1 quart cut-up rhubarb with 6 cups sugar in a heavy, 2-gallon enamel or stainless steel kettle and let stand overnight as directed. Next day, mash 2 quarts washed and hulled strawberries (you will need 1 quart mashed berries), and add to rhubarb along with ¼ cup lemon juice. Insert candy thermometer in kettle, bring mixture to a boil, then proceed as directed above. NOTE: Do not double this recipe because you will have more jam than you can cope with in your biggest kettle.

STRAWBERRIES

You can freeze strawberries and you can simmer them into jams and preserves (see recipes). Any other way you try conserve them will be a waste of time (to say nothing of strawberries).

TO FREEZE: To preserve as much of the strawberries' inherent goodness as possible, slice them or crush them, then pack with sugar. Puréed berries freeze commendably, too, and are perfect for shortcakes and dessert sauces. But berries frozen whole turn limp and drab after thawing. *Amount of fresh strawberries needed to fill a 1-pint freezer container:* About 1½ to 2 pints depending on whether berries are sliced, crushed, or puréed.

Sliced or Crushed Strawberries:

1. Pick plump, firm, bright red berries in the cool of the morning. Wash well in cold water, drain, and hull. Slice about ¼" thick or, if you prefer, partially crush with a potato masher (don't overdo the crushing–there should be good-sized lumps of berries).

2. Measure the total amount of sliced or crushed berries and to each quart, add ¾ cup sugar. Mix thoroughly.

3. Pack berries into 1-pint freezer containers, shaking them down for a more compact fit and filling the containers to within ½" of the tops. Snap on lids, label and quick-freeze.

Puréed Strawberries:

1. Gather, wash and hull the berries as directed in Step 1 (above). Press the berries through a fine sieve (do not purée in a blender because you will beat in too much air).

2. Measure the strawberry purée and to each 1 quart, add ⅔ cup sugar. Mix well.

3. Pack strawberry purée tightly into 1-pint freezer containers, filling to within ½″ of the tops. Cover containers, label and quick-freeze.

KEEPING TIME: About one year at 0° F. although the strawberries will have far fresher flavor if served within 6 months.

GRANDMA'S COOKED BERRY JAM
Makes 4 Half-Pints

This master recipe can be used for many different types of berries—strawberries, blueberries, red or black raspberries, blackberries, loganberries, boysenberries. Just make sure the berries are firm-ripe—use the dead ripe ones for cobblers or pies. Lemon juice will sharpen the flavor of the jam and brighten the color of strawberry and red raspberry jams. NOTE: Do not double this recipe.

2 quarts firm-ripe berries (about), stemmed   *¼ cup lemon juice (optional)*
or hulled, washed and drained well   *3 cups sugar*

Mash the berries with a potato masher and measure; you will need exactly 1 quart of mashed berries. If you like, sieve out some of the seeds, but add enough additional mashed berries to round out the 1-quart measure. Place the berries, lemon juice, if you like, and the sugar in a very large, heavy enamel or stainless steel kettle; insert a candy thermometer and bring mixture to a boil, stirring until sugar dissolves. Boil uncovered, stirring occasionally, about ½ hour until thick and thermometer registers 218° to 220° F.

While the jam cooks, wash and sterilize 4 half-pint preserving jars and their closures. Keep closures and jars immersed in separate kettles of simmering water until you are ready to use them.

To test the jam for doneness, take up a little of the hot mixture on a metal spoon, cool slightly, then tilt the spoon; if drops slide together in a single jelly-like sheet, the jam is done. Remove from heat and let stand 1 to 2 minutes; skim off froth. Stir jam 1 minute, then pour into hot jars, filling to within ¼″ of the tops. Wipe jar rims and seal jars. Process for 10 minutes in a simmering water bath (185° F.). Remove jars from water bath, complete seals if necessary, and cool thoroughly. Check seals, then label jars and store in a dark, cool, dry place.

VARIATION: *End-of-the-Garden Berry Jam.* When you have only tag ends of berries left in the berry patch, make a mixed berry jam, improvising however you like with flavor combinations. Mash enough berries to total 1 quart, then prepare the jam following the recipe above.

STRAWBERRY PRESERVES
Makes About 4 Half-Pints

These strawberry preserves have particularly good flavor and texture because the berries have been allowed to plump overnight in their own juices.

4 pints tart, firm-ripe, medium size
   strawberries

4½ cups sugar
1 tablespoon lemon juice

Stem and hull the berries; wash in cool water and drain. Do not slice, halve or cut up. Measure the berries carefully; for this recipe you will need 6 cups of hulled whole berries.

Place the berries in a very large, heavy, broad-bottomed, enamel or stainless steel kettle, add sugar and let stand at room temperature about 15 minutes until the juices begin to flow out of the berries. Set uncovered over moderate heat and heat 4 to 5 minutes, stirring gently—just until berries are heated through. Remove from heat, cover and let stand overnight at room temperature.

Next day, wash and sterilize 4 half-pint preserving jars and their closures; keep jars and closures immersed in separate kettles of simmering water until needed. Set the kettle of berries over moderately high heat, stir in lemon juice and insert a candy thermometer. Bring to a boil, stirring now and then, raise heat and boil as rapidly as you dare, stirring only if berries threaten to scorch, for 20 to 25 minutes or until candy thermometer registers 221° F. and preserves are thick, sparkling and translucent.

Remove kettle from heat, skim off froth, then pour hot preserves into hot jars filling to within ¼" of the tops. Wipe jar rims and seal jars. Process for 10 minutes in a simmering water bath (185° F.). Remove jars from water bath, complete seals, if necessary, and cool completely. Check seals, label jars and store on a cool, dark, dry shelf.

Appendix

THE FOOD PROCESSOR'S ROLE IN PICKLING AND PRESERVING

I'm an impulse buyer, and the impulse that sent me dashing to buy a food processor was a mountain of cucumbers waiting to be sliced into Bread and Butter Pickles. I'd been hearing for months what a miracle worker the food processor was, and clearly this was the time to put it to the test.

Within half an hour of assembling the machine, plugging it in and feeding that first chunk of cucumber through the slicing disc, I became a convert, for the processor had reduced a formidable pile of cucumbers to uniform slices with awesome speed. This all happened more than ten years ago, and I have since (in the course of writing a food processor cookbook) put every major machine through its paces and learned dozens of techniques that apply to pickling and preserving.

Most Useful Blades

Today's standard food processors pack three cutting blades: *a medium-slicing disc* and *medium-shredding disc*, both of which ride at the top of the work bowl, and *an S-shaped, scalpel-sharp metal chopping blade*, which spins at the bottom.

The two most valuable for pickling and preserving, however, are the *slicing disc* and *metal chopping blade.* If your particular processor offers such optionals, I would also recommend the *thin-slicing disc,* the *thick-slicing disc,* and the *coarse shredding disc,* which quickly cuts vegetables into an acceptable julienne.

For Safety's Sake

Although food processor manufacturers have built safeguards into their machines and detailed the Dos and Don'ts for their safe operation, accidents *can* happen. No machine is failsafe, and must thus be used with alertness and respect. These general safety guidelines apply to all machines:

1. Study your processor's instruction manual until you are wholly familiar with the machine's assembly and disassembly, its use and care.

2. Always use the *pusher* to guide food down the feed tube, never your hand. And never stick fingers down the feed tube when the machine is running.

3. Never fit a blade or disc onto the machine without first setting the work bowl into place; you *might* accidentally activate the motor.

4. Always let processor discs or blades come to a complete standstill *before* uncovering the work bowl. Most new processors have braking actions to stop blades almost as soon as the motor is snapped off.

5. Never force a processor beyond its capability by applying too much pressure on the pusher as you guide food down the feed tube. This is most apt to happen when you are trying to shred or slice something tough or hard— fresh horseradish, for example. Unless you own one of the powerful new heavy-duty processors, your machine may not be able to cope with fibrous vegetables. Forcing the machine can dull or deform the blade or stall the motor.

6. Always leave the metal chopping blade in place when lifting the work bowl from the power base (this prevents leakage), but *do always remove it* before emptying the work bowl.

7. Always stop the processor before arranging a new batch of foods to be sliced or shredded. You'll minimize the risk of accidents and you'll also slice or shred food with greater precision.

8. Always disassemble and store your food processor as the manufacturer recommends. Never store the machine with the work bowl locked into place, because you may break the delicate spring-mechanism that in many processors is the On-Off switch.

9. Always handle processor blades and discs as carefully as you would your sharpest knife; place in the dishwasher where they can be seen at a glance, keep out of reach of small children and also well away from counter or shelf edges where they may accidentally tumble off and injure someone.

How to Processor-Prepare Foods for Pickling and Preserving

Apples, apricots, peaches, pears	*To Chop:* Peel fruit, pit or core, then cut into 1-inch chunks. Equip processor with metal chopping blade. Add 2 cups fruit chunks to work bowl and for a moderately coarse chop, pulse or snap motor on and off quickly 3 times (this is a good texture for most jams and preserves); for a finer chop (good for fruit butters), use 5 or 6 pulses or on-offs of the motor. *To Slice:* Peel, quarter, then pit or core fruit. Slip medium-slicing disc into place, put work-bowl cover on, but do not turn motor on. Lay enough fruit quarters on their sides in the feed tube for a fairly snug fit, hold in place by exerting gentle pressure on the pusher, then snap motor on or depress the Pulse button. *Tip:* Apples, apricots, peaches and pears all darken when cut open and exposed to the air. To retard browning, sprinkle cut surfaces at once with lemon juice.
Artichokes, Jerusalem (sunchokes)	*To Chop:* Scrub tubers in cool water but leave skins on, if you like. Cut in 1-inch chunks and place 2 cups in work bowl of processor fitted with metal chopping blade. For a coarse chop (best for radishes), snap motor on and off 2 to 3 times.
Beets	*To Slice:* Parboil *unpeeled* beets 20 to 25 minutes until firm-tender (for richer color, also leave 1 inch of stems and roots on). Trim beets and peel. Stand 1 or 2 beets (just enough for a snug fit) in feed tube of processor fitted with medium-slicing disc, then depress Pulse button or snap motor on and guide down feed tube with gentle pressure. *To Shred:* Equip processor with medium- or coarse-shredding disc. Parboil, trim, peel and fit beets into feed tube as directed above, then depress Pulse button or snap motor on and guide beets down feed tube with gentle pressure.

Cabbage	*To Chop or Shred:* This is best done by the metal chopping blade. Trim cabbage, quarter and slice off core at point of each quarter. Cut cabbage into 1-inch chunks and place 2 cups in food processor fitted with the metal chopping blade. For a moderately coarse chop (best for sauerkraut and relishes), pulse or snap motor on and off about 5 times.
Carrots, celery, cucumbers, rhubarb, summer squash	*To Chop:* For most relishes, a coarse chop is what you will want. Trim vegetables and wash or peel as needed. Cut in 1-inch chunks and place 2 cups in a food processor fitted with metal chopping blade. Pulse or snap motor on and off 2 to 5 times, inspecting the texture of the chop after each pulsing. *To Slice:* Trim and wash or peel as needed, cut in 4-inch lengths, then stand as many vegetable pieces as will fit snugly in feed tube of food processor fitted with thin-, thick- or medium-slicing disc. Depress Pulse button or turn motor on and guide vegetables down feed tube with moderate but steady pressure. *To Shred (carrots and summer squash only):* Trim and wash or peel as needed; for short shreds, cut vegetables in 4-inch lengths, and stand on end in feed tube of a processor fitted with medium- or coarse-shredding disc. For long shreds (mock julienne), cut in lengths to fit crosswise in feed tube, then arrange there as securely as possible. Depress Pulse button or snap motor on and push down feed tube with steady but moderate pressure. *To Cut in Matchstick Strips or Julienne:* Trim and wash or peel vegetables as needed, then cut into lengths to fit sideways in feed tube. Equip processor with medium- (for julienne) or thick- (for matchstick strips) slicing disc, and lay food crosswise in feed tube. Depress Pulse button or switch motor on and guide food down feed tube with moderate pressure. Remove slices from feed tube and neatly restack. Now stand on edge in the feed tube as many restacked slices as needed for a tight fit, their cut surfaces parallel to the front of the feed tube. Turn motor on or depress Pulse button and slice as before.

222

Citrus Rind (lemon, lime, orange, grapefruit)
To Chop or Mince: Using a swivel-bladed vegetable peeler, remove colored part of the rind (zest) in long thin strips. Equip processor with metal chopping blade; to work bowl add 1 cup of the sugar called for in recipe, then rind strips. Snap motor on and buzz 10 to 20 seconds until as coarse or fine as you like.

Corn
To Make Cream-Style: Cut kernels of sweet corn from cobs whole; fit food processor with metal chopping blade, add 2 cups corn and chop, using four 1-second bursts of speed.

Cranberries
To Chop: Wash and stem berries; equip food processor with metal chopping blade, add 1½ to 2 cups berries and chop moderately coarsely (best for relishes and preserves) by pulsing or snapping motor on and off 2 or 3 times.

Horseradish
To Grate: This is best accomplished with the metal chopping blade. Wash horseradish root, pare, then cut in ½- to 1-inch cubes. Place 1 cup cubes in processor fitted with metal chopping blade and grate fairly fine, using three or four 10-second churnings.

Onions
To Chop: Peel onions and if large, cut into 1-inch chunks; otherwise, cut in slim wedges. Fit processor with metal chopping blade, place 2 cups onion wedges or chunks in processor and pulse or snap motor on and off 2 to 3 times for a coarse chop (best for relishes).
To Slice: Select, first of all, onions slim enough to fit whole in processor feed tube. For most pickles, small silverskins are choicest. Blanch onions quickly in boiling water, slip off skins, then stand enough for a snug fit in feed tube of a processor fitted with thin-, medium- or thick-slicing disc (whatever thickness recipe dictates). Depress Pulse button or turn motor on and push onions down feed tube with light pressure.

Parsley and other leafy herbs
To Chop and Mince: Wash well, remove coarse stems, then pat very dry on paper toweling; dump into processor work bowl fitted with metal chopping blade and pulse or snap motor on and off 3 or 4 times for a coarse chop (best for

	most relishes), 5 or 6 times for a moderate chop (best for jellies); use two or three 5-second churnings for a uniformly fine mince (for purées and sauces).
Peppers, sweet or hot	*To Chop:* Wash, halve, core and seed peppers; cut in 1-inch pieces and place no more than 2 cups in food processor fitted with metal chopping blade. For a coarse chop (best for most relishes), pulse or snap motor on and off 2 to 3 times. *To Slice (large peppers only):* Wash, halve, core and seed as above. Equip processor with medium- or thick-slicing disc. Fit 2 pepper halves together spoon fashion, slip into feed tube, turn motor on or depress Pulse button and ease pepper down feed tube.
Purées	*Berries and Fruits:* Most are juicy enough to purée without additional liquid, but should any be needed, add a little orange or lemon juice (about ¼ cup to each 2 cups fruit). Purée by buzzing in 5-second increments, inspecting textures after each churning until you achieve degree of velvetiness you want. Press through a fine sieve. *Cooked Vegetables:* Do not attempt to purée starchy vegetables (potatoes, for instance) because they will turn to glue. Vegetables that purée to silk are carrots, beets, turnips, green beans and peas, onions, mushrooms, broccoli, cauliflower, asparagus and such leafy greens as spinach and watercress. Equip processor with metal chopping blade; add 2 cups vegetables cut in small chunks and if they seem dry, 2 to 6 tablespoons beef or chicken broth or about 1 tablespoon butter or margarine. Purée using three to four 5-second churnings, scrutinizing the texture after each churning and stopping the instant you reach the smoothness desired.
Tomatoes	*To Chop:* Wash tomatoes, core and cut into slim wedges. You can chop about 2 medium-size tomatoes at a time in the processor (or about 2 cups of wedges). Fit machine with metal chopping blade, add tomatoes, then pulse or snap motor on and off briskly 2 or 3 times—no more.

To Juice: Choose ripe tomatoes at their peak of flavor; wash, core and cut in slim wedges. Equip processor with metal chopping blade, dump in up to 2 cups tomato wedges, then reduce to juice with two to three 20-second churnings of the motor. Strain mixture through a fine sieve to remove seeds and bits of skin.

WEIGHTS, MEASURES AND YIELDS

Pinch or dash = less than ⅛ teaspoon
3 teaspoons = 1 tablespoon
2 tablespoons = 1 fluid ounce
4 tablespoons = ¼ cup (2 fluid ounces)
8 tablespoons = ½ cup (4 fluid ounces)
16 tablespoons = 1 cup (8 fluid ounces)

2 cups = 1 pint (16 fluid ounces)
2 pints (4 cups) = 1 quart (32 fluid ounces)
2 quarts (8 cups) = ½ gallon
4 quarts (16 cups) = 1 gallon
2 gallons (8 quarts) = 1 peck
4 pecks (8 gallons) = 1 bushel

1 pound granulated sugar = 2 cups
1 pound brown sugar = 2¼ to 2⅓ cups (firmly packed)
1 pound pickling salt = 2 cups

JAR AND CONTAINER ESTIMATING

Amount of Fresh VEGETABLES Needed to Fill

	A 1-Quart Preserving Jar	*A 1-Pint Freezer Container*
Asparagus	CANNING NOT RECOMMENDED	1 to 1½ pounds
Beans (Green or Wax)	2 to 2½ pounds	¾ to 1 pound
Beans (Lima)	3 to 5 pounds (unshelled)	2 to 2½ pounds (unshelled)
Beets	2 pounds (weighed with 2" tops) if packed whole, 3 to 3½ pounds if sliced or diced	FREEZING NOT RECOMMENDED
Broccoli	CANNING NOT RECOMMENDED	1 pound
Cabbage	CANNING NOT RECOMMENDED	FREEZING NOT RECOMMENDED
Carrots	2 pounds (weighed without tops) if packed whole, 2½ to 3 pounds if sliced or diced	12 medium-sized carrots = 1 pint frozen purée
Cauliflower	CANNING NOT RECOMMENDED	FREEZING NOT RECOMMENDED
Corn	4 to 5 medium ears per 1-*PINT* jar if packed as whole kernels, 5 to 6 ears if packed cream-style	4 to 5 medium ears if packed as whole kernels, 5 to 6 ears if packed cream-style
Cucumbers	Amounts vary hugely depending upon whether cucumber pickles are packed whole, sliced or ground into relish (see individual recipes).	FREEZING NOT RECOMMENDED
Eggplant	CANNING NOT RECOMMENDED	FREEZING NOT RECOMMENDED
Okra	½ to ¾ pound per *PINT* jar when packed whole (as pickles)	About ¾ pound
Onions	CANNING NOT RECOMMENDED	FREEZING NOT RECOMMENDED
Parsnips, Salsify	CANNING NOT RECOMMENDED	FREEZING NOT RECOMMENDED
Peas (Black-Eyed)	3½ to 4 pounds (unshelled)	2 pounds (unshelled)
Peas (Green)	4 to 6 pounds (unshelled)	2 to 2½ pounds (unshelled)

A 1-Quart Preserving Jar	*A 1-Pint Freezer Container*

	A 1-Quart Preserving Jar	*A 1-Pint Freezer Container*
Peppers (Hot)	See pickle recipe.	FREEZING NOT RECOMMENDED
Peppers (Sweet)	See individual pickle relish recipe.	2 to 3 medium peppers = 1 pint frozen minced peppers
Potatoes (Irish)	1½ to 2 pounds (2″ potatoes)	FREEZING NOT RECOMMENDED
Potatoes (Sweet)	1½ to 2 pounds	See special recipes.
Pumpkin, Winter Squash	See special recipes for canning and freezing.	
Spinach, Other Greens	CANNING NOT RECOMMENDED	1 to 1½ pounds (untrimmed)
Squash (Summer)	CANNING NOT RECOMMENDED	See special recipe.
Tomatoes	2½ to 3 pounds if packed whole. See special recipes for juice, paste.	FREEZING NOT RECOMMENDED
Turnips, Rutabagas	CANNING NOT RECOMMENDED	FREEZING NOT RECOMMENDED

227

Amount of Fresh FRUITS Needed to Fill

	A 1-Quart Preserving Jar	A 1-Pint Freezer Container
Apples	2½ to 3 pounds if packed as slices or quarters, 3 to 3½ pounds if packed as applesauce	About 1½ pounds
Apricots	2 to 2½ pounds	¾ to 1 pound
Avocados	CANNING NOT RECOMMENDED	2 to 3 large avocados = 1 pint frozen purée
Blackberries, Boysenberries, Dewberries, Loganberries, Raspberries, Youngberries	4 pints berries = 1 quart juice	1⅓ to 1½ pints if packed whole; 2½ to 3 pints if packed as purée
Blueberries, Elderberries, Huckleberries	CANNING NOT RECOMMENDED	1⅓ to 1½ pints
Cherries	2 to 2½ pounds	1¼ to 1½ pounds
Cranberries, Currants	See special recipe.	½ to ¾ pound
Figs	See special recipes.	¾ to 1 pound
Gooseberries	CANNING NOT RECOMMENDED	1⅓ to 1½ pints
Grapefruits, Oranges	CANNING NOT RECOMMENDED	1 medium grapefruit if packed as sections; 1½ if packed as juice; 2 to 3 medium oranges if packed as sections; 4 if packed as juice
Grapes	See special recipes.	FREEZING NOT RECOMMENDED
Melons	CANNING NOT RECOMMENDED	Balls or cubes from ½ large melon
Peaches, Nectarines	2 to 2½ pounds	1 to 1½ pounds
Pears	2 to 3 pounds	FREEZING NOT RECOMMENDED
Plums	1½ to 2½ pounds	¾ pound if packed whole, 1 to 1½ pounds if halved, quartered or puréed

	A 1-Quart Preserving Jar	A 1-Pint Freezer Container
Quinces	CANNING NOT RECOMMENDED	FREEZING NOT RECOMMENDED
Rhubarb	CANNING NOT RECOMMENDED	About ¾ pound if frozen as chunks, 1 pound if puréed
Strawberries	CANNING NOT RECOMMENDED	About 1 pint

AT-A-GLANCE PROCESSING GUIDE

FOOD THAT MUST BE PROCESSED IN A STEAM PRESSURE CANNER (AT 10 POUNDS PRESSURE):

All canned vegetables (with the exception of tomatoes, which are actually a fruit, and rhubarb, which is naturally high in acid)

All canned meats, seafood and poultry (and mixtures containing them)

All canned soups and stews, also mixtures containing milk

FOODS THAT MUST BE PROCESSED IN A BOILING WATER BATH (212° F.):

All canned fruits

Canned high-acid tomatoes, tomato juice, paste and sauce, etc., not containing additional low-acid vegetables

All catsups, chili sauces and chutneys

Pickles

Relishes

FOODS THAT MUST BE PROCESSED IN A SIMMERING WATER BATH (185° F.):

Fruit butters
Fruit conserves
Jams
Marmalades
Preserves

FOODS THAT REQUIRE NO PROCESSING AFTER THEY HAVE BEEN PACKED INTO JARS:

Jellies

CANNING AT HIGH ALTITUDES

All processing times, temperatures and pounds of pressure given in this book are for altitudes of sea level up to about 1,000 feet. If you live at a higher altitude, you will have to lengthen the time of processing in a water bath or increase the amount of pressure in the steam pressure canner to compensate for the lower atmospheric pressure. Follow these guides:

When Processing Food in a Simmering or Boiling Water Bath

ALTITUDE WHERE YOU LIVE	Increase in Total Processing Time Needed if That Time Is . . .	
	20 MINUTES OR LESS	MORE THAN 20 MINUTES
1,000 feet	1 minute	2 minutes
2,000 feet	2 minutes	4 minutes
3,000 feet	3 minutes	6 minutes
4,000 feet	4 minutes	8 minutes
5,000 feet	5 minutes	10 minutes
6,000 feet	6 minutes	12 minutes
7,000 feet	7 minutes	14 minutes
8,000 feet	8 minutes	16 minutes
9,000 feet	9 minutes	18 minutes
10,000 feet	10 minutes	20 minutes

When Processing Food in A Steam Pressure Canner

Ten pounds of pressure (the equivalent of 240° F. inside the pressure canner) may be used up to altitude of less than 2,000 feet. However, if you live at an altitude of 2,000 feet or higher, you must increase the pressure inside the canner in order to achieve the necessary 240° F. (the processing times will remain the same, only the pressure will change).

ALTITUDE	INCREASE PRESSURE IN STEAM PRESSURE CANNER TO:
2,000 feet	11 pounds
4,000 feet	12 pounds
6,000 feet	13 pounds
8,000 feet	14 pounds
10,000 feet	15 pounds

Note: If your pressure canner has a weighted gauge instead of a pressure dial, you may need to have it adjusted for use at high altitudes. Contact the manufacturer's representative in your area, or write the manufacturer directly.

When Making Jams, Jellies, Preserves and Marmalades

Use a candy thermometer and cook the jam, jelly, preserves or marmalade until the thermometer registers 8° to 9° F. above the boiling point of water in your particular area.

TEMPERATURE GUIDE TO FOOD SAFETY

°F

250

240 — Canning temperatures for low-acid vegetables, meat, and poultry in pressure canner.

Canning temperatures for fruits, tomatoes, and pickles in waterbath canner.

212

Cooking temperatures destroy most bacteria. Time required to kill bacteria decreases as temperature is increased.

165

Warming temperatures prevent growth but allow survival of some bacteria.

140

125 — Some bacterial growth may occur. Many bacteria survive.

DANGER ZONE
Foods held more than 2 hours in this zone are subject to rapid growth of bacteria and the production of toxins by some bacteria.

60

Some growth of food poisoning bacteria may occur.

40

32 — Cold temperatures permit slow growth of some bacteria that cause spoilage.

Freezing temperatures stop growth of bacteria, but may allow bacteria to survive. (Do not store food above 10°F. for more than a few weeks.)

0

FOR FOOD SAFETY
KEEP HOT FOODS HOT
COLD FOODS COLD

UNITED STATES DEPARTMENT OF AGRICULTURE • OFFICE OF COMMUNICATION • 1975

Index